ROCK
KEYBOARD

Edited by
Bob Doerschuk

Foreword by
Keith Emerson

Quill/A Keyboard Book
New York

GPI Books

Art Director
Dominic Milano

Art Associate
Christina Holt

Darkroom
Cheryl Matthews, Paul Haggard, Mark Medalie

Typesetting
Leslie Bartz, Director; Birgit Byrd,
Pat Gates, Lea Milano

Indexer
Marjean Wall

Editor: Keyboard Magazine
Tom Darter

President/Publisher: GPI Publications
Jim Crockett

Associate Publisher: GPI Publications
Don Menn

Director: GPI Books
Alan Rinzler

Contents

Foreword

I am reminded of that corny advertising phrase, "We've come a long way, baby." This certainly applies to the keyboard, which has in the last ten years or so made a transition far greater than that of any other musical instruments. Certainly the sales figures for keyboards have shown a dramatic increase. And no wonder, since today's instruments encompass the full sound spectrum of the orchestra, and all sorts of timbres and effects present themselves for the player to mold into whatever shapes his or her imagination can envision.

Bear in mind that I am, of course, biased as I confess a certain smug satisfaction about all this. I still remember my early days of humping an L-100 Hammond organ around from gig to gig and being laughed at for playing a piece of furniture, for that's how most people saw it. My mother would dust and polish it religiously. It was obviously an object of embarrassment to other band members, who accepted it just for its sheer novelty value.

So there you'd sit, comping away while being drowned out by the exhibitionist up front who played guitar. As if this indignity were not enough, the roadies would have their fun by "losing" the organ stool, forcing you to stand and play your piece of furniture in a pose so unnatural that it would have caused your dear 80-year-old piano teacher to throw up her hands in horror.

It's a wonder those early gigs didn't transform us all into "Hunchbacks of Notre Dame," although perhaps the "Phantom of the Opera" image is closer to the mark. One had only to tinkle the opening motif to the *D Minor Toccata and Fugue* to win a knowing sympathetic smile from the other keyboard players in the audience.

Of course this ignominy couldn't last forever. The little spark that got you going in the first place grew into a sizable flame that made you accept the best of a bad lot to the extent that now, in retrospect, you could hug that roadie for losing your organ stool. Your newly-found poise gave you a freedom that was never before possible and a confidence that you could hold your own against that twanging egocentric out front, even though you did break your back trying to make a 300 lb. instrument look as light as your opponent's guitar. Never mind, you'd made your point, and technology has since stepped in to complete your dreams and make things a little easier for you.

Bob's book traces the "long winding road" from early rock piano to today's synthesizer bands, allowing you, the keyboard player, to remember your heritage. So even if that guitarist is still around trying to drown you out, you can smile and remind yourself that we have indeed come a long way, with still more technological and musical promise awaiting us in the future.

Keith Emerson

ntroduction

In the beginning, there was the piano—usually a beat-up, banged-out upright, but a piano nonetheless. You could hear it tinkling or pounding behind the slap bass, the riffing horns, and the metronomic whack of the drums. It was seldom mixed very high among the other instruments; rather, it stayed in the background, providing a roadhouse ambience and bridging the infant rock and roll to its boogie-woogie ancestry.

Keyboards have gone through some strange changes in rock since those early days. They've moved up front, and multiplied in form and number. They don't just send hammers banging against strings; they shoot electric juice through oscillators, filters, tone wheels, transistors, and dozens of other high-tech devices. Some of them are bulky monsters nearly as big as pianos—come to think of it, some of them *are* pianos. Others you can tuck under one arm and tote out to the beach for some lightweight jamming.

And the players have changed too. The pioneers were a breed in themselves. Many of the most important early rock pianists were anonymous session men hidden away in the shadows behind flashy featured performers. But the ones whose names most of us remember—Jerry Lee Lewis, Little Richard, Fats Domino—were nearly mythological creatures even in their own time. Their styles were not identical; Lewis' wrist action had the impact of a Gatling gun on the keys, Richard flailed away like an asylum escapee, and Domino was by comparison an introvert, beaming happily as he bumped his peripatetic piano toward the wings. Yet they and their lesser-known colleagues left a single mark on the nation's musical consciousness, identifying the piano as an integral ingredient in the recipe for rock and roll, and those who played it as swaggering maniacs.

Sooner or later this was bound to change. Few could challenge the pianistic force of this unholy trinity, or dredge up enough cash to nurse battered strings, frames, and actions back to health. As the music began to catch on, so then, did an alternative, somewhat less fragile keyboard instrument. When Jimmy Smith brought the Hammond organ out of its radio soap opera milieu and into the steaming funk of gospel jazz, people like Paul Tesluk of Johnny And The Hurricanes and Dave "Baby" Cortez realized that they could use it within a rock context too, to produce much more sound than you could coax from a piano, and with much less effort. Soon eager young ex-pianists were pulling all stops out and revving their Leslies into high gear from coast to coast.

For those who dug the organ sound but lacked the money and muscle to cart 400-pound B-3s from gig to gig, a new streamlined breed of electric organs offered a compromise. These chrome-plated specials lacked the raw grinding guts of the warhorse Hammonds, but they did have a distinctive sound of their own—piercing rather than overwhelming. The whiny sonorities of the Vox and Farfisa models were already familiar to fans of Del Shannon and the Telstars when the first English wave changed the face of rock and roll and brought these instruments into prominence. Unlike the '50s rockers, these new performers were not awesome superstars; they were simply gangs of kids who put their own bands together in their various neighborhoods and became millionaires overnight. They were accessible, much of their equipment was affordable, and many of them were keyboard players.

I remember how amazing it was to turn on the radio and hear things like the Animals' "House Of The Rising Sun," with the classic Alan Price organ solo, or Rod Argent's skitterish electric piano break on the Zombies' "She's Not There." The door was opening for keyboard players, and you didn't have to look like a teen idol to push through it. In fact, if you were a skinny bookish kid with glasses, the only way you could get into a rock and roll band was by being a keyboard player. Just ask Manfred Mann. Or me.

Over the next few years we keyboardists saw our horizons broaden even further. At first all the energy continued to center in the Hammond organ school. Al Kooper borrowed from it on Bob Dylan's behalf and came up with the unforgettable tone colors on "Like A Rolling Stone." Booker T. Jones wove his tasteful funk into the fabric of the Stax soul sound. Billy Preston spiced up *Shindig* each week with another fix of the church spirit. Felix Cavaliere of the Young Rascals needed just 16 bars to blow us all away with his "Good Lovin'" solo (while mystifying one interviewer by likening his B-3 to Aldous Huxley's sense organ in *Brave New World*). Mark Stein took Cavaliere's approach one step further with Vanilla Fudge. And Lee Michaels outdid everybody, turning "Stormy Monday" into a Hammond orgy.

All these guys were Americans, and they all shared a fondness for bright registration, rich vibrato, and gospel phrasing. In England they had a kindred spirit in Steve Winwood, whose keyboard and vocal work as a 14-year-old prodigy with the Spencer Davis Group stunned the musical community. But in general it was a different

Keith Emerson's chops, charisma, vision, and forays into the new world of synthesizers set the standards for keyboard performance that still apply to this day.

scene over there, downplaying the American tendency toward razzle-dazzle, and concentrating instead on more technically demanding experiments. Leslie speakers most often rested in the slow speed or, as was the case for a while with Deep Purple's Jon Lord, were replaced entirely by regular guitar amplifiers. Brian Auger looked back toward jazz for his inspiration, but it was the progressive rock movement that stirred the imaginations of most young players. Tony Kaye of Yes, his successor Rick Wakeman, and most of all, Keith Emerson of the Nice embarked on a series of attempts to blend rock with the complex structures of classical music. Their goals were laudable, their talent and technique frequently very impressive, but the results of their explorations were, in the final assessment, mixed. Still, every keyboard player in the business benefitted from the contributions of the progressive school. Specifically, Keith Emerson's chops, charisma, vision, and forays into the new world of synthesizers set the standards for keyboard performance that still apply, and finally won the keyboardist equal footing with the guitarist in the echelons of rock.

Meanwhile, other ideas were brewing, particularly among those using Voxes, Farfisas, Ace Tones, and other portable electronic organs. These smaller instruments couldn't match the power of the Hammond tone wheel, so new ways of playing had to be formulated. In his work with the Blues Project, Al Kooper demonstrated that this liability could translate into a kind of liberation from the thrilling but already cliched vocabulary of the B-3 style. Rather than do thinner imitations of stock Hammond licks, Kooper concentrated on developing a more subtle sense of melodic and tonal interplay with his band. These efforts had a strong effect on Ray Manzarek of the Doors, whose milky-smooth solos in "Light My Fire" and "The End" provoked a revolution in rock keyboard improvisation. You can hear Manzarek's impact in dozens of psychedelic period-piece records, the ultimate example being Doug Ingle's undulating Gothic masterpiece with the Iron Butterfly, "Inna-Gadda-Da-Vida."

Manzarek, Ingle, and company represent a fulcrum on which rock keyboard history balances. Everything that came before them, and much that would follow, was romantic in essence, as one would expect a fusion of bluesy earthiness, churchy ecstasy, and street-corner rebellion to be. The cooler, less physical style inaugurated by Manzarek was something of a reaction against romantic excess. In this reaction rock and roll experienced the birth of its classical ethic, which demanded a new simplicity and an end to the emotional self-indulgence that was already trivializing much of the music of that period. It is this ethic that prevails in new wave rock and its aftermath.

The new classicism also helped push keyboardists to their current position of supreme importance in modern rock. To understand why, we need to look back once more to the era that spawned rock and roll in its original form. Three short decades ago Bill Haley, Elvis Presley, and their contemporaries exploded into a restlessly romantic time. Despite the first signs of the kind of regimentation we take for granted now, or maybe because of them, the image of the guitarist, implying both the loneliness of the James Dean delinquent and the unsettled mobility of Jimmie Rodgers and the American hobo balladeer, fit the mood perfectly.

That image lost a lot of relevance through the '70s and into the '80s. Young musicians learning their trade today live in a more rigidly structured world. Feelings, like information, are broken down and computerized by complex systems of institutions and machines. Rather than revolt against this depersonalization, the modern rockers buy into it and feed back their frustrations in a musical language that echoes the heartless cacaphony of a video game arcade. The new rock masks powerful emotions behind its blank facade. It's the old spirit sifted through an electronic filter.

Nobody brings that spirit to urgent life better than today's keyboard player. Just as the white-smocked, slide-ruled, science class nerds of the '60s have unexpectedly replaced their hippie predecessors as role models for the electrified young, so have the keyboardists, cooly tweaking dials and flipping switches like company men juggling accounts, jumped past the guitarists to the forefront of rock. In extreme cases they seem to parody themselves with deliberately robotic choreography, jerking the music as far from the cathartic heritage of Janis Joplin and Jimi Hendrix as it can go. Their synthesizers and effects racks surround them like desks and profit charts, yet they resist the romantic temptations of old-fashioned virtuosity. For them, the keys are not ends in themselves, no more than calculators are for the maestros of finance. Instead, they are tools to use in creating a musical statement, pure and simple.

But what tools! Thanks to the incredible advances made over the past ten or fifteen years in keyboard design, the latest generation of rock keyboardists has a greater latitude than any other instrumentalists have ever enjoyed in being able to cultivate their own individual styles. They can bend notes with all the nuances of the best guitarists, borrow from any melodic and harmonic tradition that appeals to them, and pull off aural tricks the old-timers couldn't have even dreamed of. It's no wonder that the modern musical utopians embrace technology rather than avoid it, unlike their romantic older brothers and sisters, for each step forward in instrument capability gives the keyboardist that much more freedom of self-expression in sound.

Anyone who can get around a keyboard and into the electronics attached to it can learn to create this freedom for themselves. The new classicists—Gary Numan, the Human League, Soft Cell, Devo—do it routinely. The neo-romantics—Seth Justman of the J. Geils Band, Jimmy Destri of Blondie, Greg Hawkes of the Cars—use their digital/analog hybrids to evoke the organ sylphs of the '60s. Even the composer/performers like Elton John, Billy Joel, Leon Russell, and Randy Newman, who continue to remind us of the piano's importance, have discovered the wonders of the synthesizer. In the end, however, the rock keyboard story belongs to all of them, the people playing the machines, from this year's superstars to the forgotten juke joint boogie men with their mothballed uprights. It is the players, not the products, that keep rock keyboard music alive.

Keyboard Magazine has been documenting this story since the premiere issue hit the stands in 1975. Just about every important character in this colorful drama has been interviewed, or at least discussed, in our pages since then. Of course we've also been covering the greats of jazz, classical music, and other genres, yet it's only with the kind of rock articles compiled in this book that you get a peculiar roller-coaster sensation, partly because of the personalities involved, but also because the most dramatic musical surprises seem to happen in rock. New artists come along almost every month, shaking things up a bit and setting the stage for someone else's entrance a few weeks down the road.

Bob Doerschuk

I. The Early Years

Rock Piano

Jerry Lee Lewis, Fats Domino, Little Richard, and Other Pioneers

Classical musicians played it, jazz musicians played it. Even little old ladies and their pigtailed pupils played it. But rock musicians pummelled, battered, banged, bashed, smashed, axed, danced on, *and* played it.

From the very beginning, rock and roll revolved around the piano. For one thing, the electric guitar was a relatively new item; people like Chuck Berry were still helping to define just exactly what its role would be in the evolving music of the day. The piano, on the other hand, was a longtime fixture, an intact survivor of the shifting musical tides. Its roots dug directly into the rich earth of the blues, gospel, and other traditional styles, sending the nutrients of the past straight into the body of rock and roll without any technological detours.

And the piano was a sturdy creature. Berry may have played his Gibson hollowbodies behind his head or coyly tucked between his legs, but it took a few more years for guitarists to embrace the idea of destroying their axes onstage, either as schtick or as statement. It was different with the pianists. One can almost see Jerry Lee Lewis rolling up his sleeves, shoving past his guitarist ("Get them wimpy little strings outta my way!"), and venting his version of true rock and roll on the next hapless piano that dared cross his path. Rock meant conflict and rebellion to fans as well as detractors, so the more resistance an instrument could offer, the harder it pushed the player, and the meaner it made the music.

By this time, the boogie woogie style of blues piano playing had more or less defined itself. Partly because of the ragtime precedent, and partly because of its urban roots, its adherents played with a more insistent rhythm than their rural counterparts, most of whom concentrated on guitar. And much of that rhythm foreshadowed patterns that would later be categorized as rock. For example, as Eric Kriss points out in his book *Six Blues-Roots Pianists,* Jimmy Yancey, perhaps the most influential of the great Chicago boogie pianists, frequently used the following bass pattern in his left hand:

The pattern can be heard in many classic rock performances. However, it would show up more often in bass lines rather than in piano parts. In Little Richard's "Slippin' And Slidin'," for instance, the saxes and bass carry this Yancey line while the piano provides a rhythmic counterpoint. Boogie woogie was mainly a solo piano style, but rock has always been geared toward ensembles, so the functions of the piano and the kinds of parts it played differed.

More relevant to the growth of the rock piano style was the work of Leroy Carr. Born in Tennessee in 1905, Carr was raised in Indianapolis, where he learned to play on a piano his mother had bought for his sister. In his many recordings — in four years and 15 sessions, he cut nearly 100 tunes — Carr emerged as a synthesis of the rural and urban blues. Carr did most of his work in a duo with guitarist Scrapper Blackwell, who often wound up playing walking bass on his low strings, freeing Carr to augment the rhythm with his left hand, much the way rock bands provided a bass line that allowed pianists to concentrate on the beat with both hands. On many tunes, like "Gettin' All Wet," recorded in 1929, and "Barrelhouse Woman #2," you can hear how he kept the rhythm closer to straight eighths than dotted eighths, while riffing on a right-hand figure.

One pianist who was strongly influenced by Carr was Champion Jack Dupree. Dupree had heard Carr play several times in Indianapolis, and for a while he performed at the Indianapolis Cotton Club, where Carr had worked earlier. But there were other aspects to Dupree's playing that would have an impact on rock piano, mainly due to his New Orleans background.

New Orleans has always been a rich musical garden, with the diverse sounds of its many ethnic groups twining together in alluring new combinations. Jelly Roll Morton had referred to the "Spanish tinge" in the city's music, and while there is a world of difference between what he and the New Orleans pianists of more recent years played, this was a fairly consistent quality, and its impact would affect the development of both jazz and rock in their respective eras.

Dupree reflected this aspect of his heritage in his move away from the regularity of the boogie woogie bass. His freer left-hand rhythms in some ways betrayed a jazz or Latin influence, but this was countered by a more punchy right hand. Seldom a graceful soloist, he preferred a pounding attack, whacking out the beat with such force that he would often stand up at the piano and throw the weight of his entire body into the attack. In Dupree's approach, the piano became a percussive instrument, a rhythm-generating device, rather than a source of melody or texture. He was, in this sense, a direct spiritual ancestor to Little Richard and Jerry Lee Lewis.

Dupree, who still performs today in Europe, made his first records in 1940, on the Okeh label. By that time, other antecedents of the rock piano style were in full development. With the decline of the big bands, many black musicians and listeners were exploring the rougher edges of rhythm and blues, a heavier-riffing, more emotional style that had been growing among small ensembles in nameless and numberless roadside joints while the better-known swing groups played their polished jazz uptown. In Los Angeles a community of R&B artists from Texas and Oklahoma was beginning to make an impact, and much of what they were doing would affect the future of rock and roll. They included the innovative electric guitarist T-Bone Walker, saxophonist Eddie "Cleanhead" Vinson, and the singer/pianist Charles Brown.

One writer referred to Brown as the father of "club blues," a hybrid born of the Southwestern blues style and the slick showbiz scene in L.A. Most of his fans knew him as a singer of sad romantic songs; Ray Charles, for one, was heavily affected by Brown's vocal performance of "Merry Christmas Baby" and other tunes. But he also was a seminal R&B pianist.

What Brown contributed was a restrained piano style, based on fills behind the vocal line, that would come to characterize the rock ballad piano style. On most of his early records with the Three Blazers, a jazz influence predominated on the up-tempo sides, while the slower tunes were unadulterated blues, though played in a some-

Jerry Lee Lewis, c. 1957. "The Killer" has antecedents in gospel, Western swing, R&B, and boogie woogie, spiked with incredible endurance, frenetic energy, and a vicious vocal style.

what reserved fashion and almost rigidly straight rhythms behind Moore's lush guitar chords. His delicacy and avoidance of syncopations helped set the style for slow rock piano fills of the future.

Another major figure in early R&B piano, Amos Milburn, played and sang in a somewhat stronger style. However, Milburn was never able to crack the rock and roll market in the '50s, despite his attempts to update his sound. On slow tunes, Milburn tended to play fast background piano runs out of rhythm, winding in and out of the upper range of the keyboard as the tempo rolled inflexibly on; this approach can be heard on tunes like "I Love Her," "Let's Make Christmas Merry, Baby," and "Please, Mr. Johnson." On the faster songs he stayed within the beat. On "I'm Going To Tell My Mama," for instance, his left hand unwaveringly plays between the upbeats to match the drummer's insistent jump rhythm pattern. In these two characteristics — the free approach to rhythm at slow tempos, and the tight adherence to faster beats—Milburn is in tune with the phrasing of many subsequent rock piano performers.

Of course not all rhythm and blues was low key in the Brown and Milburn mold. A more fiery school, more oriented toward dance than listening, was blossoming on the West Coast at the same time, led by artists like Roy Milton and Joe and Jimmy Liggins. Some jazz notables borrowed from the excitement of this music; vibraphonist Lionel Hampton's "Flying Home" is an early R&B classic. Others took a full plunge into the new style, like bandleader Johnny Otis.

Probably no one will ever be able to compile a definitive list of the great R&B pianists of this period. To often the personnel on these long-forgotten records were never listed. There are some golden moments — the incredibly heavy pedalling and thudding left-hand fourths by T.J. Fowler in saxophonist Wild Bill Moore's "We're Gonna Rock, We're Gonna Roll," to name just one of many dozens — but most of the names and dates are lost to us; only the essence of their collective styles remains.

But rock piano has more roots than this. Country music contributed enormously to our concepts of execution and phrasing in rock and roll. The piano was important both in the music itself and in the lives of many who listened to it. In many respects this style paralleled blues piano, in the melodic slides from minor to major thirds, the steady left hand, and the basic three-chord progressions. But there were differences too.

The country piano lineage dips back into the

western swing and honky tonk music of the late '30s. Al Stricklin of Bob Wills' Texas Playboys, Papa Calhoun, who played with Milton Brown, and John "Knocky" Parker, whose credits included work with the Light Crust Doughboys and the Cowboy Ramblers, borrowed heavily from jazz but kept their music close to its folk traditions at the same time. As a group they were important in popularizing the rhythmic piano tradition for their predominantly white audiences. There was one man, though, who summarized figure in country piano.

Aubrey "Moon" Mullican was born in Polk County, Texas, in 1909. His church-going parents bought an old pump organ in hopes that their son would learn to play hymns at home. Instead, he used it to develop the blues licks a black farmworker taught him. At the age of 21 Mullican caught a freight train to Houston and began playing a long string of all-night gigs—hence the

nickname "Moon." He performed throughout the Texas and Louisiana areas in the '30s, recorded with Leon Selph's Blue Ridge Playboys in 1939, and made himself a national reputation by the '40s. In 1947 he released his version of an old Cajun tune, "Jole Blon," on the same King label that recorded Ivory Joe Hunter, Bill Doggett, and other black and white innovators. The tune sold a million copies within three years, and was followed by other hits, including "Sweeter Than The Flowers" in 1948, "I'll Sail My Ship Alone," "Mona Lisa," and "Goodnight Irene" in 1950, and "Cherokee Boogie" in 1951.

Mullican's work anticipated the merger of country music with the reinvigorating force of rhythm and blues. Moon constantly reflected black piano styles in his own playing and arrangements. The triplets in the guitar part behind his spare piano lead in "Farewell" are straight out of the R&B ballads. In his live recording of "Pipeline

Fats Domino, as he appeared in the Warner Brothers picture "Jamboree," also starring Jerry Lee Lewis, Buddy Knox, and The Four Coins, in 1957.

Blues" he runs an energetic boogie bass while constructing his right-hand solo in octaves. And in the first two choruses of "Bottom Of The Glass," Mullican pretty much approximates what would become known as the rock piano style, especially in his right hand, though the *boom-chuck* pattern he uses in later choruses to accompany the guitar solo reaches back to Texas swing.

Mullican died on New Years' Day, 1967, but he left as a legacy a generation of pianists who would alter the face of popular music. Some, like Floyd Cramer, eventually settled more in the country field, though Cramer did play on a number of early Elvis Presley sessions. Others carried Mullican's ideas a few steps closer toward rock, retaining enough of a country flavor to affect Jerry Lee Lewis and the other Sun label pianists. Perhaps the most important of these was Merrill Moore.

Moore's big sellers were remakes of older tunes. In 1953 he recorded "House Of Blue Lights," which had originally been cut by bandleader Freddie Slack in the early '40s. After that Moore laid down his versions of Ray McKinley's "Down The Road A Piece" and another Slack title, "Cow Cow Boogie." The latter song was one step beyond Mullican, a bit closer to rock; he played with a very light attack in the high end of the keyboard, keeping his eighth notes undotted and relying on a clean, almost pecked-out attack, with practically no glissandos. He did echo Western swing once in a while—his "Hard Top Race," complete with steel guitar, had a powerful rockabilly flavor—but basically Moore was a rock pianist, a prototype Jerry Lee Lewis minus the fury and frenzy.

Moore came along just as rock was about to emerge on the charts. Also thriving at that time was another equation in the formula, the latest incarnation of the New Orleans piano school. Styles had changed since Champion Jack Dupree. A new line had emerged, still tinted by Morton's "Spanish tinge," but playing with a different feel. The typical 1940s ensemble pianist in New Orleans was playing R&B at medium tempos, with rolling left-hand patterns similar to the Jimmy Yancey riff notated earlier, and triplet eighth-notes in the right hand, somewhat more forcefully played than the slow triplets that R&B pianists had been playing on *doo-wop* vocal records.

You hear this style in the work of dozens of New Orleans pianists from the late '40s. Huey "Piano" Smith, one of the top keyboard artists on the scene, once declared, "What was typical about my style is the heavy left-hand rhythm," yet this could be said about most of his colleagues as well. It was a unique sort of style—not as static as the hammerings of Jerry Lee Lewis and Little Richard, who usually let the low horns and bass carry the left-hand lines without doubling them on the keys, but not as mobile as the earlier stride and boogie players.

In John Broven's excellent book, *Rhythm And Blues In New Orleans*, trumpeter Dave Bartholomew, the bandleader who gave Fats Domino his first big break, comments on the pianist's significance as an exponent of the New Orleans piano style: "Fats always did the triplet piano himself, [but] he got this from a guy called Little Willie Littlefield. He had a record out years ago ('It's Midnight,' on Modern in 1948), and that was where Fats got the triplet piano. . . . He did not originate this, but he made it popular. Once he made it popular, naturally, he couldn't leave it."

Born in 1928, Antoine Domino studied piano with Harrison Verrett, a veteran of the local jazz scene, who introduced him to the keyboard by writing the names of each note directly on the white keys, and on white tape which he placed on the black keys. By the age of 10 Domino was working for hand-outs in various clubs. Eventually he supplemented his earnings with lawn mowing jobs and factory work. Finally, in the late '40s he landed a gig with bassist Billy Diamond's band at the Hideaway Club.

The young pianist's break came when Dave Bartholomew heard him and arranged for his first recording session. In October '49 Domino cut eight titles. One of them, "The Fat Man," became his first hit, a million-seller by 1953. Compared with many of Domino's later releases, "The Fat Man" is unusual in that the piano is mixed so prominently in the foreground. In Brover's book, Bartholomew explains why: "The sax sound was too harsh, and I really was responsible for it. . . . So what happened, Fats played loud at the piano, we made a mistake and sent the record out. The piano was much higher than everything else. We didn't really want it that way, but at the time we couldn't do anything about it."

This accident gives us a close look at Domino's style. From beginning to end, it is emphatically rhythmic; the left hand pumps out open fifths right on the beat while the right hand plays bluesy licks on top. Midway through the piece Fats breaks into the trademark New Orleans triplets against the stomping 4/4 meter. Overall it is much simpler than some of the work done by some other New Orleans piano instrumentalists—

Jerry Lee Lewis in 1957. "The father of bringing the piano into rock music" played his first gig at 13 after dropping out of the Bible Institute of Waxahatchie.

notably Professor Longhair—but it is nonetheless direct, punchy, to the point, and first-rate rock and roll.

In his book *A Jazz Retrospect*, Max Harrison sums up Fats' keyboard style, in comparison with the inimitable Longhair: "[Domino] retained Longhair's walking bass, but finessed the cross-rhythms into uniform triplets, and though he can be as cavalier about the distribution of beats, his results are invariably smoother." Somewhat more succinctly, Domino's producer, Cosimo Metassa, tells *Keyboard*, "I guess you could say that Fats' style was typical of a lot of New Orleans players, but the outstanding thing about the way he played was that he sounded so much like himself. All he had to do was play one chord—*boingg!*—and you knew it was Fats."

Although Domino was the most famous of the New Orleans pianists, Longhair was probably the most important stylist, and the one whose contributions most strongly affected the direction that rock piano would take. Without Longhair, the flavor of New Orleans would never have been injected into rock piano. His rhumba-like rhythms—again, the Spanish tinge—affected Huey "Piano" Smith in songs like "Barbara" and "Rockin' Pneumonia," and every other R&B pianist to some greater or lesser degree as well.

The legendary pianist was born in Bogaloosa, Louisiana in 1918, but raised in New Orleans. There, young Henry Roeland Byrd—not yet Professor Longhair—listened to pianists like Sullivan Rock, Kid Stormy Weather, Buck Sullivan, Isadore Tuts Washington, and Bertrand. His reputation began to grow after he sat in with Bartholomew's band at the Caledonia Inn in 1949; that same year he formed a group, the Four Hairs (hence his nickname), and cut his first records, including the hit single "She Ain't Got No Hair."

In the many records Longhair issued up until his death in 1980, he displayed an erratic technique, with wrong notes peppering even his medium-tempo solos, but his joyful rhythm never slackened. As Harrison noted, the Professor seldom played the triplet figures that his colleagues would make a New Orleans trademark, but he shared their fondness for doubling the low saxes and bass with a left-hand ostinato, a preliminary step toward the rock idea of leaving the bass line to other instrumens and devoting the left hand to reproducing the pounding figures of the right. A choice example of Longhair's unaccompanied keyboard work can be found in the opening chorus to "Willie Fugal's Blues," from the album *Crawfish Fiesta*. The lush Latin influence, the tin-

kling right hand, the rolling left hand, the relaxed syncopation, and effortless groove are all typical of his work, and of the legacy he left to rock.

Many of the New Orleans R&B greats did their recording at J&M Studios, run by Cosimo Matassa; the pianists played his six-foot Baldwin into a ribbon microphone. As word began to spread about the quality of his productions, artists from outside of town began to show up, in search of the same spirited sound. They often recorded with local musicians, and the results were usually exciting, often electrifying, and every now and then historic. Such was the case when Little Richard and Ray Charles came to town.

Both men brought a gospel touch on the piano to their New Orleans sessions, a sound that didn't surface too much in the work of Longhair, Domino, and the other locals. In Charles' case, the church made itself heard through melodic and rhythmic nuance, in a relatively polished style that betrayed his interest in jazz. But with Richard, the feeling came through like a keyboard explosion. Charles, even at his most transcendent, seemed always in control of his own phrasing, while Richard tended to slam away like a man possessed.

Their gospel roots were similar; Richard Penniman was born on December 5, 1935, in Macon, Georgia, and raised in the Seventh Day Adventist faith. As a young man he sang in choirs and learned to play the piano in church. Charles was born five years earlier in Albany, Georgia, and before losing his sight he began piano studies with a neighbor, Wylie Pittman. Both had breathed in the ecstasy of the piano as it was played in the black churches.

Time has shown that Ray Charles is much more than a rock musician alone, but perhaps his impact has been felt more strongly in rock than in any other idiom. In his hands the piano—and the electric piano with the release of "What'd I Say" in 1959—was liberated from the stylistic constraints of rock and roll. He didn't tie himself down to boogie, New Orleans, or any other formulas; he covered the entire keyboard, kicking the beat in whatever was the most appropriate way. This was due partly to his facile chops, but even moreso to the energizing touch of gospel music.

Like Charles, Little Richard Penniman was a rhythm dynamo on the keys. Where jazz ensemble pianists tend to augment the beat as laid down by the rhythm section, Richard helped set the style for the rock players who used the piano

as the prime source of rhythm. Rock drummers and bassists generally avoided the flexibility that their jazz equivalents cultivated; instead, they stuck rigidly to upbeats and riffs. It was often up to the piano to provide spontaneity and variations on the unrelenting beat, and at this task Little Richard had no peer.

Richard made his first records in 1951 for RCA, and he did a few sessions on the Peacock label as well, backed up by Johnny Otis, but it wasn't until he sent his tapes to Specialty Records in California that he began to be heard. Bumps Blackwell, Specialty's producer, met Richard in New Orleans, where they had a trial session at Matassa's studio. They cut a number of straight R&B tunes with Huey Smith playing piano behind Richard's singing, but on the last song Richard moved over to the keyboard, and in two or three takes a rock classic, "Tutti-Frutti," had been cut.

Blackwell, who had recorded both Ray Charles and Fats Domino (as Lloyd Price's accompanist) beforehand, believes that people like Richard and Domino were masters of rock piano because they focused on feeling rather than technique. "Finished [trained] piano players were all wanting to play jazz," he explains, "and they looked down on anybody who played simple rhythmic things like Fats or like Richard, who brought the piano more into the foreground. The rock guys were limited in their technique, but they were good because they had a feel and a simplicity no one else did. You couldn't get a learned piano player to give you that simplicity with so much energy and excitement."

Surprisingly, both Matassa and Blackwell remember that on some of Richard's and Domino's most popular records, other piano players, like Edward Frank, Huey "Piano" Smith, or James Booker, were brought in to do the session; the piano part of "Slippin' And Slidin'," for instance, wasn't played by Little Richard. Blackwell points out that on some songs Richard's singing was too overpowering; even when a cardboard sheet might be placed between him and the vocal mike, he would still drown out the piano signal. In those days before overdubbing, the easiest solution was sometimes to bring in another pianist and put Richard somewhere further away in the studio.

"But it didn't really matter who we used, because they all played Richard," Blackwell adds. "You're gonna hear exactly Little Richard. Richard would play the part, and the other guy would have to copy it identically or I wouldn't use it."

Whether it was Little Richard or a forgotten substitute laying down the piano part on "Good Golly Miss Molly," "True Fine Mama," and his other early hits, these discs had an immediate impact. Some artists, like Larry Williams, a New Orleans product who did most of his recording on the West Coast, played in a nearly identical style; unlike Richard, Williams even took a few piano breaks. The left-hand syncopation in the first bar of Williams' solo in "You Bug Me Baby" betrays his New Orleans background, but the rest of the improvisation centers around percussively pounded straight eighth-note chords in the Little Richard fashion.

Rock and roll was a fact of musical life by the mid-late '50s, but already it was following a path that earlier forms of American popular music had explored. As in jazz, ragtime, and Stephen Foster, the initial innovations in a new genre were made largely by black musicians, whose ideas were picked up by white imitators for the larger white public. This usually meant the second-hand performances, though often merely shades of the originals, were by far the bigger hits.

Little Richard helped break this pattern—his "Long Tall Sally" outsold Pat Boone's antiseptic cover—but it was broken in other ways as well when a new fusion took place between the raw kindred spirits of R&B and country. Historians call the by-product rockabilly, and one of its leading lights may be the ultimate rock piano player of all time.

Jerry Lee Lewis was the culmination of all of rock piano's antecedents. Strains of gospel, Western swing, R&B, and boogie woogie mingle in his keyboard work, spiked by an endurance and frenetic energy worthy of Little Richard himself. Born in 1935, Jerry Lee was raised in rural Louisiana, and he began teaching himself to play his father's guitar at age eight. He discovered his Aunt Stella's piano a year later, however, and displayed such enthusiasm for it that his parents mortgaged their home to buy him a used Stark upright.

Jerry Lee only took one or two lessons on the piano, though. He preferred learning about music at Haney's Big House, a local club where an underage kid could listen to people like Ray Charles and B. B. King a while before being thrown out. At 13 he played his first gig, and after a futile attempt at pious study in the Bible Institute Of Waxahatchie, he was out on his own, hustling a music career. When Lewis first heard about Sam Phillips' Sun Records in Memphis, where folks like Elvis Presley and Carl Perkins were starting to make it big, he packed up at once and headed out to west Tennessee.

Jerry Lee's visit was perfectly timed. "At the time Sam ran into Jerry Lee, he had been thinking for a long time about incorporating another instrument into rock and roll," says Knox Phillips, Sam Phillips' son and now head of the Sun studio and his family's publishing companies. "Sam was interested in the piano from the beginning, because he was into vocal quartets. When he began recording R&B people, he formed a close friendship with Ike Turner, who played piano during that time. Ike was one of the keys in Sam's search for a way to bring the piano into urban blues."

When Jerry Lee arrived in Memphis, Sam Phillips was out of town. "So Jerry Lee said, 'I'm staying here till Mr. Phillips hears me, and that's it, I don't care, period.' He was the same Jerry Lee even then," Knox laughs. Eventually Phillips did return, and after hearing Lewis' tapes, he realized that he had found what he had been looking for—the man who, as Knox says it, was "the father of bringing the piano into rock music."

Lewis helped solidify the Sun sound, which basically meant rock in all its power with a country slant, some echo on the voice and guitar, and relentlessly pneumatic piano playing. Of course much of this playing happens on Jerry Lee's own records. Rhythm is paramount; nothing in his piano style places even a close second. Lewis almost never lays down a walking or boogie bass line in the left hand, since straight-ahead pounding does the job more directly; note the thudding fifths beneath his solos on "Hound Dog," "Jailhouse Rock," and "Let The Good Times Roll."

There was more than one pianist in the Sun stable, and several of them actually played more sessions there than Lewis, like Charlie Rich. Compare the piano solo in Rich's version of "Break Up" with Lewis'; though less flashy, it nearly matches Jerry Lee's in sheer drive. But the most frequently used Sun pianist was the enigmatic Jimmy Wilson, whose credits are listed in *The Complete Sun Session Files* [Martin Hawkins, 229 Godinton Rd., Ashford, Kent, England].

And of course there were many other rockers behind the keyboards with other acts. Joey Welz, whose credits include Bill Haley And The Comets and Gene Vincent's Blue Caps, notes a change in the rock piano of the late '50s, with a return to left-hand movement as opposed to the relatively static punched-out chords of Little Richard and Lewis, and a new emphasis on right-hand melodic and chordal playing. "It was Walter Gates, the pianist on 'At The Hop' and 'Rock And Roll Is Here To Stay' [by Danny & The Juniors], who opened up that melodic top thing in the later '50s of chords changing around the blues left hand," Welz points out. "The triplets were still there, but they changed with the left hand rather than staying with the same chord. Little Richard would play that same chord for 30 seconds."

In other words, Welz states, a greater musicianship was creeping into rock performance, though not at the expense of the music's spirit. "You had to develop a complete left-track and right-track head," he says. "You walked the left-handed boogie chops while doing completely different things with the right hand, just like a stride pianist doing honky-tonk or jazz. Today's players have trouble playing rock and roll because they've got their two hands set for chords."

As more sophisticated players began to appear, one got the feeling that it would be only a matter of time before the priorities of the classic rockers—feeling and rhythm first, subtleties somewhere toward the bottom—would be reversed. Of course there are many who believe today that this is exactly what happened. But before the demise of the rock piano era, there was one brief swan song, envisioned and put together by an unlikely non-keyboardist from Los Angeles.

"I always thought the guitar was an overrated instrument," says legendary rock producer, composer, and entrepreneur Kim Fowley. "There were very few innovative guitar players back then, yet there were so many guitar instrumentals. The guitar was for the great unwashed, but the piano was for thinking, sensitive people. There should have been a keyboard Duane Eddy or a keyboard Ventures, but there wasn't. So we decided to create some. Just like that."

Fowley's idea was to adapt a classical theme to rock piano. Similar things were happening around that same time; a pianist named Kokomo recorded "Asia Minor," based on the Grieg *Concerto* theme, though it was orchestrated into more of a pop than a rock setting. Another pianist, Jack Fina, had cut several adaptations of Rimsky-Korsakov's *Flight Of The Bumblebee*, in solo format, with a trio, and with Tony Martin's orchestra. But as far as rock piano was concerned, Fowley's vision was still fresh.

His first effort along this line was "Like Longhair," a take-off on Rachmaninoff's C# *Minor Prelude*, with a young pianist named Paul Revere at the keys. Revere, later a mainstay on Dick Clark's *Where The Action Is* as leader of the Raiders, had already enjoyed regional success in the Northwest with "Beatnik Sticks," a rock version of "Chopsticks." But "Longhair," the first rock piano hit instrumental, made it into the national Top 10.

Fowley followed this with the even bigger "Nutrocker," which borrowed the "Sugar Plum Fairy" theme from Tchaikovsky's *Nutcracker Suite*. He originally recorded it with Jack B. Nim-

ble & The Quicks, but the remake by B. Bumble & The Stingers is the one that topped the charts in the early '60s. Another B. Bumble record, "Bumble Boogie," using the same Rimsky-Korsakov theme that Fina had used, also enjoyed success.

The piano sound was delightfully tacky on these records, a buzzing effect reminiscent of honky-tonk uprights. Fowley claims to have gotten the sound by taping empty Coke bottles to the strings. And the pianist played with an unsyncopated deliberation that demanded attention. All in all, it was maybe the last great gasp of classic rock piano.

But who was B. Bumble? Fowley answers, "There was no such person. It was a fictitious name. We gave a guy, Hal Hazen, some cash and had him play it. He was real embarrassed; he told me, 'I feel guilty taking the money, because this isn't very interesting.' And he got even more embarrassed when "Nutrocker" was a hit, but he did put out his own instrumental on Phillies Records under the name of Ali Baba."

Since those glory days, rock has matured, entered a relatively dignified middle age. Perhaps it was different at one time. Revere, maybe the last of the classic rock pianists, recalls his first years with the Raiders as a club and bar band: "You never heard the piano in the old swing bands. The piano player was there, very impressive with his big grand, but you never heard a damn thing he played. So when I started out, to make sure the piano didn't get lost, I gave it the brightest, clangiest, banginest damn sound I could. I put it way out front and cranked that mother up, then let my boys try to keep up with me.

"We used to buy pianos at each gig for like $50," he laughs, "just old uprights that were half-assed out of tune. I'd thumbtack it, put on a contact mike, and then we'd destroy it onstage! Mark [Lindsey, singer] would get up on it and kick off the black keys, and I'd wad up paper, lift the lid, throw it down in there, and light! It'd start burning and blazing and smoking, and we'd put it out with a fire extinguisher. Then we'd tip it over and crash it onto its back, and I'd get on top, kick off the keys, and finish it off. We were nuts."

Was it music? Was it for real? Was it "significant?" Kim Fowley believes "that's for some boring scholar to figure out," and he's right. That's my cue to sign off, stack up the old King 45s, put on the headphones, loosen up the wrists, and practice those triplets. Rock piano lives after all.
Bob Doerschuk

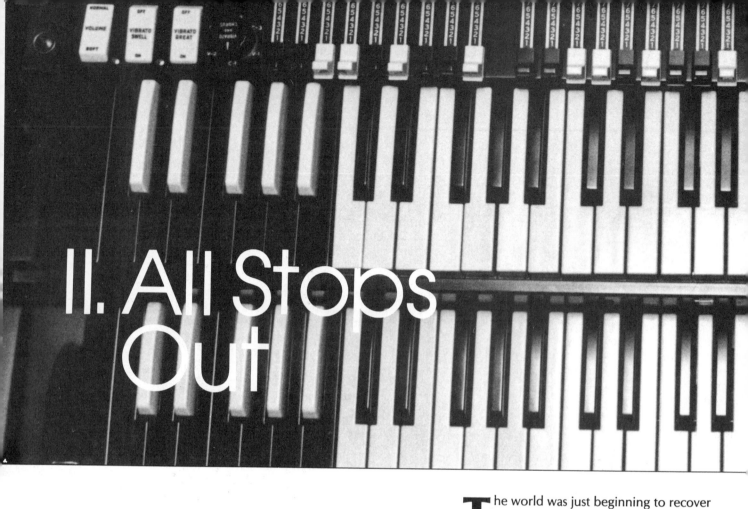

II. All Stops Out

The Rock Organ Romantics

The world was just beginning to recover from rock and roll's piano-bashing pioneers when the Rock Organ Romantics struck in the early '60s. To many, it was an unexpected shock, something like two consecutive killer waves ripping through a bevy of wiped-out surfers. As a commercial and cultural phenomenon rock was barely eights years old, yet it already seemed to have spent itself out. The radio was filled with mush teenage *recitatifs* about boyfriends and being totalled in motorcycle wrecks, and bouncy little hits ground out by assembly-line tunesmiths in the Brill Building.

In retrospect, the bridge between Jerry Lee Lewis and Alan Price appears much longer than it actually was, because it spanned two quite dissimilar worlds. One end was rooted in pre-JFK America, the other in those first numbed days after Dallas. Young people in both eras were suffering turgid emotions under difficult circumstances. Significantly, it was rock that came to their rescue, rousing them from the epidemic snooze of the Eisenhower years, then helping them to focus their outrage at the dawn of the Vietnam period. It would later play a similar role in the '70s as we shall see.

So when that unexpected wave of Beatle clones washed through the *Ed Sullivan Show* and into our national consciousness in early '64, the music and the people listening to it got the quick fix they both needed, and out of the maelstrom, unnoticed at first, stepped the Rock Organ Romantics.

What qualfied these clean-cut young Brits and their American cousins as Romantics? Like Liszt, Berlioz, and their nineteenth-century contemporaries, the new rockers were more concerned with feeling than form, too transfixed by the power of their music to worry about straitjacketing it into sophisticated "adult" configurations. Historically, this is the Romantic view, and it flourishes especially during times of great youthful turbulence. Despite its flirtation with Tin Pan Alley, rock was still a new music, its audience still young in spirit. Idealism, or if you prefer, naivete, was gushing through adolescent America's lifeblood, propelled by the upbeat optimism of the New Frontier. That idealism didn't simply disappear with the events of November '63 and related sobering traumas; it found release in a Romantic rebirth of the rock and roll spirit.

When the organ began to replace the piano as the predominant rock keyboard, musicians found that gospel music offered an effective inspiration for their Romantic instincts. The ecstacy and release of black church music expressed itself in relatively accessible musical terms, and the Hammond organ was the instrument that best put out that message. Some purists in both the secular and religious music camps were distressed at the marriage between their two styles, but these objections were quickly drowned out by the transcendent playing of people like Billy Preston, the first and the best of the gospel-rock organists. "I enjoy playing rock," he told *Keyboard Magazine* in 1977. "I don't

think it makes me a sinner. Some people don't like you to mix it up (with gospel music), but it doesn't bother me, because I find God in all music."

Preston, born in 1946, was a church music prodigy. By the age of ten he had accompanied the queen of gospel singers, Mahalia Jackson, and a few years after that he would play behind her male counterpart, Rev. James Cleveland. When he made the move to rock as a member of Little Richard's band in 1962, his style remained essentially the same, as it did through his years of performing with the Shindogs, the house band on the popular *Shindig* television show, and in his many appearances as a soloist and accompanist with the Beatles, Ray Charles, and other giants of rock. He was not a subtle player by any means. Unlike many jazz organists, who gave at least lip service to the melodic and harmonic innovations of their jazz piano colleagues, Preston went straight for the gut, with screaming glissandi that shot to the top of the keyboard, and Leslie speakers gunned to full speed. A transcribed Billy Preston solo would look embarrassingly simple— very little, if any, left hand; lots of very long held notes in the right—but this only proves that not all rock solos translate well onto paper, especially if they exploit Romantic intangibles like tone, texture, and inspired interaction with the other players. To get the full impact of Preston's work, you have to go back to the record and listen as unanalytically as you can.

There are, of course, exceptions to this rule. A

number of rock keyboard players were laying down solos in the mid-'60s that still read well when notated. More than any other instrumentalists in rock, the keyboardists have always been more willing to delve into the kind of jazz style that lends itself well to transcription, partly because of the proliferation of instruments, from pianos and electric pianos through organs and, later, synthesizers, which allows them a freedom of multifaceted expression that guitarists, stuck for so long on the treadmill of emulating Chuck Berry and B.B. King, couldn't enjoy. Back in 1964, for instance, a guitar player might have alienated his rock audience by breaking free of their expectations and whipping off the sort of solo that Rod Argent played on electric piano that year in the Zombies' "She's Not There."

Yet Argent was a Romantic at heart. Eventually he would drift back to that flagship Romantic keyboard, the organ, with his group Argent. Other jazz-influenced Hammond specialists on both sides of the Atlantic, from Manfred Mann, leader of the group that bore his name, and Dave Greenslade of England's frenetic fusion band Colosseum, to Earl Van Dyke, the house organist at Motown, and Al Kooper, the versatile visionary behind the Blues Project, early Blood, Sweat & Tears, and Bob Dylan's *Highway 61* sound, kept themselves grounded in the Romantic traditions of emotional expression and reliance on the Hammond's grinding power; Kooper's unaccompanied abstract organ improvisations of the late Sixties and early Seventies even hinted at the dissonances of post-Ornette Coleman free jazz.

Brian Auger, a promising young English jazzer who cast his lot with rock through his work with Steam Packet, the Trinity, and Oblivion Express in the '60s, remembers that the leap from one style to the other wasn't nearly as easy then as it is today. "I got a lot of flack because the jazz purists thought I'd ratted and gone commercial," he recalls in the April '77 issue of *Keyboard.* "But by the end of 1969, music had changed so much that there were two areas of influence which rock fed from. One was classical, the other was jazz. ELP (Emerson, Lake & Palmer) and Yes did a number on the classical side, and I was from the jazz side."

As diverse as all these artists were, they all established themselves through their work on the Hammond organ, so it seems ironic now that each of the five people profiled in this section has severed, or at least weakened, his ties to that instrument. Booker T. Jones plays it only sporadically now, most often on sessions he has pro-

duced. Steve Winwood still utilizes it, though on his latest LPs it lies buried beneath layers of synthesizer overdubs. Felix Cavaliere lives in amiable seclusion in Connecticut, coming out now and then to do a session, but most often preferring to watch scene from a comfortable distance. Lee Michaels has forsaken his bulky old A-100 organ for two small synthesizers wedged into a shopping cart. And in his heyday with the Band, Garth Hudson eschewed the Hammond altogether, preferring to paint his aural masterpieces at the Lowrey console.

Yet these performers stood at the forefront of the Romantic movement. Booker T. was sixteen years old when he and three other musicians who called themselves the MGs (for "Memphis Group," after their home town) recorded an improvised blues called "Green Onions" as the B side of a 45 rpm single. Much to their surprise, it became a hit, and established them as the most popular instrumental rock group of the Sixties, with Jones standing out as one of the most important style-setters in the organ world.

Like Booker T., Steve Winwood was a rock prodigy. He was born in 1948 in Birmingham, England, the son of a semiprofessional saxophonist. At the age of 15 he joined his brother's jazz band. In 1964 they both signed on with the Spencer Davis Group, then working at a local pub called the Golden Eagle. Within a year they had recorded "Keep On Running," a chart-topping hit in England. By late 1966 one of Steve's compositions, "Gimme Some Lovin'," had reached number two in England and broken into the American top ten. It was his gift for writing memorable riffs, his startlingly soulful vocal style, and authoritative grasp of the Hammond that made that record and its follow-up, "I'm A Man," instant rock classics—in spite of the fact that prior to the "Gimme Some Lovin'" session he had never played a Hammond before.

Already outgrowing the band's R&B style, Winwood began rehearsing with other musicians in 1966, including Eric Clapton and Jack Bruce, with whom he attempted to form a band called Powerhouse. After his final gig with Davis on Cliff Richards' television show in April '67, Winwood moved off to a country cottage to live and practice with the musicians who would comprise his next and most successful outfit, Traffic. Their debut album, *Mr. Fantasy,* released in June '67, displayed Winwood in a more complicated setting. Where the Davis Group showcased his thrilling keyboard solos and vocals, Traffic demanded more teamwork, fewer fireworks. The four gifted and strong-willed players in Traffic were challenged from the start to find and maintain a careful balance of egos and ideas. The band's discography reflects the many successes they achieved along this line before finally calling it quits in the early '70s.

Winwood's most recent work blends his earlier showpiece attitude, briefly resurrected with the all-star quartet Blind Faith in the late '60s, and the taste he developed through Traffic. His 1981 solo album, *Arc Of A Diver*, effectively mixed these two elements of his musical personality in the three areas of songwriting, singing, and keyboard work. Better than most '60s veterans, Winwood has been able to move with the times; his effortless virtuosity as a synthesizer soloist makes him as much a voice for the '80s as his steaming organ licks enshrine him among the giants of the past.

Meanwhile, back in the States, Felix Cavaliere was contributing some memorable moments of his own on the Hammond. The frenzied performances of his band, the Young Rascals, were largely sparked by his organ work, which mixed solid rhythm with an unprecedented immensity of tone and volume. Cavaliere's gospel-tinged solo on "Good Lovin'" took Billy Preston's style a step further; though they shared a tendency to rely on dramatic registration rather than on melodic subtlety to make their points, Cavaliere moved beyond Preston's treble-heavy fills to evolve a wall-of-sound approach, in which he surrounded and smothered audiences with the rich roar of his B-3. He was one of the pioneers of the art of orchestral keyboard playing in rock. Under Cavaliere's hands, the Hammond transformed itself from just another solo instrument in the band to the fundamental power source, the critical element in a group's collective sound.

Mark Stein of Vanilla Fudge and other young organists would further develop this concept of enveloping the listener with the voice of the Hammond organ, but none would run as far with it as Lee Michaels. He was easily the most audacious of all the Romantics. No one else had the moxie to go onstage with no bass and no guitars; all Michaels needed was a drummer and a modified hot-rod Hammond A-100. He drove his organ like a sky jockey in a fighter jet, with dives and spirals that swooped as far as the machine would allow. He steamrolled the senses, always backing off the volume pedal just short of the breaking point, only to regroup his resources and plunge forward once again. Michaels took the Hammond as far as it could go in the Romantic realm. There was nothing left to say on the instrument after he had finished.

But there is one more name in this Romantic pantheon. Garth Hudson, the soft-spoken virtuoso behind the Band's best keyboard work, defies the Romantic stereotype through his disinterest in the conventions of the Hammond sound and style. He developed his unique rock organ conceptions in London, Ontario, Canada, where he was born on August 2, 1942. There he helped his father restore old organs, listened to the country stations on the radio, studied voice-leading and counterpoint in the music of Bach and the Anglican Church, and began playing accordion in a country band at the age of twelve. His shimmering tone blends, rolling rhythms, and pitch-bending tricks became familiar to thousands of Bob Dylan fans when Hudson and the rest of the Band backed the legendary singer on his 1965-'66 world concert tour. Though a brilliant soloist, Hudson worked most effectively in the background, making good songs sound great and breathing life into even mediocre material with his intriguing textures. In rock's pre-synthesizer era, Hudson stood alone as a master of electronic phrasing and orchestration.

They were a colorful crowd in their great days, the Rock Organ Romantics. Their fervent styles and investigations of timbre would leave a permanent mark on rock and roll. The stories of these five pacesetters add up to the story of this entire movement.

Bob Doerschuk

Booker T. Jones

"Green Onions" and Other Soul Spices

January, 1980 — *Although you are perhaps best known as a keyboard player, you can hold your own on a number of other instruments too. What, in fact, is your first instrument?*

Well, my very first instrument was the clarinet, which my parents bought for me when I was ten years old. I moved from that to oboe, and from that to saxophone. I went through all the saxophones, and I stayed on that through college. I was a general music major at Indiana University, which had a reputation for being an overall good music school. Mainly they had good theory, arranging, and composition, but I also took strings, percussion, woodwinds, composition. I took a little bit of everything, but I was a trombone major.

Did you take any keyboard instruction there?

You know, I think that the only thing I didn't take at Indiana was keyboard. I took theory, so it wasn't required.

What led you to pull out of a promising recording situation in order to go to college?

I was 16 years old when I went to Indiana, and it was when I was 16 that "Green Onions" went to the top, so I had to choose. Basically, I wanted to be an overall musician. I wanted to be able to stand in front of an orchestra, or a jazz band, or a combo, and know what was going on, be able to talk to anyone, to communicate my ideas, to be able to arrange and conduct. I wanted to be an arranger, mainly, and I felt that I had to do it then, because I couldn't see myself going back to school at 21.

It must not have been an easy decision.

It wasn't. It eventually caused a split between me and Stax. It was our first major argument.

The elegant Booker T. Jones at the piano, with a Hohner Clavinet resting on a Rhodes electric piano. "I've always been the little guy alone in the practice room, trying to learn this lick . . ."

They said, "How the hell are you gonna leave now? You're gonna make a million dollars, and you're gonna go to *college*?" And I said, "Yeah." And I did. They never forgave me for that. But if I hadn't done that, I wouldn't be able to communicate with an oboe player, I wouldn't be able to play the bass. I would have been limited to leading that group [the MGs].

When exactly did you start learning keyboards?

My second music teacher was a piano teacher. I studied with her for about six or eight months when I was a little kid; I was throwing papers to pay for it, so I must have been 12 or 13. She was a real finger-tapper; I mean, she would take that stick and tap my finger when I wasn't doing it right. She also had a Hammond B-3 organ in her dining room, and during my visits, I kept looking at it and looking at it, until finally I convinced her to teach me on both piano and organ.

Did you use the foot bass often onstage?

When I improvised with the MGs, I would play foot bass. Sometimes when I took solos, they would just let me go on my own; they'd walk off-stage! It started as a trick. They pulled that on me while I was holding a chord or something, so I just kept playing. It worked, and people liked it, so they kept doing it. Sometimes I would even go classical, kind of like Keith Jarrett, although this was way before Jarrett came along, but that was really the only time I ever used the foot bass in concerts.

When you actually started working professionally, did you feel most comfortable at the keyboard, or did you still think of yourself as a horn player who doubled on keyboards?

Well, my first studio job was playing baritone sax on a [singer] Rufus Thomas session, but my first professional live job was playing piano, so I felt comfortable both ways. I spent so much time practicing in the band room with horns and, at the same time, at home with the piano, that I really could go either way.

Did you listen mainly to horn players or to keyboard players as a kid in Memphis?

When I was a kid, the first record I bought was by [singer] Roy Hamilton, on Epic. It turned out to be mostly jazz I listened to in my teens, although I also enjoyed [country singer] Hank Williams. I listened a lot to Ray Charles, to the solos he played on that live album (*Ray Charles Live*), and to the way he played electric piano on his first records. I also went through a Jimmy Smith phase, even to the point of sometimes simulating in the studio his sound and his style.

The key to it was in the tremolo, the fingering, and the attitude—aggressive, real pushy. As far as the organ goes, though, my real inspiration was Jack McDuff. He was my man, if you want to know who was on top at the organ for me. When he came to Memphis I sat underneath his organ and I couldn't believe it. He came without a bass player, and he was all over those pedals. He really made sure that I was going to be an organ player.

How did the MGs get together?

Like I said earlier, I got that job at Stax playing baritone sax with Rufus and Carla [Thomas, singers], and then they found out I could play piano too, so I got another session on keyboard. Eventually I was doing a country session with Al Jackson. We were introduced to country music through Chips Moman, who was a partner with Jim Stewart and Estelle Axton, the onwers of Stax. Chips is famous now in Nashville as a record producer. Anyway, the other people he called for the date were Steve Cropper on guitar and Lewis Steinberg, a Jewish person of black descent, on bass.

The MGs sound like an odd lineup for a country session.

Well, for some reason, it just wasn't happening, so we started to jam. The thing we were playing was a blues, because that's what Steve loved and because Lewie was a big blues bass player around Memphis. Jim [Stewart] said, "Let's put it down," so we taped it, and it was "Behave Yourself." He said, "this would make a nice record," but we needed a B side. Steve and I had an idea, and it turned out to be "Green Onions."

So it was just knocked out at your first session, with no real rehearsal.

Right, and it was just a B side. They decided to call us Booker T. And The MGs, and the next day they took it to the radio station. Dick Cane at WLOK played the blues side, liked it okay, and then flipped it over. People started calling in then, saying they liked "Green Onions." It became a hit, and that started the whole thing.

In your subsequent work with the MGs and all the famous singers who recorded at Stax, did you have any idea of the impact you were making on the music scene?

We were so unaware of the way we were influencing the rest of the music world, because all we did was what we did. We were closed in, so we couldn't see the effect of it. We were very happy for a good while—I mean, really happy. We had a good time after I got back from college. We had Otis [Redding] by that time. We had Sam And Dave, we had Wilson Pickett, and we had Eddie Floyd, a lot of great singers. We had even a better time than we might have had otherwise, because I was able to write string tracks, so they didn't have to depend on other people for a lot of things. But in a way, it was like being enclosed in a shell. Bad feelings were still there because I had been gone for four years at Indiana. Maybe if I had been able to see how influential we were at the time, I wouldn't have been so anxious to break away.

Was the organ your main keyboard axe at that time?

At first it was organ and piano. The first few years I felt like I was a piano player, and the organ was a little toy I would slip in. Later, though, the organ became my major instrument. Since then, I've really been into organ in a lot of different ways. I even got into the German pipe organ and Bach in school. In my theory studies I spent a lot of time transcribing Bach fugues for the school symphonic band. It taught me a lot about arranging, but it also taught me all about organ fugues. Even listening to a Bach fugue gives you a ready-made theory lesson.

Even on the early Stax records you were experimenting with a wide variety of registrations on the Hammond too.

I did that a lot with the MGs, but I did have one basic sound, one basic setting that I usually started with. It worked off the drawbars. I generally would pull out the first four drawbars to start with, before I started playing, and then according to what was happening, I would move them in and out, maybe moving the second one in and bringing the others on more strongly. But I would usually start with that setting, unless I was going for a happier feeling. Then I'd push the second one in, and pull the next two and the very last drawbars out.

What electric pianos do you favor?

I love the Wurlitzer and the Rhodes. I pick one or the other depending on the song. The old Wurlitzer and the new one are different stories, you know. I recorded "Chinese Crackers" on an old Wurlitzer that I gave to [singer] William Bell. I was stupid. I gave it to him because he didn't have a piano, but I didn't know Wurlitzer was going to stop making those old models. He still has it down in his little studio in Atlanta.

When you record, do you work out your solo lines in advance, or do you improvise more or less freely?

Lately I have been working them out more, because I've found that I can make them more interesting that way. Usually I don't lay the solos out that much; I just put a little bit of thought into them before I do them. In the old days, like

with "Green Onions," it was totally spontaneous, but now records are a little more sophisticated and people don't want to be bored.

What was your toughest session as a backup keyboard player?

As far as the keyboard goes, my very first session in L.A., which was with [singer] Bobby Darin in 1965, was real hard for me, because it was mid-'60s pop music, "Mack The Knife" type of thing, which wasn't really jazz and wasn't quite rock either. It was at Sunset Sound, the studio I'm still working at. I was kind of nervous. I mean, here I was from Memphis, young, away from home. My sister even had to drive me there; I didn't have a driver's license. And there was the New York producer, the Hollywood musicians, the charts, and that's the way it was. The place was full of people: Ahmet Ertegun was producing, Darin was singing, there were two bass players and two guitar players—Al Jackson was playing guitar, Hal Blaine was on drums, the Blossoms were singing in the background, I was at the organ, some short guy was at the piano, and there were five trumpets and trombones. I was so proud. And when we left the studio, people were on the street with machine guns; it was the first day of the Watts riot! Martial law was declared the next morning. That was probably my most difficult session.

How do you assess your own keyboard technique?

It's not up to par, but I have more spontaneity in my playing now than I did before. I know more appropriate things to do, because I'm older. But the other things I'm doing in music are more important right now than having technique. I'm dealing more with the whole. I can hire guys with technique when that is what is required.

You've started playing again in public after a long absence. Are you excited about your return to the stage?

Yeah, I am. I feel like I never really knew how to perform before. I was too young the first time out to really know how to do it. I had the talent, but not the experience. Live performing is being into people, and I've always been the little guy alone in the practice room, trying to learn this lick or whatever, and it's just lately that I've been into people. And that's what live performing is— not necessarily making sure every note is right, but that every one is played for the people.
Bob Doerschuk

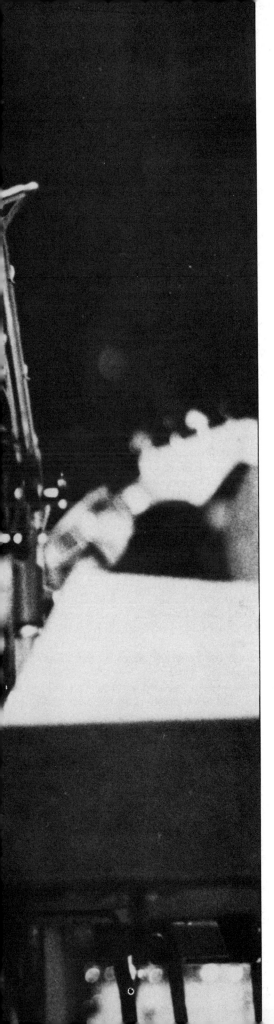

Steve Winwood
The Prodigy Prince of British R&B

June, 1981—*Why did you decide to do* Arc Of A Diver *by yourself? This was the first album you've ever done with no sidemen at all.*

That's right. The first one I didn't use an engineer on as well. It's something I've always wanted to do, but I'd never been able to. I always found it difficult. Also, I'd built this studio in my house that finally enabled me to do it myself. I don't think I would have been able to do it completely alone in a commercial studio.

Because of the costs?

Because of the costs and the pressure and everything. I've always enjoyed messing around with tape machines and overdubbing, but it's very difficult to do that if you're working with other people, because they need the patience of Job. If an artist is doing all the overdubbing, it's a long time before anybody who isn't directly involved can see that there's anything worthwhile happening. A producer is not going to sit around for three days with nothing happening, then suddenly wake up when it comes together on the third day and say, "Oh, yeah!" He's going to keep saying, "Why don't you do this? Why don't you do that?" That's why I prefer working totally alone if I'm going to overdub.

How many of the bass lines were done on bass guitar, and how many on keyboard?

It's keyboard on all of them, even the ones that sound like a bass guitar.

What instruments did you use for the bass?

I used a Multimoog, and I think I used a Minimoog on a couple of the cuts. My basic education on synths was with the Minimoog. It was one of the first mono synthesizers, and I got used to it. I did get the Multimoog, which I suppose is

Previous page: Steve Winwood and bassist Rick Gretsch in an old publicity photo for Ginger Baker's Air Force. Winwood made extensive use of the RMI electronic piano (pictured) and the Hammond C-3 during this period.

just an updated version of the Minimoog. It has more voices, and the triggering is not always from the same place; it goes up the keyboard. It has a ribbon instead of a pitch wheel too, but that was basically the only mono synth I used.

For solos as well as bass lines?

Yeah.

Were you trying to phrase the bass lines like a bass guitarist?

The answer is yes. Had there not been a synthesizer that sounded like a bass guitar, I would most certainly have played bass guitar. I wouldn't have been able to play the stuff I did on the album, but I certainly would have had a go at it. I did play bass guitar on some Traffic stuff, but I could never play it with the technique I know and understand on the keyboard.

To bend notes with a string-vibrato effect, did you prefer the Multimoog ribbon to the Minimoog wheel?

Yeah. I'd gotten used to the Minimoog technique, and going to the ribbon was a bit of a changeover, but now the ribbon feels a lot better, in fact, than the wheel. I only use Minimoogs for patching into sequencers now. I play very little on them now, because the Multimoog ribbon just seems so much better; when you let go, the pitch goes straight back to center without you having to push it back. It's a lot quicker.

Did you use a Multimoog for that solo with the hard-edged tone in "While You See A Chance?"

Right. I can't remember the wave shape. It was fairly square. But I did use a filter pedal to give it kind of a phased texture. I've found that synths can very easily lack natural sounds, so you need some kind of chorus effect to fatten the tone up and give it some life. Basically, a synth is not an actual instrument. It has sounds of other instruments. Even people like Klaus Schulze, who do abstract music, base their sounds on strings or voices, things you're familiar with.

Did Schulze, whom you worked with in Go, and other modular synthesists influence your work on this album?

Well, at first, yes, because I think they're fantastic and I love to listen to them, but secondly, no, because I don't know what the hell they're doing or how they do it. I think it's amazing that someone can take a Debussy piece and orchestrate it for the synthesizer. It's a fantastic achievement, but I don't use things like oscilloscopes and voice prints. To a certain extent I think you can't reproduce certain sounds so exactly unless you use that kind of equipment,

but I still go by ear.

One of your earliest synthesizer solos was on the title cut of The Low Spark Of High-Heeled Boys, *with that buzzy tone. Or was that a saxophone going through a fuzztone?*

Actually, it was an organ through a fuzzbox.

Fooled me twice!

Yes! But I think that was the idea. We had been looking for something like synths for a long time, I suppose. I wish they had been around ten years ago. I suppose they were, actually.

Now that they are around, do you find them effective as tools to bring out your musical ideas into sound?

Absolutely. In fact, I find that I'm able to do things that I otherwise might not have been able to do. I've always made vague attempts to produce different sounds on instruments, like you mentioned on the *Low Spark* album. I've even tried to do that on instruments I can't play! There's one track on that album, in fact, where I played sax with Wood, and I've never ever played saxophone in my life!

Which track was that?

"Rock & Roll Stew." I played a line where I just stayed on one note. I just found it, and then Chris and I played the line: *bupbupbup,* or whatever it was [*laughs*]. I'm still trying to find simple music where I can do things like that. I mean, I can't play the drums, but I was able to make it sound like I could by writing the drum parts on *Arc Of A Diver* within my limitation on the instrument.

You also used rhythm boxes on that album, didn't you?

Not on every track, and even when I did use a Roland CR-78 I overdubbed drums on it. On one track I used the sequencer, and on another I used a tambourine loop.

How has your synthesizer work affected your keyboard chops?

In some ways it's simplified them, but it's also become necessary for me to learn different licks. I've had to get used to one-handed playing, for instance, and to the fact there's a totally different touch technique, not only with regard to mono synths, but to poly synths as well. I used the Yamaha CS-80, which demands a completely different approach than the Prophet or Polymoog. It's amazing that you just lean on the notes and you get some other sound or effect. I mean, playing notes and then leaning on them is a kind of technique you don't traditionally use for keyboard. You can also play a chord and bring out certain parts of it by leaning on one note.

Winwood in his studio at home, playing a Yamaha CS-80. In the background: a Hammond B-3, a Mini-moog, and a Linn LM-1 drum computer.

Did you use the CS-80 for many of the violin sounds on Arc Of A Diver?

Yes, quite a few of them. I used the Prophet as well.

What do you see as the real challenge of producing quality rock and roll?

Well, I know this is a musician's magazine, but I personally have an ultimate faith in the listening public. That's not to say that I'll do anything as long as people say it's good, but I think I'm saying that people who aren't musicians somehow know instinctively what is good music. I think it's wrong when music, or any kind of art for that matter, gets so complicated that it becomes a plaything of some elite intelligentsia. Music is a very natural thing that's inside everybody; it just happens to be something that some people are able to make and some people aren't, but that's only a question of organizing sound.

So if one of your records never made it into

the charts, would that affect your own feelings about it?

Let me put it this way. If only musicians came up to me and said, "Your album is great," and other people didn't say anything, I would probably think something was wrong. It would make me reassess my situation.

When you listen to your old records, do you hear any major changes in your keyboard style?

Strangely enough, I think I've changed the least in my keyboard playing. There are changes in the way I sing, the way I write, and the way I produce, but my organ playing sounds very similar to the stuff I was doing ten or fifteen years ago. Obviously I can hear a development in my keyboard playing. I'll play a piano solo or an organ solo on an old record, and I'll realize that I was hung up on something then which I'm not hung up on now. But it's hard to pinpoint exactly what it is that has changed. I'd like to think that

Steve Winwood on the Minimoog. "Given a choice,
I'd rather be a synth player than a piano player.
My piano technique was never what I would have
liked it to be."

now I have more awareness of doing things more tastefully.

And of course you've got more instruments to develop on.

Right. I've got the same full-sized Steinway concert grand I had ten years ago; I bought it as an investment, and it seems to have paid off. I recently bought a Jupiter-4 from Buzz Music, which is quite a big keyboard store in London. That's a fantastic instrument. It has a bend lever I like, which you can use to determine how much bend you've got on the tone, and to bend either way. But I didn't use it on *Arc Of A Diver;* I've only gotten it since I finished the album. I also got a Roland CQ-100 sequencer at the same time, and a Sequential Circuits sequencer. I used to have a Rhodes electric piano, but I sold it.

Are you using the same organ you had back in the '60s?

Yeah. In fact I'm using the same C-3 I brought over with me on my first trip to the States in 1969. It's not in very good shape. It's held together with gaffer tape [*laughs*]. I've got a B-3 as well, which I've boarded for some time in L.A.

Didn't you used to have an RMI electric piano too?

That's right. I had an RMI for a long time. It was great, but to a certain extent the touch was too organ-like for me. There was no touch sensitivity, and it was a bit light. It tends to sound like a rather limited organ. Another thing I've had for a long time is the Wurlitzer electric piano. It has a distinctive, lovely sound. I've just recently started to play it a bit more. It had been stuck in the corner for years, but I needed to get a piano upstairs, so I brought it out again, and now I've gotten used to writing and messing around on it.

Have you kept up your piano playing while acquiring all your electronic hardware?

Yeah, I did. I play the piano a fair amount. I haven't consciously said, "Well, I must keep playing the piano or I'll forget how," because given the choice, I'd rather be a synth player than a piano player. My piano technique was never what I would have liked it to be. In certain cases I've been unable to achieve what I might have liked, but still, I love playing the piano.

If you come across a new keyboard instrument you like, does that affect the way you compose? Do you write songs with a particular instrument in mind?

No, I don't. I try not to be taken by certain instruments, although there again I don't like formulas or rules. On some occasions it might happen that I would record a keyboard and then put some vocal line over it that sounds good, so in that respect, yes, but I don't think generally that a certain kind of keyboard will affect the way my songs come out. And for that reason I try to write on different instruments, on guitar, on keyboards, even drums. I sometimes write with no instrument at all. Writing all the time on keyboards can get you imprisoned into doing certain changes naturally, although maybe that's because my piano technique isn't as varied as I would like it to be.

Do you have any impressions of what the differences are between rock audiences of today and those you encountered 15 years ago?

Well, it's been so long since I've played in front of an audience that I really don't know yet, but basically I would say that not a lot seems to have changed, except that the standards have risen. You have to work harder. I'm sure that you can get away with less now than you could back then.

In terms of musicianship?

Musicianship, showmanship, everything. You have to work. Equipment has gotten better, which probably cancels out that first difference. Basically, rock is an entertainment medium anyway. I know lots of artists I talk to think that "entertainment" is a dirty word, but basically that's what I do, and that's what people who perform do. *That* hasn't changed.

Bob Doerschuk

Felix Cavaliere
Blowing Hard, Blowing Fast

October, 1983—Perhaps more than any other keyboardist from the mid-'60s, you can take credit for popularizing the Hammond sound in rock. There weren't many organs being prominently used in the music back then.

We were the first ones to use a B-3 in a pop group. When I worked with Joey Dee And The Starlighters, I played a Lowrey. As a matter of fact, they used it for both the bass lines and the top, the way we [the Rascals] ended up using it too. But I found the Hammond to be a far superior instrument. I was turned on to it at a black club in New Rochelle, New York, where I heard my first jazz organ trio. I just went into bliss! I couldn't believe what I was hearing from just three guys—drums, organ, and sax. I had to play that instrument. That really was a major turning point in my life.

You played piano up to that point?

Oh, yes. I took lessons for eight years, and I was pretty good. I didn't have the feel for classical music, though, because my creative urges made me want to change it, and my teachers wanted me to play it as it was written, so I ran into some real static. But even though that caused me a lot of problems, I'm glad I had the lessons. I feel sorry for people who don't have the proper training technically.

Do you think that playing rock and roll had a harmful effect on your technique?

Absolutely. It hurt me. I was a lot better when I was younger. Most of the people doing sessions in the '60s were rebelling against written music. They were trying to come up with excitement in the studio rather than a programmed arrangement, so, at least in my case, the written note

Previous page: Felix Cavaliere at the Hammond
B-3, which he used extensively with The Rascals.
Cavaliere popularized the organ sound for
rock music in the mid-60s.

became less used, except when we would be
working with additional instruments like horns
and strings. That made me slip away a little bit.

*What is it that attracted you toward playing
the organ, then?*

Well, it was so much easier. You could fly
across the organ keyboard. I just found this kind
of peace with the instrument. It was like the
whole thing was there. I used to hang around
Macy's in New York and go into their organ
showroom. The salesman knew I couldn't afford
anything—I was about three feet tall at the
time—but I was totally enamored of this instrument, so he'd let me fool around with it. I kind of
abandoned the piano for a while. For a long time
I didn't play it as much as I'd have liked, except
when we were recording.

What model organ did you first get?

I think I started with an M-model Hammond.
It wasn't the one I wanted, but it was a question
of expense; that was the only one I could afford
at the time. My first professional experience with
an organ was with the Lowery that Joey Dee had.
I never really cared for it, but it fit his music and
his sound. I was the third organist to join that
group; I came along after they had really had
their success.

*Were you listening to any particular organists
at that time for insights into how to use the
instrument?*

Mostly I listened to the jazz guys. Of course
the first organ player I tried to emulate was
Jimmy Smith. I couldn't believe the sound he
could get out of that instrument. I also dug
Jimmy McGriff, even though he really played
with just one setting. Shirley Scott was good, and
Jack McDuff. The rock people, with the exception of Brian Auger, were not really experimenting with it. Some of them got a little crazy with
the electronics of it, like when the Cream and
other groups started phasing Leslie speakers. I
didn't care much for that.

What is the ideal Hammond sound for you?

If I can get the whole spectrum of sound from
the depth of the bass all the way to the top percussion, that's the one. A lot of times with Hammonds I've found that the bottom kind of dies
off. I can never get an explanation why it does
from any of the technicians, but it just fades and
loses its punch, and the top end is either too
sweet or a little distorted. I don't like it too distorted; I want to be able to put the distortion in
myself if I want it.

*Your sound was seldom distorted, but you
really went for massive tone, much bigger than*

*anything else that was happening in rock when
the Rascals came along.*

For a while there I really did believe that the
power of that instrument was unique. I don't
know where my head was at the time, but I
wanted to encompass the rooms we played in
with its sustained sound. If I held down notes at
certain frequencies and volumes, it seemed to
grab the audience subconsciously and hold them.
When I released the notes the people would go
back to doing whatever they had been doing
before. I didn't play the Jimmy Smith style at all
onstage. He used the B-3 as a solo instrument,
with rhythm accompaniment. I used it more or
less in the way they use synthesizers today, like
string and horn sections. I don't know, we might
have gotten a little carried away with that, but we
never became a Blue Cheer type band.

*What kind of drawbar registration did you
favor?*

I don't remember exactly how I learned about
the drawbars—maybe someone showed me how
to use them, or maybe I used a book or something—but I found myself using a few more or
less standard settings as starting points many
times. The sound I liked best was the Jimmy
Smith sound, with the first three drawbars out
and the last one in percussion, but it was a problem cutting through the band with that one.

*That setting didn't seem to show up much on
your older records.*

Well, we tried to put it on there. We did on a
lot of songs, but it just wasn't powerful enough
when the other instruments were playing loud.
For sweet sounds I would make a concave circle,
with the middle drawbars pushed in. And I had a
trick of manipulating the drawbars to the rhythm.
I would take about four or five of them in my
fingers and flex them in and out to the beat. I
usually did that live; it was so subtle that it didn't
come off on record. I was able to manipulate the
settings and get what I thought were some pretty
interesting sounds from it, but I was only scratch-
ing the surface.

*Frequently you coincided your drawbar
adjustments with growling clusters that crawled
up out of the Hammond's low register. Did
you move the drawbars with your right hand
while playing the smears with your left?*

I did it the opposite way. I used my left hand
on the drawbars, and my right hand to play the
chords, especially if it was at a place where I
could sustain the bass note and not have to worry
about too much movement. That was a tremendous effect. It created another motion in the

room, like a wave.

And you timed it with an accelerating Leslie tremolo too.

That's right. It all worked together, if I was using my own equipment. If I was on the road and renting other people's equipment, I'd have very serious problems, because the timing would be completely off. I took that effect from Jimmy Smith's *Who's Afraid Of Virginia Woolf?* album. He did the same thing, much more subtly than I. He created a rising crescendo sound pattern that was tonal, by just putting his hands on the keys and moving up. I magnified that to the '60s level of monster sound, and I think my way of doing it had a very strong effect on the music of the Beatles.

How so?

Well, all of us were very aware of each other in those days. We took plenty from the Beatles, and I'm proud to say that they took something from us. We were working in a club in London, and Paul (McCartney) came down to see us. It was a small room, and in that kind of a place, a Hammond organ with two Leslie speakers and full reverb is quite an experience. You can't get away from it. It fills every corner, because the sound from the Leslie isn't straight; it's *around.* At the end of our set we played this jazz/rock number called "Cute," and at the end I did this effect, going from the complete bottom of the second manual to the midpoint and all the way up to infinity. I remember that Paul was very taken aback by that. He felt it. The next time they put out an album, it was *Sgt. Pepper,* and they did the same thing, using a whole orchestra [in "A Day In The Life"]. He took it another step. From Smith to Cavaliere to McCartney; that's how that one went. Where Smith got it from I have yet to find out.

You played bass pedals with the Rascals in lieu of having a bass guitarist. Was it hard for you to master pedal technique?

No, it really wasn't. Someone told me it's like learning to walk or ride a bicycle. There's a little stiffness for a while, then all of a sudden it comes along naturally. I would say that within three weeks I was able to develop the coordination I needed to do it.

Why didn't the band include a bass player?

Because I never learned to play Hammond organ *without* playing the bass. In my opinion, if you want to play an organ without playing the pedals, you should use a different organ, because the Hammond is just not made to be played only on the manuals. If the pedals are not attached, I

feel very uncomfortable even sitting at the instrument. I feel off-balance; I don't know how I'm supposed to play. It's like wearing long pants instead of short pants as a kid. Somehow it just doesn't feel right.

Did you ever run the whole Hammond through straight speakers?

We tried that, but I really didn't like it. The Hammond and the Leslie just go together very well. I did like to take the tremolo completely off the Leslie so the horns didn't move at all, though. I had a switch built into my foot pedal that would bring the rotating horns to a quick halt.

Rather than the gradual slowdown you usually hear on Leslies.

Right. We used it in all kinds of ways. I liked to kick it in right at the end of a big crescendo. It was a lot of fun in the beginning, then after a while it took a back seat to some things we were trying on other keyboards that were coming along, like the Rhodes and Wurlitzer electric pianos. I was one of the first people to realize that those little toys that were being hooked up to guitars—phasers, wah-wahs, and things like that—could also work on keyboards. These guitar tricks were a lot simpler to use on the new keyboards than on the Hammond. I had always wanted to wire those effects into the Hammond somehow, but we never quite got that together.

Did you get into an extensive multi-keyboard setup with the Rascals?

Compared to what you see today, no, but I was trying a few things out. The first addition I made was a [Hohner] Clavinet, which I put on top of the organ. It helped me out a lot. Next came the RMI electric piano, which was good for certain bell-like sounds. After that I tried the Rhodes, but I found it to be too frustrating. If I had been able to work on it and get it to sound the way you hear them today, I would have been happier with it.

Why didn't you add more keyboards to your collection?

The problem was that I was locked to the organ because of the bass. I couldn't expand too much because I had to keep my foot on the pedals. Eventually I came across a keyboard bass unit that you could play with your left hand, but the group split up too soon after that for me to really get free with it. So my whole time with the Rascals I was stuck in one position; I could only sit, and every now and then turn just a little ways.

You didn't have any synthesizers?

I had an ARP 2600, but there were maybe two or three effects I was able to program with it, and that was it. I used it mostly for solos or effects. We had another keyboard in those days, an Ondioline, which we used on one of our earlier records, "Lonely Too Long." I often felt frustrated because I couldn't bend notes on the keyboards I had, or kick the tunings down to semitones. I did what I could with what I had. In those days we used a little spring unit for reverb, and I would get explosions by tapping it with my feet. I would also turn the organ off while holding a note down, and let it drift out of pitch. Most of my effects came from the organ. I had owned it much longer than the other instruments, so I really learned about it top to bottom. The Hammond was a special, special instrument to me.

Atlantic Records was mainly putting out records by black jazz or R&B artists at that time.

We were the first white act on their red and black label, yes.

And the Rascals were being hyped a lot as a "blue-eyed soul" band. You even opened a concert for James Brown once at Madison Square Garden. Did that gig and the expectations of the audiences make you nervous at all?

We were nervous only in the sense that we weren't prepared for it. That gig was sort of a surprise to us. In those days music business managers worked kind of like baseball clubs trading players back and forth. Free agency among musicians didn't really mean anything then. If your manager and the other fellow's manager got together and made some kind of a deal, the act only found out about it later. That's how the James Brown thing happened. I tell you, we were frightened that night. We were just four little white guys who probably weighed 400 pounds total. But we did okay. Everyone got into it after a while. Another night I'll never forget was a benefit concert we played for Martin Luther King at Madison Square Garden. Again, we were the only white act on the bill, but that kind of cross-over was more established by then. What a great night. Aretha Franklin was there, the King Curtis band was there. And we had to follow Sam And Dave—oh, my God! They took the whole show. Even Aretha couldn't touch 'em that night. But everybody dug it, man. They knew we were trying our best, and we were doing okay, there was no doubt about that. They knew we weren't jive. There was a respect for us that I could feel. I mean, even now I feel more recognition in black communities than I do in white communities. In the white communities I'm old-fashioned, an old-timer, now. The black communities are more loyal.

Do you feel that avenues of communication between the black and white musical communities are more open or more closed now than they were in those days?

I tell you, I'm very confused and concerned with the situation today. It's gone backwards. Both at the radio station and the record company, there is a definite segregation. The blacks have their department, and the whites have theirs. There's no co-mingling, and that's crazy! I don't understand it at all! For example, there's an AOR (album-oriented rock) radio station in my area that is probably the number two or three station in Connecticut. The program director is a very good friend of mine. He calls me up from time to time, and we chat. I asked him if he had heard the new Marvin Gaye single, which had reached number one on the charts. And he hadn't heard it! The number one record, by a guy who's a legend. I just cannot figure it out.

During the Rascals' last years, after you had switched labels from Atlantic to Columbia, the band began bringing some of the top black jazz artists into its sessions. That was a pretty daring move in those days, since so few of our fans had ever heard of people like bassist Ron Carter.

That's true, although when we hired Ron Carter I was so in awe that I couldn't even play. He had to put me at ease; otherwise we would never have gotten out of there. But the public still doesn't understand. Most of them have never been exposed to these people the way we were, or the way I was early in my life. For some reason these people's names were more important then than they are today. When you mentioned a name like Miles Davis, you knew that he was the best at what he did, even if they don't sell that many albums. But that respect is gone, even in the musicians' eyes. Nowadays they look at the bands with the big sales figures—the Bostons, the Foreigners—with the same awe that we felt for the people who were doing new things in music. It's not their fault; it's a question of who gets most of the press and the exposure.

By the time the Rascals split up in '72, as you were getting ready to cut your solo albums, the organ was pretty much a thing of the past for you.

That's right. I tried writing at the Hammond at home, but I found that it made it hard for me to adapt to modern rhythms. I'd play the same rhythms I had always played on the organ in the past, because I was locked into them by the bass. Also, you just didn't hear many organ solos by then. The synthesizer was becoming the main keyboard instrument, and I find it very difficult to sit in a studio and play a basic track on a synthesizer. I use them on overdubs; I prefer having full command of the whole 88 piano on the basic track. People do know me, to a degree, as a keyboard player, but if some dynamite keyboard soloist is available to play on my record, I'll give it to him. I don't feel like I've got to play every darn note.

Do you think that the synthesizer knocked the Hammond out of fashion in rock and roll?

I think the guitar displaced it even before that. The guitar took over completely, and there was a big lapse in keyboard work. The fact that you could bend the strings, and the cutting edge you could get from a guitar tone, gave it a strength the organ just didn't have. The weight of the Hammond was a problem too; that turned a lot of people off, because it was so bulky and hard to move. But the keyboard sound is what's happening now.

What are your thoughts on the current electro-pop synthesizer style?

It's very interesting. We're all products of our times, and since the beginning of time music has always reflected what's happening. The music I hear from these English synthesizer bands is a perfect representation of what's happening over there. There's a tremendous depression in England, a tremendous lack of hope for the future. The last time I was in England, I kept thinking of *A Clockwork Orange.* That's where a lot of people are at. They feel like, "Hey! We've got no money, we've got no jobs, the bomb isn't even three hours away, so screw it! The hell with it!" Bands like the Police are an exception to this, but in most English music you don't hear any of the joy that you hear in the gospel churches over here. It's missing in a lot of American music too. I don't even hear it on the R&B stations. They're just trying to *lull* you into some kind of rhythmic pattern. But we've already been through this in my lifetime. Since music began there have been periods where nothing is happening, then all of a sudden something starts to drift through. I think some of that is starting to happen now. I don't know if it's quite hit the scene yet, but there's a little bit of disco, made a little more melodic and palatable, with some of the hardness from the anti-emotional music coming into it.

Is there talk of a Rascals reunion?

There's always talk. In one way it's flattering, and in another way it's very annoying to me.

Why?

It's just that I would rather not do it. Dino [Danelli, drummer] is really the only member of the group I would still like to work with. I feel as inspired in his musical presence as I did then. Unfortunately, I just don't feel that same spark of enthusiasm with the other fellows. I was always the experimental party in the group. I always wanted to try new things, and to go for new sounds, new equipment, new beats. It's still like that now. The people didn't want to go where I wanted to take them, and that was twelve years ago.

Are the other guys interested in getting the Rascals back together?

Yes, but for reasons that are a little embarrassing. They're more financially motivated, and that puts a tremendous burden on me, because I have to say no to people I know very well. Every time we start talking about the subject, somebody says, "Well, this is worth a lot of money," and it gets kind of like that's the most important part of it. We've been approached with the idea of going back and cleaning up these tapes of us playing at the Barge [in Long Island]; that was our first attempt at recording for Atlantic. The bass was a problem because we just couldn't get the separation it needed from the rest of the sounds in the band, but we may go back and overdub a bass part and somehow release it in conjunction with a video. The idea is to not make a real big deal out of it, maybe just rent a hall for a party with some friends or old fans, and record it for posterity.

How do you feel about the fact that you may always be mainly remembered for your solo in "Good Lovin'," even after all the projects you've been involved with since then?

As far as I'm concerned, it's an honor to be remembered for anything in musical history. If you have any part in that big picture, you're joining some heavy company. It doesn't matter whether it's a solo or a song or whatever; I've always wanted my music to live after me, even if for only one solo. The trouble comes where people are exposed to the luxuries of fame and fortune. That's not what's important. What did you contribute? *That's* the important thing. Without that, it just stops cold.

Bob Doerschuk

Lee Michaels
Sensory Overkill

Keyboards were a rare enough feature in rock bands when you began giving concerts as half of an organ-and-drum duo. What led you to attempt such a radical experiment?

Money. Around '64 or '65 we'd go to little bars that would hire bands for a hundred a night, and we'd offer to play for fifty because there were only two of us. Later, when we made my first album [*Carnival Of Life*], I started working mainly as a stand-up singer. I wrote all the songs, played all the organ solos and the harpsichord stuff, and showed our organ player, Gary Davis, a lot of the organ parts, but Gary played all the background keyboard things. We did that album, mixing and everything, in five days—three days recording, two days mixing. We sounded exactly like the album onstage; the only overdubs were the solos.

How did that band devolve from five pieces to two?

It happened at the Avalon Ballroom in San Francisco, where we were doing two shows a night. [LSD pioneer] Augustus Owsley came in and gave me some really great acid, and I was totally out of my mind. We were doing our first song, and I was running around with my microphone, when I looked up at the light show on the wall and I thought, "What am I doing being a stand-up singer? I'm an organ player! How did I ever get this messed up?"

Why had you become a stand-up singer?

My organ had gotten repossessed right about when I was starting this band, so I had to hire an organ player [*laughs*]. But anyway, I left the stage in the middle of the first song, went into the dressing room, sat in the corner, and started cry-

Previous page: Lee Michaels. "I listened to all the guitar players turning their amps up and said to myself, 'Wow! I wonder what would happen if I turned my organ way up?'"

ing. The guys came in and said, "Don't worry, you'll come down in a little while." A couple of hours later I felt basically the same, and they said, "You've got to do something. You missed the first show." I was so loaded, I said, "The only thing I can possibly do is go out with just the drummer and play some organ." The whole band is there, five guys ready to go on, and I told them that just the drummer and I were going out. I was really bombed. I could barely see the organ, but when we started playing, it was the best. I could hardly believe how good it felt. So in between shows we instantly changed the whole format, and from that night it started clicking.

Was it hard to find work with that sort of lineup?

I remember going a year trying to get gigs. My manager would call people up. They'd say, "How many guitars in the band?" "No guitars. Just drums and organ." "No way. We've got to have some guitars. This is rock and roll!" All the keyboard players working those days were in guitar-based bands. Even keyboard players who were lead singers were in guitar-based bands, even if they were really good on the keyboard. It was really a hassle. Even the crummiest places hiring the crummiest bands wouldn't hire us. I went for almost a year without one gig until, finally, this one promoter decided we were great and put us on a bunch of shows.

With no other keyboardists doing what you were doing, who did you listen to for ideas?

I listened to all the guitar players. That's how I got into the big power setup. I'd go see the Cream or Hendrix, all those early bands who were doing real loud guitar things, and I'd say, "Wow, listen to these guys, man! They're turning their amps way up! I wonder what would happen if I turned my organ way up?" Fender had given me eight Showman amps and a bunch of other equipment when I had my four-piece band, and I had two Super Beatle amps, so one day after I had fired my band I was down at A&M Records with all these amps, and I got this idea. I said, "I wonder what would happen if I hooked up all these amps to my organ?" So I did, and it was the most tremendous thing I'd ever heard! Everything was mismatched, but it was a huge sound! I started getting into turning everything up until it was roaring like guitar bands roared. I figured that if Blue Cheer could do it, I could plug in twice as many amps to my organ, so people would *have* to listen to it. I would force them to hear keyboards like they'd never been heard before. That was the only way to do it, because I was opening shows at big concerts, and you know how that is—everybody's just coming in

from getting their popcorn, finding their seats, talking to their friends. My only chance was to play so loud that conversation was impossible. If you were in the building, you either listened to us or put your fingers in your ears, because there was no way you could ignore us. We literally plowed our way through the barriers they put in front of keyboard players.

There really was nothing quite like it in rock and roll.

"Big-time wrestling on the drums and organ." That's what Frosty [drummer Bartholemew Smith-Frost] and I used to call it when we were working together. It was like a lot of explosions. See, everybody was just holding chords on organs in those days. There wasn't much rhythmic playing, so I was trying to run the Hammond volume pedal real hard to capitalize on that built-in gargantuan monster organ sound. I still like to play real loud, but it's a different kind of loud now. Synthesizers don't have that Hammond growl.

Do you still play the organ?

No. I haven't used a Hammond in ten years, except for one or two little things. The Hammond was great in the old days, but what else was there? You had the Rhodes and the Wurlitzer electric pianos, so it was the best alternative. The choices are huge now. I've played some little things that are supposed to sound like Hammond organs, and they do. I got rid of my Hammond last April [1983], the same one I had all those years. It just became so impractical. I don't think I'll ever own another one.

Your organ bass lines were quite solid. How did you develop your pedal technique?

I didn't use pedals. I used my left hand. That's why I had Keyboard Products put a Hammond BC generator into an A model cabinet for me; it runs the organ an octave lower. If you pull out the lowest drawbar on a B-3, you'll hear that the last two octaves are identical. The BC generator runs the lowest octave all the way down. That's why I used to get such tremendous bass out of the organ.

How did you get your bass guitar-like attack?

Keyboard Products put percussion on both manuals for me. The drawbars are all harmonics, but I'd only engage the percussion on the first and third drawbars while keeping all three pulled out for the bass on the lower keyboard. Later I started adding a little high with the fourth drawbar.

What kind of registration did you use on the upper manual?

I generally used only two tones. I had a full setting with all the drawbars out, and I had a setting with the first four out and the last one about three-quarters of the way out with some percussion on the high harmonic. Those are the only two tones I ever used.

Did you take piano lessons as a kid?

I didn't start playing piano until I was a sophomore in high school, but I played accordion when I was seven, and that's how I got all my basics together. The neighbor kid had an accordion, and I was so infatuated by this thing that I got one. I even was in a band with it in fourth grade. Get this, man, my first keyboard-drum band! You'll love this! There were three of us: One guy had a pair of drumsticks and a breadbox, the other guy had something else he beat on, and I had an accordion. We went down to a Mexican theater in Indio down by Palm Springs, where I was living, and asked if we could play between shows. The guy thought we were so out of it that he gave us a job. For a dollar apiece, we'd play between the movies. My mother still has my first dollar; it's her prized possession. I was one of those little kids who plays accordion every second. I mean, I played it nonstop for about four or five years until I found out how lame it was. I didn't play music after that until high school because for some reason I was all hung up with wanting to play sports, even though I was the world's worst athlete. It didn't take long to find out that I really wanted to play music.

How did you familiarize yourself with synthesizer?

I bought an ARP 2600 when they first came out. I used it on some of the old albums. There are some French horn parts and some lines that really sound like a Fender bass that I did on the 2600. But it took two hours to get a sound out of it. I'd have to sit there screwing around with it until I was about to go crazy. I never could zone in on the 2600, but the Polymoog I had was neat for the time. It was a real playable axe, rather than just an effects instrument. That's my biggest complaint about synthesizers; you have to have all these different models, one for each effect you want. It seems like everybody has five or six of them, and none is a main axe. The [Yamaha] CS-80 came close. I liked the overall tone of the Polymoog better, but the CS-80 was so well laid out. In terms of making adjustments, the Polymoog was a nightmare to deal with; all the little sliders were too sensitive.

How do your old Hammond records sound to you now?

The old songs don't do nothing for me. I can't listen to my old records. I actually hate them! I hated each one by the time I was finishing them up. By the time every one of those albums was in the stores, I loathed them! It's nice for nostalgia if somebody wants to drag his old lady out and say, "Remember that song from the first time we took acid?" But how many times can you sing "Hidey-Hi"? I do a couple of the old songs live just to keep everybody off my back. You'd be surprised how many promoters insist I do these old songs. This one guy said to me the other day, "Lee, why should I book you if you're not going to do any of your old hits?" Well, what can I say to this guy? Some of these people used to go to my shows when they were younger, so they have this thing: "Well, I'll book Lee Michaels, and he'll come to play 'Hidey-Hi'." What they're really saying to me is, "I'm interested in you because of what you did then, not because of what you are now, because you're nothing now." I can't accept that! Maybe it works in pop music, but I still consider myself a rock player, not a pop musician.

What is the essential difference between the two?

The absolute dividing line between rock bands and pop bands is contempt. Contempt is the common denominator in rock; it is now, and it always has been. The second that a band loses it, it becomes a pop band. The guys in pop bands would never utter a negative word. The lyrics, the music, everything is very careful. If there is any anger, they won't show it to you. To me that's what pop is all about.

So part of your return to music involves bringing that aspect out in your personality, which is hard to do with old boring songs you've done a million times.

That's right. I'm full of contempt as a person, you know. It's not like I feel like spitting on everybody, but I just have sort of a contempt for things.

Is there a danger that young audiences won't be interested in your work because you're older than they are?

I really haven't thought about that, but you're probably right. If I was 19 and some 37-year-old guy showed up onstage, I might think, "What is that old fuck doing here?" But the audiences that go to rock shows in LA are really your classic rock audiences. They seem pretty much like the audiences from the old days. They still come for a certain catharsis, so I don't know if they'll be expecting anything that different from what I can play for them.

And you won't be giving them some tightly-controlled evening of pop tunes, will you?

There's no control like out of control. That sums it all up for me—turn it up to ten and stand back, you know?

Bob Doerschuk

Garth Hudson

Tone Color Artistry with the Band

December, 1983—*Since your work with the Band reflects so many diverse influences, what kind of music were you specializing in when you first began working with bands back in Canada?*

I did both rock and jazz when I started, playing piano and saxophone. I played in a little rock group, the Capers, and I also played piano with big bands in the '50s, some very good bands around London, Ontario. We did all the old charts. I saw 'em all, from "In The Mood" to "Paradiddle Joe."

I don't remember "Paradiddle Joe."

Not many people do, but the members of Johnny Downes' band will [*laughs*].

You were also playing organ back then, weren't you? In fact, you and your father would restore old organs together.

My dad bought a reed pump organ and began fixing it, then I began to get into it and repair things. All these little wooden parts were always breaking, and the reeds needed cleaning. When you buy an antique like that, you find that there'll always be dirt in the reeds, so you have to go through and clean all of them to begin with. Then you wait till one stops sounding, go in, pull that one, clean it out, and so on. They need repair constantly.

Were those organs the first keyboards you had ever played?

No, I started with piano and accordion. My mother had an accordion.

What kind of lessons did you receive as a child?

I took private lessons in theory, harmony, and counterpoint with Thomas Chattoe, composition with John Cooke, and piano with Clifford Von

Previous page: Garth Hudson, mondo-guru of The Band, playing the Yamaha CS-80 with a Rhodes Chroma in the background.

Custer. I can still recommend certain exercise books to young keyboard players. I would recommend reading a Bach chorale every other day, and continuing on to improvise to maintain an awareness of four-part voice leading. I'm continuing to devise my own exercises, a whole study in illegitimate techniques, techniques that are not taught.

Can you share some of them with us?

Not yet. It can't be put into any form now, but I've made notes with the idea of passing it along someday. If it can't be passed along, it's worthless.

What kind of techniques did you develop beyond your classical lessons that later served as foundation for your rock style?

I watched a tabla player, which made me begin to think about other ways of developing dexterity. The tabla technique does help in loosening the hands. Also, one should think about separating the hand into two or three areas. One exercise that helps do this on the keyboard is to play for half an hour using just two fingers, then play for ten minutes using the thumb in the left hand only.

Which keyboard did you feel most at home on in the early days?

Piano, of course.

What were your first electric keyboards?

I played a Minshall organ. I worked for the Minshall electronic organ company—in Canada, it was a branch of Minshall/Esty from Brattleboro, Vermont. I did everything with them. I worked in the factory, and I demonstrated their instruments at fairs and at churches.

When you played the Lowrey with the Band, you often seemed to be using a theatre organ, tremulant-type vibrato.

Well, every maker—Thomas, Lowrey, Gulbransen, Baldwin—made some attempt to put in a moderately priced Doppler effect, which was a kind of Leslie sound that was similar to the wide vibrato of the Tibias, but at that time I wasn't really looking for a theatre organ sound at all. There were other organs that got that sound — Gulbransen, I thought, did it very well. But the Lowrey had enough bite, and I could make it distort enough, to fit in with what we were doing. The early Lowries had a nice little growl. I began with a Lowrey Festival, which had something like ninety or a hundred tubes in it, and that gave it a great distorted sound when you turned everything up.

Do you still have your old Lowrey at home?

Yes, I still have the Festival, and I got another Lowrey that was new in 1974.

Have you done many modifications to them?

Yes, we did do some things to them, along with Ed Anderson, who was our technical person for years on the road. We also kept in touch with Alberto Kniepkamp at CMI, the Chicago Musical Instrument company, which became Norlin. He's a brilliant technician and designer. We'd talk to him a lot on the telephone, and he'd send us extra parts and so on. One thing we did was to modify the pitch-bend so it began a semitone lower than on the factory preset. There was a little switch on the left side of the volume pedal, and when you pressed it and released it, that allowed the pitch to fall and return to normal. On the original Festival they had an automatic preset rate at which you would return to normal pitch, but there was also a switch where you could vary the rate of return by moving your foot carefully to the right. The return to pitch rate was either factory preset, or based on the speed at which you moved your foot back and let the spring-loaded switch return to normal.

And that's how you did the pitch-bending that so many people associate with your organ style?

Well, Lowrey always had that feature. It worked best on string sounds. I liked the Lowrey strings. They were a little softer than some of the string units that came out later on.

So many organists were playing Hammonds in the '60s. Did you ever use those instruments?

Here and there. Never owned one, though. When you play a Hammond organ, it sounds like a Hammond organ. I thought that the strings, some of the brass sounds, and the little pitch-bend thing on the Lowrey made it worth investing in a "maverick" company. I mean, Lowrey organs are well accepted as a home organ in mid-America, and they're great toys. Electronically they're very well designed. But nobody was using them in bands.

You're playing synthesizers now onstage instead of the old Lowrey. How long has that been going on?

The Yamaha CS-80 prototype had been brought out before we stopped touring. I was aware of it before we did The Last Waltz. I even had the prototype, but I didn't know how to use it. I tried a couple of things with it, but I had not fitted in with it, so I stuck mostly with the Lowrey for The Last Waltz. I can very easily do things now that I always wanted to do on the Lowrey as far as texture is concerned, and I play along with the bass more easily, so it remains a constant source of amusement. We have certain basic sounds that I've found when we're recording or playing that will always be in those tunes, but I never play the songs the same way twice.

Do you try to approximate the kind of pitch-bend phrasing you got on the Lowrey when playing the CS-80?

No. I know how to do that, but I really haven't been too concerned with that in the last ten concerts. The instruments I have will do that, but they encourage me to do other things too.

What do you like about the CS-80?

The CS-80 is polyphonic, and I can come up with a strong section sound. It has a wide variety of sounds, and one interesting thing about the instrument is that you never really return to a particular preset sound, because most of the controls do not have detentes, so that you can move a control to within an eighth of an inch of where it was to get a particular brass sound, and it'll be a little different. It won't be a tuba this time, it'll be more like a trombone. And you can't really see where you're moving the little green filter tab, just to the right of center, or the red resonance tab to the right of the filter, so you do get a varied performance.

It gives you a sense of adventure, then.

Oh, sure. That's the whole deal. I also need an instrument that has presets and digital memory, so that I can work out a sound and then tailor it over a period of time, however long it might take to get the thing to respond right, until I have what I want right there on number 42, or whatever. So I have a Rhodes Chroma.

Do you like to blend the CS-80 and Chroma sounds?

Oh, yes. All the time.

How would you characterize the difference in sound between the two?

The Chroma is more transparent. It doesn't have the rough edge or cut through quite as much. It hasn't the midrange quality, but it does have a very good high end, so it's more like the digital synthesizers.

Do you keep many of the original factory programs on the Chroma?

I've selected 50 from the 150 factory presets to use with the Band and with country music. Most of them are safe, you know. Nothing really odd there [laughs]. Four or five strings, five brass, five Clavinet sounds, five piano sounds, five sounds to complement a steel guitar, and so on.

You must take a very different approach to sound selection when doing more new-wave-oriented music with the Call.

It is quite a bit different. I like their music, because I've liked the distorted guitar sound ever since I heard "Wild Thing" [by the Troggs]. I don't know what year that was but I think that was probably for me the beginning of new wave.

How did you get involved with the Call?

The members of the Call had been aware of the Band's work for a long time. They knew a whole lot of our songs, and had apparently performed them. In fact, they once asked me about the bridge of one song we did on *Cahoots* that I had forgotten and that they couldn't quite figure out. Anyway, they wanted me to play on their demo, so I played five songs on their demo, which went to Mercury/Polygram, and Polygram picked up the group. I wound up doing five songs on the first album, *The Call*, and five more on their second album, *Modern Romans*. I also played various places with them. We played in the Veterans' Hall in Santa Cruz for a flood relief fund, and we were playing this tune that I didn't recognize at first. We got into it, and I began learning it as we went along, and it turned out to be "Knockin' Lost John," from *Islands* [laughs].

Your work with them differs from that of most young synthesists in that style. The prevailing idea seems to encourage repetition of a certain riff or sound, where your work emphasizes constant shifts in texture and structure.

Well, repeated phrases are an old device, going back to the Jazz At The Philharmonic tours. They're part of the art of the tenor saxophone player, and it's just going on now in keyboards with sequencers and people who play passages that sound like they're being played by sequencers. Now, I have worked up certain sequences as kind of a challenge to find things a sequencer cannot do, but that won't fit with the music. I don't know whether the majority of the young players see it that way or not, but you try to devise real-time exercises that somebody cannot program with an Apple Computer, or that can't be done easily in real time on a Fairlight or whatever other digital instrument may be around.

Are you concerned about losing a sense of spontaneity by over-relying on sequencers in performance?

Well, there are people who perform onstage who press a button and their sequencer memories get going, and that's a wonderful effect. I may do a couple of those myself. I have a little sequencer, an early Roland, and it's a great toy. I use it at home mostly with my [Sequential Circuits] Prophet, just to play around. You can hear it back, or you can do three or four or five tricks

Garth Hudson on the accordion. "I started with
piano and accordion.... I would recommend to
young keyboard players reading a Bach Chorale
every other day."

with it.

Was it easy for you to get into synthesizers when they first came out?

Well, I didn't find it a great source of entertainment to develop the type of memory you needed to remember what each of those little holes meant on the old patch-cord synthesizers. I had an ARP 2600; still have it. But I mainly learned about synthesizers on my Minimoog. I still have it too. It needs a little service; it could use some new components.

Do you play many synthesizer leads with the Band?

Yes. I favor the CS-80 for solos, then I'll bring in the Chroma for a little variety later on, or possibly the Rhodes. I use a small 54-key suitcase model.

You seem to like envelopes with slow, gradual attacks in your synthesizer programs.

Yes, for the complementary work, for the backgrounds and textures. Slow envelopes allow you to snake in and out easier. Now, a lot of that comes through my focus on the pedal board, the volume pedals and effects you gradually bring in.

What effects do you use?

I have an Ibanez floor unit that has a limiter, compressor, tube-simulated distortion, chorus or chorale, and a master on/off. I only use that on the Rhodes. I've been using a [Roland] Boss Chorus 1 on the CS-80, and another one I use occasionally on the Chroma.

Richard Manuel has a number of keyboards closer to the front of the stage. Do you ever go out there and play on his stack?

I play the [Yamaha] CP-80 on a couple of numbers. I leave everything on it set up just the way he has it.

How do you and Richard work in dividing the keyboard parts?

He's great at organizing, very good with chords, so he works closer at the beginning with the guitar players and the bass. Then later on I come in and do whatever I can figure out. I come up with a riff or a sound that suits the tune after I've heard it a few times.

You've also been playing accordion on the Band reunion tour.

I've even done a couple of gigs with Greg Harris and the Bandini Brothers on accordion only. I hadn't done anything like that in . . . oh, forty or fifty years [*laughs*]. That was good.

What kind of accordion music do you like?

I listen to the norteno players, and I admire many of them. My favorite group is Los Tremendos Gavilanes; Solomon Prado plays guitar and

sings, and Juan Torres plays accordion. I have a collection of records by all these groups that work six nights a week, and that's their living.

What do you look for in choosing an accordion?

Well, I have to have a musette tuning; musette is accordion language, and it means two sets of reeds on each note that are basically in unison, but one is tuned a little sharp so that there is some beating. The ideal musette is three sets of reeds, one dead on, one sharp, and one flat, so you get your chorus effect, which is pipe organ terminology. Almost all accordions have three or four sets of reeds, but a lot of them do not have a musette select button; they'll have an octave above, an octave below, and the fundamental.

The Band also backed up some important singers in concert and on record. When you played behind Van Morrison, for example, how did you adjust your playing to fit his style?

Van sings very well with horn parts, you know, and he plays saxophone himself, so I played parts that were more in that vein, attempting to imitate a horn section a little bit, to bring that out.

Of course you also performed extensively behind Bob Dylan. Was there anything about the Band's work with him that was out of your ordinary approach?

No. Everything seemed to be right in line. The wonderful thing in working with Dylan was the imagery in his lyrics, and I was allowed to play with these words. I didn't do it incessantly; I didn't try to catch the clouds or the moon or whatever it might be every time. But I would try and introduce some little thing at one point a third of the way through a song, which might have something to do with the words that were going by.

What about some of the classic Band keyboard sounds—the jaw harp on "Up On Cripple Creek," from The Band, for instance? Originally you played that on a Clavinet run through a wah-wah pedal. Do you still play it that way?

We play that tune, but Ernie Cates [who supplemented the Band's lineup on their reunion tour] plays the Clavinet sound now. I just add the occasional note or two with the Clavinet sound in the Chroma, and do some of an organ-like part, which seems to fit with the vocals more.

At the end of the chorus on "This Wheel's On Fire," from Big Pink, there are some real fast repeated chords. How did you do that effect?

It could been the mechanical reiteration on

"The wonderful thing in working with Dylan was the imagery in his lyrics. I would try and introduce some little thing which might have something to do with the words that were going by."

an RMI [Rocky Mountain Instruments] keyboard that we had then; I can't remember the name of the instrument. But it also could have been a telegraph key. I had hooked up a telegraph key to whatever the instrument was, a very nice key. I had picked up a couple of them in a war surplus store. I still have that key. It has a reiteration feature, so that if you move the key in one direction, you would get one dot or dash, and if you move it the other way, you would get reiterated dots. I got a little box and mounted some quarter-inch receptacles into it through which you could connect the key to the instrument. Then you set the reiteration rate, and you were ready to play.

Did you do a lot of modification work in those days based on odds and ends you would find in surplus stores?

Oh, yeah, but they're all still top secret [*laughs*]. I got everything I needed from hardware stores, military surplus, old music stores, and pawn shops.

Do you still take time to gather materials from these places?

Not too much recently. The instruments I work with now keep me going. I had a shop set up in Woodstock, though, where I hooked up with an excellent technician, designer, and craftsman named Bill Putnam. We designed a lit-

tle miniature pipe organ together. I also bought a dude ranch near Malibu where I began designing and building acoustic instruments, mostly keyboard instruments. I bought a theatre organ that was only partly there. A lot of the pipes were missing, but the toy counter [percussion effects] was pretty well all there, with the drums and the marimba and the xylophone and the orchestral bells. These were actuated by electro-pneumatic devices. Some organs have been made with direct electric action—a solenoid that would open the pallet that allows air to enter the pipe—but I don't believe they are really that popular. There's still a preference for the old feeling you get from the electro-pneumatic action, and of course there's also been a revival of interest in tracker action because of new materials. You can build a tracker organ now that doesn't need as much service as the old ones did.

You've been involved in a lot of other outside activities over these past few years, like the electronic music you composed and performed on tape for Tony Duquette's sculpture exhibition. How did you get into that?

Tony and I had talked about music, then I didn't see him again for two or three years. I rented this little ranch from him, and I can't begin to describe it: cactus, plants, little environments here and there. It feels like a Shangri-la type of place. Tony had one of his angel statues set up in his studios, along with several tapestries and models, incredible little models that were not just angels, but other characters as well. As a set and costume designer, he would make a model first, so he had a model of the entire exhibition floor in a little glass case about three feet wide and five feet long. It was an amazing little display. He told me about his whole project, and he thought I could do music for it. It was a wonderful challenge to work with those people.

You've also been involved with an organization called the Visual Music Alliance.

This is an organization that Tom Seuffert founded for young people involved in film special effects, video work, and combining video with music. They meet every month, and I go there and talk. I've also worked with Tom on his piece for Triple I, Information International Inc., an agency that does commercials. We applied music to their demo tape, which they take to product manufacturers to show the quality of their work.

That sounds somewhat similar to the Producer's Music Organization, another video music group that you've been working with in L.A.

No, not really. Producer's Music is much smaller than Tom's studio, which is built into a house. Gary Chang, who was with Fairlight, is behind them. I visited with him occasionally, and we talked about what could be done with music and video, but I never became involved with the typewriter keyboard on his Fairlight because I could see that Gary was very fast with it, and it was fun for me to sit back, think of something, and watch him come up with it—you know, try to trick the machine. He did some tricks with it that were amazing. We've worked together on various little projects. Gary is now independent, and he has a wonderful little studio in Santa Monica that allows you to think that maybe you can do the same kind of thing in your own garage or living room.

*You've done some film music of your own too—*Raging Bull, *for instance.*

I just did a little section there where they had a band in the background of one scene. Martin [Scorsese] wanted some music from the mid-'40s, so I listened a bit to Count Basie's "One O' Clock Jump" and Harry James' "Two O' Clock Jump," and we came up with something from that period.

Did you write charts out for that scene?

No, it was improvised on a chord progression.

For other film music you've done, do you generally write the music out, or compose by playing onto tape?

Both of those methods, the traditional scoring and several other ways of going about it that I've worked up in my home studio, where I do something in my living room and take it back to my studio. In a couple or three years I suppose a wonderful toy will appear on the scene where you will be able to carry an attache-size digital thing with a video screen, headphones, and possibly a little keyboard, and score a film as you fly off to Keokuk, Iowa. You can already see these devices that sync a recording machine to a copy of the film or video cassette. I'm interested in all the little toys that the kids will be dealing with in four, five, or six years.

It doesn't bother you that many young players are learning their way around the keys on electronic or even portable mini-keyboards, rather than the piano?

I don't care. Who wants to win the game? The young people will know that in order to become strong in this whole endeavor, they may have to go back to the piano and do a lot of hard work, other than just rehearsing with a group and remembering patterns and arrangements. There are many people who get by on that, but the ones who really want to learn will see that it really takes a lot more than that.

Bob Doerschuk

Grand Designs, Noble Visions

All throughout Europe and America, keyboard players were waiting for a sign as the '60s wound down. Thanks to Alan Price, Felix Cavaliere, and the other Romantics, they had found a niche in rock and roll, but it was only a niche. Restless minds were racing and reeling at the prospects of playing "96 Tears" and "Double Shot Of My Baby's Love" forever. Desperately, they reasoned that there must be more to rock keyboard than this. But what?

The answer came in part from the laboratory of Bob Moog, a brilliant young physicist and musician in Trumansburg, New York. At the request of composer Herb Deutsch, who was exploring the possibilities of electronic music, Moog designed a modular synthesis system, with voltage-controlled oscillator, filter, and amplifier wired to an electric organ keyboard in an *ad hoc* breadboard configuration. Pleased with the results, Moog exhibited his hand-made prototypes at the 1964 Audio Engineering Society convention. By 1967 his products were being referred to as synthesizers, and in 1969 he was contracted to design his first live-performance model. One year later, Moog was back at the AES show, displaying the first Minimoog.

III. Progressive Rock

Not many people realized it then, but Moog, Alan R. Pearlman of ARP, who unveiled his ARP 2600 at the same 1970 AES show, and a handful of other far-sighted manufacturers had just blown the lid off the keyboard industry. They had figured out a relatively inexpensive way to take the principles that governed the electronic music laboratories in Cologne, at Columbia University, and in other high-tech centers, and apply them to a traditional keyboard triggering system in such a way that anyone with some proficiency on the keys could begin building sounds and making music the likes of which had never been heard before.

Electronic music was nothing new, and for that matter neither were keyboard controllers on electronic instruments; home console organs, the gigantic Ondes Martenot keyboard, and the very same organs with which several rock stars had already made their fortunes, all qualified as electronic musical instruments. But their control over the parameters of sound was limited by comparison to those early synthesizers. Where the Hammond's drawbars enabled the player to adjust the volume ratio of the overtone series, most new synthesizers went much further, with oscillators

that offered choice of sound wave shapes, filters that blocked out selected bands within the frequency spectrum, controls that molded the attack, sustain, decay, and release contours for any sound in the instrument's capability, and such tasty extras as true glissando and guitar-like pitch-bend.

The synthesizer was in its infancy, yet it was already stimulating keyboard players in all styles of music to look at their art in a fresh light. Many conservative performers would remain relatively unaffected, but others, especially those whose musical ideas had seemed unattainable only a short while before, were intrigued by the vast range of sounds that now lay open to them. For those who loved the varied colors of classical music as much as the physical thrill of rock and roll, the synthesizer was a godsend that promised to make their old dreams come alive in sound even while pushing them on to yet higher goals.

Nowhere was the impact of the synthesizer more dramatically felt than in England. There were probably more brilliant rockers per square foot in London than anywhere else in those heady days, and as Brian Auger noted earlier in this book, many of them were testing formulas

47

on their keyboards for capturing rock's gutsy essence in the refined structures of classical form. Mike Pinder was using his Mellotron, a keyboard that drew its sound from pre-recorded tapes of actual orchestral instruments, to layer lush violin textures onto the songs of the Moody Blues. Venerable themes from Bach were being dusted off by Gary Brooker and revived as stately melodies for his group, Procol Harum. Vincent Crane's blazing solos on the Hammond nearly stole the show from his wild-eyed singer, Arthur Brown. Rick Wright's forays into free-form improvisation and abstract electronic keyboard effects helped build an underground following for Pink Floyd during the group's early gigs at the Marque Club, the Sound/Light Workshop, and the UFO Club. And one young man whose keyboard technique and imagination had no precedent in rock was getting ready to show the world just how far he could stretch the boundaries of his chosen music.

In terms of his impact, Keith Emerson was the first and greatest of the progressive rockers. He was the catalyst and focal point of the keyboard revolution. A lithe, menacing figure in sleek leather, he did what no one before him had been able to pull off; he made the bulky, stolid Hammond organ as sexy as the guitar. In his performances with the Nice, and later with Emerson, Lake & Palmer, Emerson jumped on it, wrestled it to the ground, even seemed to assault it with a knife. All that brought in the crowds. But when he took time to play it, that brought in the musicians. All histrionics aside, Emerson was a musical breathtaker. He shouldered his way through complicated arrangements with an astonishing muscular facility, not only on organ, but on piano and, with ELP, synthesizers as well. He nonchalantly peppered his improvisations with snippets from Bach, Copland, and assorted composers in between. He topped Pete Townshend, Jeff Beck, and the rest of the guitar virtuosos by adapting their feedback techniques to the organ. And most important, he showed thousands of young keyboard players throughout the world that they would no longer have to hold anything back to play great rock and roll. Emerson knocked down all the barriers. After him, no keyboardists, from your basic boogie-woogie variety to conservatory graduate, ever needed to be ashamed to express himself or herself in the language of rock.

Emerson was born on November 2, 1944, in Todmorden, Lancashire, England. Although he began piano lessons at the age of eight, he never received advanced training; most of his chops evolved from playing on his own. After leaving high school, he went to work as a bank teller, spending his evenings at local gigs with different bands, among them Gary Farr And The T-Bones and the VIPs, who later became Spooky Tooth. Soon Emerson was a full-time musician. In 1967 he joined bassist Lee Jackson, guitarist David O'List, and drummer Brian "Blinky" Davison in the band backing up P. P. Arnold, a black British soul singer. The quartet split off in October that year to begin performing on its own as the Nice.

They began attracting attention immediately. With Andrew Loog Oldham, formerly manager to the Rolling Stones, briefly handling their business, they put out a debut album on his Immediate label, *The Thoughts Of Emerlist Davjack*, in February 1968. By the release of their second LP, an ambitious four-part megawork titled *Ars Longa Vita Brevis*, a year later, O'List had departed, and Emerson stood out clearly as the showpiece of the band. Jackson and Davison quickly faded into supportive roles as Emerson's pyrotechnical style blossomed. He gathered material from a melange of musical sources, imprinting his stamp on everything he played, from Bob Dylan to Bela Bartok. Though a fluent improviser, he put most of his energy into devising elaborate settings for his arrangements and original compositions, never sacrificing the pile-driving power that would become synonymous with his style.

The Nice enjoyed great popularity throughout Europe, but some of the extra-musical controversy they provoked seemed to operate against their interests across the Atlantic. When they brought their rendition of Leonard Bernstein's "America," from *West Side Story*, to a climax at a June 1968 Royal Albert Hall concert in London by unfurling and burning an American flag, the composer angrily responded by blocking their plans to release that record in the U.S. Perhaps the Nice would have broken through in the New World anyway, given enough time, but they were already on their way to splitting up when they embarked on their first American tour in 1969. Jackson and Davison were weary of being swamped by Emerson's brilliant displays on the keyboard, and Keith was getting restless as well.

Fate intruded in the form of a chance encounter between Emerson and Greg Lake in San Francisco late that year. Lake was then playing bass and singing with King Crimson, another early progressive band whose Mellotron-saturated album, *In The Court Of The Crimson King*, had become a hit in both England and the States. When King Crimson fell into as much disarray as the Nice in 1970, he and Emerson decided to start their own band. With drummer Carl Palmer, fresh from engagements with the Crazy World Of Arthur Brown and Atomic Rooster, they united as Emerson, Lake & Palmer, and made a stunning debut at the 1970 Isle Of Wight rock festival.

In ELP, Emerson was at last able to perform with colleagues whose flashy chops could keep pace with his. Yet throughout their long career, which lasted nine years and is documented on eleven albums, he remained the focal point. It was his siren-like solo that breathed life into Lake's "Lucky Man" on their first LP and brought the sound of the synthesizer to the surface of the rock mainstream. His classical-rock experiments grew more daring than ever. After thoroughly remodeling Mussorgsky's *Pictures At An Exhibition*, an album-length undertaking, he blasted Aaron Copland's *Hoedown* and Maurice Ravel's *Bolero* into the electronic age on *Trilogy*. Solid backing from Lake and Palmer challenged Emerson to compose some bedevilling works of his own as well, from the semi-programmatic *Tarkus* in 1971 to a one-movement piano concerto, complete with symphony orchestra, on *Works, Vol. 1* in 1977. By that time he was playing the GX-1, Yamaha's awesome $50,000 polyphonic synthesizer, and making the final arrangements for a blowout tour of the U.S., in which the group would hit the road with a 59-piece orchestra, six-voice choir, and assorted personel adding up to an entourage of 115 and a weekly budget of $250,000.

That project brought ELP to its apogee. Emerson's musical concepts were gigantic in scale, and reality finally caught up with his imagination when, after 15 dates, the tour fell apart due to the prohibitive costs. Subsequent ELP albums seemed to diminish in scale and vision, ending in *Love Beach,* a hodgepodge of trite tunes with only occasional echoes of the band's grand days. Shortly after that album's release in late 1978, "the show that never ends" came to a finish. Emerson withdrew to a beach house in the Bahamas with his family, where he wrote a soundtrack for the movie *Nighthawks* and did some sporadic recording with funky local musicians. By 1983 he had returned to England, his future plans uncertain.

What was certain was the fact that Emerson had single-handedly opened the floodgates. Even if he were never to play another note in public, his contribution to the keyboard world would have to be considered immeasurable. Rock historians will hopefully disregard his awkward attempts to play honky-tonk jazz, his occasionally uncomfortable extemporizations in simple one-chord settings, and his rare failed endeavors, like the basically straight lift of Henry Mancini's "Theme From *Peter Gunn*" on the *In Concert* album. What counts in the end with Emerson is the extent to which he inspired other rock keyboardists to chase after their own musical dreams, and to realize that the technology and creative climate of the modern age had placed those dreams within reach.

Though Keith Emerson was the driving force in progressive rock, it would be a mistake to dismiss the other keyboard giants in that style as merely derivative. Jon Lord, for one, hacked out a trail for himself that followed quite a different, if sometimes parallel, course. Born on June 9, 1941 in Leicester, England, Lord studied both classical piano and drama, two discipines that would fuel his organ work and stage performances with Deep Purple. With guitarist Ritchie Blackmore and drummer Ian Paice, two highly individualistic and inventive rock veterans, Lord put the nucleus of the band together in Hamburg, Germany in February 1968. They added bassist Nick Simpe and singer Rod Evans, recorded a cover version of the Joe South song "Hush," and watched it clamber to the top of the American charts. Stateside tours in late 1968 and early '69 further established Deep Purple as a major force in rock.

Like Emerson, Lord brought a fascination with classical themes to the rock format. He, too, indulged himself in a few orchestral projects, including his concerto for rock band and symphony orchestra, presented on September 24, 1969 with the Royal Philharmonic Orchestra in Royal Albert Hall, and again at the Hollywood Bowl a year later. But he and Emerson looked at the progressive movement with differing senses of proportion. Where Emerson could be preoccupied with intricate counter-rhythms, contrapuntal lines, and other primarily classical devices, Lord stuck closer to rock basics, seldom expanding too far beyond the familiar verse-chorus tune structure. Lord was not as much of an orchestrator, yet he was in some ways a more dramatic soloist, using the percussion and vibrato effects of his Hammond/Leslie setup to full effect in "Hush," "Hard Road," and other tunes. His growling tone, stark voicings, and solo exchanges with Blackmore steered one wing of the progressive school toward the heavy metal style, wherein powerhouse guitarists reign supreme and only the strong keyboardists — like Lord — survive.

Closer to the baroque soul of progressive rock was Rick Wakeman. Though he rose to prominence a few years after Emerson and Lord, he quickly carved out a place for himself at the forefront of rock as perhaps the first true multi-keyboard virtuoso. He had developed a formidable technique through years of classical training, but his strength was more as a background player than a soloist, with a sense of texture and a knack for intricate orchestration that would permanently affect the rock keyboard world.

Where Emerson was primarily self-taught, Wakeman, who was born on May 19, 1949 in West London, began years of arduous study at the age of three. By the time of his admission to the prestigious Royal College of Music at 16, he had resolved to become a concert pianist. His extra-curricular performances at various London pubs for weekend spending money soon attracted the attention of music industry executives, however, and the session gigs they began sending his way soon proved an irresistible distraction from his classwork. After a year and a half of skipping lectures to fulfill studio obligations, Wakeman was dismissed from the College and propelled headfirst into full-time rock and roll.

Luckily he was already a top-call studio player by then. Wakeman contributed organ, piano, and other keyboard parts to records by T. Rex, Cat Stevens, and David Bowie, among many others, before accepting an invitation from guitarist Dave Cousins to join the Strawbs, an arty folk-oriented outfit that wound up heavily exploiting his classical background. His performance on their live album, *Just A Collection Of Antiques And Curios,* recorded in July 1970 at the Queen Elizabeth Hall in London, won him his first widespread critical acclaim and provoked the first inevitable comparisons to Keith Emerson. For this reason, Wakemans's decision to sign on as keyboardist Tony Kaye's replacement with the group Yes in August 1971 was some of the hottest music news of the season.

With Yes, Wakeman was at last in his idiom. Already considered one of the preeminent classical-rock fusion bands, Yes had been together for three years when Kaye quite to form his own group, Badger. Kaye had been an early advocate of synthesizer use in rock, but with Yes he remained first and foremost an organist, spiritually akin to Jon Lord in his forceful style. What the band needed, though, was a keyboardist who could weave exotic tone colors into their soaring harmonies, support their difficult polyrhythmic episodes, and spin out symphonic sounds that would envelope, rather than puncture, their finely-wrought compositions. Wakeman, en-

circled even then by a cluster of keyboard instruments, precisely fit the bill.

Beginning with *Fragile,* the first of his six albums with Yes, Wakeman stepped forward as a certified rock superstar. In 1973 *Time* named his debut solo LP, *The Six Wives Of Henry VIII,* one of the year's ten best recordings. A 45-piece orchestra, 48-voice choir, and narrator were recruited in January 1974 to augment his musical impressions of a Jules Verne classic in his next project, *Journey To The Centre Of The Earth.* On his 25th birthday, one month before *Journey* was released, Wakeman left Yes, citing musical differences as the reason for his departure. By this time his solo career was in full swing, and he was establishing a reputation for classical references and grandiose gesture that surpassed even Emerson's. *Myths And Legends Of King Arthur And The Knights Of The Round Table,* his third solo endeavor, was unveiled in a May 1975 gala at a London ice pageant, with Wakeman leading his new group, the English Rock Ensemble, and the usual massed gathering of orchestral musicians and singers. He undertook two American tours that year, the first at the head of a 100-person entourage, the second with a more modest seven-piece version of the Ensemble. And in 1976 he scored director Ken Russell's latest mega-movie, *Lisztomania,* and the Winter Olympics film, *White Rock.*

To the surprise of many, Wakeman also rejoined Yes that year. Following the departure of their third keyboardist, Patrick Moraz, the band asked Wakeman to help out with their next album. What was supposed to have been just one session turned into an extended reunion, and Wakeman would stay with them until the summer of 1980. He is an independent artist today, his orchestral and keyboard concepts perhaps too vast to be confined within any single group.

Not all progressive rockers subscribed to the Wakeman doctrine that it is better to surround yourself with keyboards than to specialize on just one or two. Kerry Minnear of Gentle Giant, for one, worked toward the opposite extreme. "Simplicity is what I'm after," he stated in the May/June '76 issue of *Keyboard.* "I don't want to do what Wakeman is doing, which is having a dozen or more keyboards and the kitchen sink at hand." But Minnear also reflected the growing preference of many players to follow Wakeman's understated use of those instruments rather than Emerson's more extroverted solo-oriented approach: "You know," Minnear complained, "I find that it's expected of me as a keyboardist to be somewhat flamboyant and show off occasionally. It seems totally wrong. I get a lot of pleasure from just playing drivel sometimes."

By the time the shock waves caused by Emerson had worn off, conscientious players were exploring synthesizers not so much as vehicles for ego-inflating solos, but as tools for sensitive, though large-scale, accompaniments. Tony Banks, a founding member of Genesis, has worked since 1967 at avoiding ostentatious display with the group in favor of carefully conceived foundation work on a relatively modest array of keyboards. "I don't like using a lot of instruments onstage," he insisted to *Keyboard*. "I use four as it happens, and even that's too many." Patrick Moraz, the Swiss-born former classical piano *wunderkind* who succeeded and preceded Wakeman in Yes during the mid-'70s, accumulated a greater number of synthesizers —"Being in a band like Yes," he explained in the November '81 *Keyboard*, "there was always someone around telling me that I had to try this instrument or that instrument. I lost a lot of money in 1975 because of that kind of thing." —yet he too sought to meld into, rather than to dominate, the Yes sound.

Lean financial times in the early '80s were reflected by the scaled-down approach to instrumentation among new wave musicians, but for young followers of the progressive gospel, cutting corners on keyboard orchestration could be painful surgery. One of the brightest new stars in the progressive firmament, Eddie Jobson, whose credits already included stints with Curved Air, Roxy Music, and Frank Zappa before he formed his own band, U.K., at the age of 22, professed a desire to keep his setup "as small as possible," but when guitarist Alan Holdsworth left U.K. in 1979, Jobson admitted that he had begun adding new gear because "now I've got a good excuse for making it bigger." Yet even at his most extravagant, he never came close to matching Geoff Downes' gargantuan tastes. At the time of his *Keyboard* interview, Jobson confessed to using four keyboards onstage, a number he described as "really quite large." But when Downes hit the road with his band Asia in 1983, he had 21 of them in tow.

Downes is the last of the distinguished line of Yes keyboard alumni. When Wakeman made his final withdrawal from the group in the summer of 1980, they recruited Downes from the Buggles, a vocal/keyboard duo that had released one hit record, "Video Killed The Radio Star," in 1979–80.

He handled the keyboard parts on the last Yes album, *Drama*, with an organ-heavy approach that reminded many listeners of Tony Kaye's work with Yes more than ten years before. But Downes' solid touch wasn't enough to rescue the band; crucial personnel changes and the exhausting challenge of meeting their own high standards had drained them of their creative resources, so in 1981 they quietly called it quits. For Downes, however, new opportunities lay just over the horizon. Only a few months after the Yes *gotterdammerung*, a new group appeared, uniting four progressive veterans — drummer Carl Palmer from Emerson, Lake & Palmer, Yes' longtime guitarist Steve Howe, bassist John Wetton of U.K., and Downes. Under the name Asia, they exploded into the charts with a solid debut album, and established themselves almost overnight as a top concert attraction.

Some may argue that Asia, with its glossy arrangements and accent on instrumental dazzle, is an anachronism, a throwback to a departed era. Undeniably the progressive heyday is past, yet its forceful voice refuses to be silenced, as the triumphant reunion of Yes, with Kaye again in the lineup, proved in early '84. While new wavers decry the Sixties superstar ethic, Downes pirouettes among his keyboards in grand dervish display on a platform high above the stage at his concerts. Almost defiantly, he and the rest of Asia have planted the banner of progressive rock in the arid soil of the '80s. If record and ticket sales are an accurate barometer, that flag will fly for some time to come.

Bob Doerschuk

Jon Lord
Keyboards in Transition

March, 1983 — Before Deep Purple came together, you had already done a lot of recording and club work in London, much of it with some very good players. Why do you think it was Deep Purple, rather than any of these other groups, that attained success?

I think it was the first hard rock band to use keyboards in another way than just as a cosmetic background effect, particularly in the earlier parts of the '70s, when Ritchie and I were trading licks and swapping solos and doing things like that that were taken from jazz but were unusual in rock. My style evolved through my playing with Ritchie, who is a very forceful personality. His guitar playing is very full; it fills most of the spaces. So I had to evolve a style which was kind of a rhythm organ, rather than a rhythm guitar. Through having a fight like that I think I might have come up with a rather unique way of playing. It wasn't until I got into Deep Purple that this began to happen. What I was doing before was pretty derivitive. I was a Jimmy Smith freak.

So in the beginning as an organist, were you more concerned with duplicating Jimmy Smith sounds than finding your own style?

At the very beginning, it was difficult *not* to play Hammond like Jimmy Smith or Jimmy McGriff or all those '60s organ stars. But if you've got any kind of searching mind at all, copying somebody else gradually becomes very unsatisfactory. After a while I wasn't doing anything fulfilling. I desperately wanted to sound like Jimmy Smith, but then I thought, "What's the point? I'm not going to achieve that on my L-100 anyway." That's when I started to search around the organ and find other ways of using it. It was really a process of learning by example.

53

Previous page: Jon Lord playing (l. to r.) a Rhodes electric piano, two ARP Odyssey synthesizers, a Hammond C-3, and a Hohner Clavinet.

Did you play organ from the beginning, or did you start on piano?

I started with piano at the age of seven. We'd been given an old piano by an aunt of ours who was better off that we were. She had bought a new piano and dumped this old one on us when I was about five. I used to plunk around on it to the point where I think my father got enraged enough by the untutored noise I was making to insist that I take tutored lessons, for which many thanks to him. I'm very grateful for that. So I thanks to him. I'm very grateful for that. So I studied for ten years in the normal classical mode.

Yes, I do. Funnily enough, my father came down to see me about a year ago with a great pile of the music I used to play, and some of it I can't play now, which is most disturbing! When I was about 15 or 16 this teacher had me playing Liszt and some of Brahms' really hard, heavy piano music. What I really most preferred playing, though, were the French composers—Debussy, Faure.

Did rock make any technical demands that classical lessons might not have prepared you for?

Not in terms of being able to move your fingers along the keys, but certainly in terms of endurance and strength. I found very quickly that large concerts were a completely different environment to sitting in the front room at home and playing the piano. Stamina became a factor, so more than ever I was pleased that I had gotten a technique. At that point, it only became a question of hardening that technique up.

When did you get interested in playing rock?

When I first heard Jerry Lee Lewis play that intro to "Whole Lotta Shakin' Goin' On." Beethoven and Mozart just went out the window for a while. I just couldn't work out how he got that effect. It was quite a shock to hear.

Was your wrist action strong enough to play that way?

No, that's what I couldn't get. I could do it from a tecnique point of view, but it sounded *wimpy*. It sounded awful, in fact. So that proves one thing: Rock and roll may be simplistic, especially in some of the early stuff, but if there's no feel behind it, it won't work. Rock is feel music as much as anything else. Technique is still a very important factor, certainly in my way of wanting to play, but I had to realize that I hadn't yet developed the feeling I needed to play it right. I had to work at my craft.

Can you recall the first time you realized that you had gotten the right feeling for playing this music?

Oh, I remember it very well. It was at a place near Portsmouth in south England, and one of Manfred Mann's early bands was playing. I sat in with them on a terrible old piano that was stuck in the corner; they miked it up, and the next hour went by in what seemed to me like 20 seconds. It was great. I enjoyed myself immensely. They came up after and said, "Hey, that was fabulous. Come sit in again." I knew I'd gotten somewhere. I recall it very strongly, actually. I recall drinking too much beer afterwards as well [*laughs*].

Was the Hammond the first non-piano keyboard you had ever played?

I had played a pipe organ in church while I was at school. My school had a big pipe organ in the school hall, and I'd gone in for a couple of organ competitions.

So you played the foot pedals too?

Yeah, in fact, in the first Deep Purple back in '68, I used to play the pedals, but I soon got rid of them because it was actually rather pointless. With the sound quality in those days, you could never hear them, and it looked like I was trying to stamp out a cigarette [*laughs*]. There was just this great amount of thrashing going on. So when I came to the Hammond, I did have some idea of organ technique—you know, the fact that there's no sustain unless you keep your fingers on the notes, and that therefore it's a good deal different from the piano. Again, this is where the ability to finger properly, which I'd learned from being taught, was of great value, especially if I was playing a slower passage with *legato* phrasing, where smoothness is essential. There's nothing worse than hearing a piano player try to play an organ like a piano. It sounds awful! The swell pedal technique is also a totally integral thing, because the organ keyboard is not touch sensitive.

What model was your first Hammond?

My first one was a small L-100, but when I got my first C-3 in '68, I was hooked. I've still got that same organ. It's a beaut; I love it. It's been around the world so many times, but it's never let me down—he said, touching wood. I've had a lot of modifications done to it, of course.

Like what?

One of the most startling ones is that there's an RMI electric piano built into it.

Triggered by the organ keyboard?

Using the same contact system, yes, as the keyboard of the Hammond, so on the top manual I can play just organ, just RMI piano, or both. That's how I get that really huge dirty sound, which is a bit of a trademark for me. There are other little refinements on the organ too. The bottom two octaves of the lower manual can be hooked up to trigger a synthesizer, so I can have my Minimoog set down on the floor and linked up to the Hammond. I just click a switch and there it is. I can't bend pitch that way, of course; it's just for when I need a straight doubling sound.

What about the rest of your keyboards?

There's a Hohner Pianet/Clavinet which I find very nice indeed. Running through the Leslie gives it an extra dimension it lacks when going through a straight speaker. For synthesizers I use Moogs, as you know, but I'm getting rid of the four or five of them I've been using, because that's too many to take on the road, and I'm going to use the new Memorymoog. I'm getting along okay with it, though I've got a lot to learn about it yet. It sounds like about eight Minimoogs all linked together. And I use the Yamaha CP-80 electric grand.

What is your approach to registration on the Hammond?

I found that I use roughly the same setting for the all-out music. In the quieter passages I experiment more with the drawbar settings. I like to use the drawbars a lot. They're such an amazing part of the Hammond sound. I used to do solos by holding down a cluster of notes and then playing with the drawbars. If I've got a few treatments on it, like echo or phasing, I can get some quite startling effects—almost synthesizer effects, and I was doing this before synthesizers. Most of my best solo work has unfortunately been onstage—I say unfortunately because it's not here anymore. It's gone, it's out in the ether. I've always found it difficult to do a convincing pyrotechnical solo on record. It's quite difficult to stand in the studio and flail away.

What was your first contact with synthesizers like?

Very strange. I think we must go back to '71. There was this guy in London named Peter Zinoviez, a mad professor type who was working with EMS. They were making the first performance-style synthesizers, where you worked with patch cords. It was really impossible; you could set one sound up, and it would take half an hour to find another one. I went round to see him because I'd heard about these new things. I was ushered into his workshop and he was in there talking to a computer, trying to get it to answer back! He gave me one of their early models, and I took it home to experiment with it,

but I really couldn't get it to do much except make odd bleeping noises, which wasn't terribly helpful to Deep Purple. In fact, I could make better bleeping noises on the organ! But then somebody introduced me to the ARP Odyssey around '72 or '73. I had a couple of them for about two or three years. I thoroughly enjoyed them, found them very useful. Then around '76, just after the band broke up, I went to see a mate of mine named Bob Papazinsky, who now is a demonstrator for Moog in Buffalo. He gave me my first Minimoog—I'd seen them used, but never actually played one myself—and I fell in love with them. I've been a Moog artist ever since.

How would you describe your relationship with synthesizers today?

I have a very particular relationship with them. I'm not an electronically minded man. Things electronic confuse me. I put the plug in the wall, and as far as I'm concerned, if it doesn't go on, it's broken. That's the limit of my knowledge. I understand the relationship between filters and oscillators and so on, but only on the most basic of levels, where I can use it as a tool for providing a sound I might not be able to find on the organ. The easier and more performance-oriented the instrument, the happier I am, because I think of the synthesizer as just another instrument in my armory. I don't see it as the keyboard of the future. Totally electronic keyboard synthesized pop I find incredibly boring. When you get to the point that the machine starts playing the musician instead of the other way round, then that musician is in trouble. I like to be its master, rather than let it be the master of me.

When working with Deep Purple, you have been credited with helping to lay the foundation for the heavy metal sound, although I've never been able to understand why some people categorize Purple purely as a heavy metal band.

I'm pleased to hear you say that, because I don't understand it either.

Your music seemed much less simplistic than the music we associate with heavy metal, and yet because of Deep Purple's approach you usually had to keep your ensemble parts pretty simple, with open fifth voicings and unison lines with the bass. Did you find your role harmonically restricting in any way?

That's a good question, and one that will take a lengthy reply, rather than just a simple "Yes," which is in fact the answer. Okay, yes, it was difficult, and perhaps initially harmonically

Jon Lord with Deep Purple. "When I first heard Jerry Lee Lewis play that intro to 'Whole Lotta Shakin' Goin' On,' Beethoven and Mozart just went out the window for a while."

restricting. But one of the great joys about Purple was that this forced me into searching for ways to make it more interesting for myself, and therefore for the listener. That's why we could never be classified as a heavy metal band. It might have spawned a lot of heavy metal bands, and it was loud and raucous, but it was more than that. It could also be soft and tender, it had dynamics, and it had humor. And incidentally, I don't consider Whitesnake a heavy metal band at all. If you like, I consider us a modern R&B band. We have tendencies toward what people might call heavy metal—it's loud and it tends to be aurally exciting—but playing heavy metal music to me is like giving somebody a strange pill that pins their ears back and produces a kind of numb lethargy. Constant grinding riffs are not my idea of rock and roll.

A lot of bands in that genre play nothing but I-IV-V progressions, but Purple in particular was never that restricted.

No. We really felt we were doing something different. There was a lovely feeling of experiment and adventure at the beginning, and it lasted a good long time. We were blazing trails in a way. Okay, other people were doing the same things in other directions. We weren't alone, but because we had that almost missionary zeal to spread the gospel according to St. Purple, it gave us a kind of freshness that I don't think can be locked in as heavy metal. And part of that freshness was the knowledge that I had to contribute in a way that was fulfilling for me, or I'd be lagging behind the guys who were making the band great. I feel the same way with Whitesnake in a slightly different area. I've got to find it interesting. If I don't, I wouldn't be able to give it the shot in the arm it might need.

What do you think about the role of keyboard instruments in contemporary rock?

I think the revolution in keyboards has been great, if not greater, than any other that I've seen in the music business in the last 20 years.

What are your opinions as to how they're used?

I have a couple of small misgivings that nag away at me. The revolution in the keyboard industry has provided the musician with a startling range of products, which is making it easier to sound very competent and brilliant with a minimum of involvement, and I'm just wondering whether this will result in a lowering of actual standards of ability, because with some of the keyboards that are now so readily available, you don't really have to fight to sound amazing. This is not sour grapes; I'm not saying that it isn't fair that we didn't have this when I was starting out. I just think that sometimes it's good to really have to work at something. Don't get me wrong. I believe that if you really do work at these instruments, you can get them to sound even more marvelous, but the ratio between required ability and resultant effect is very narrow. Jan Hammer can make a synthesizer talk, but no one doubts his immense technical ability. In actual fact, I sometimes doubt the ability of the new young keyboard players. I'm not suggesting that it must be a prerequisite in rock and roll or pop that the player be a technical genius. I mean, was Ringo Starr a technical genius? No, but he worked fine for the Beatles. I sound like Methusaleh here, but I've seen a lot of changes in the music world, and the one thing I haven't seen is a continuing supply of unusually gifted keyboard players. I would like to see someone come out of the woodwork and make me sit back in amazement. I worry that good keyboardists may already be a vanishing breed because of the technical advances. I would like to occasionally see someone who makes me say, "Jesus, he's good!" rather than. "Jesus, his machine is wonderful!"
Bob Doerschuk

Keith Emerson
The Triumph of Virtuosity

October, 1977 — *When did you first start playing organ?*

I was about 18, I think. I got fed up with playing pianos with the hammers broken off of them. That seems to be a fairly typical thing that happens to players. I saved up for about two years and bought the L-100.

Did your technique change to fit the organ?

Yes, it did. I realized it was obvious that you couldn't do all of the styles that you could do on the piano, so it was a bit limiting. Unless you're playing in a classical style on the organ, there's really no other use for that left hand. It gets a bit too boggy. You've got to comp with it. It is not as challenging as playing the piano.

When did you add the C-3 to your setup?

It was about 1968, I think. It was always the L-100 before that.

What gave you the idea of using the two organs together?

Well, at that particular time I was into throwing the L-100 around and making it feed back. I had developed this stage act and it seemed to go down quite well. I couldn't do that with the C-3, you see, and it was a necessary part of the act at the time. I liked the C-3 sound. It was far superior and the octave range was greater than on the L's.

Did anyone strongly influence your rock organ style?

There was an organ player in London by the name of Don Shin. I don't know where he is today. He was a weird looking guy, really strange. A very twittery sort of character. He had a schoolboy's cap on, round spectacles, really stupid. I just happened to be in this club when he was playing. He had an L-100. The audience—you

know there were a lot of younger chicks down at the Marquee—were all in hysterics. Giggling and laughing at him. No one was taking him seriously. And I said, "Who is this guy?" He'd been drinking whiskey out of a teaspoon and all kinds of ridiculous things. He'd played an arrangement of a Grieg Concerto, and I'd already played things like that with the Nice, the Brandenburg and all [from *Ars Longa Vita Brevis*]. So my ears perked up. Somebody else was doing these things. Playing it really well, and he got a fantastic sound from the L-100. But halfway through he sort of shook the L-100, and the back of it dropped off. Then he got out a screwdriver and started making adjustments while he was playing. Everyone was roaring their heads off laughing. So I looked and said, "Hang on a minute! That guy has got something." He and Hendrix were controlling influences over the way I developed the stage act side of things. Nobody really went for the organ in those days. The L-100 looked like a piece of furniture. I think Georgie Fame was the first to use it in England, and Graham Bond came along doing a heavier sort of thing. But most people's reaction to seeing an organ in the band was, "Yuk." I mean, people hated the sound of it. What I wanted to do was change people's image of that, make the organ sound more attractive. It didn't look that good, and the player usually sat at the instrument, so it didn't have any visual appeal at all. I guess seeing Don Shin made me realize that I'd like to compile an act from what he did. A lot of people hated it, said it was totally unnecessary. They thought that was all I could do. Some people still think that.

What drawbar and percussion settings do you use on the Hammonds?

It's pretty standard. My favorite is the first three drawbars pulled full out with the percussion on the third harmonic. The vibrato is on chorale 3. Depending on the acoustics of the hall, I'll add a slight touch of the top drawbar. I like a tacky-sounding organ. One that spits a bit, you know. I'm still searching for the ideal organ sound. It's still a bit too hard at the moment.

How much did jazz organists influence your sound.

Well, it was the Jack McDuff organ sound that really turned me on. I didn't really like the Jimmy Smith organ sound, though I liked what he did.

**Previous page: Emerson playing a Yamaha GX-1.
Opposite: Emerson demonstrating his mud-wrestling technique with a Hammond L-100 organ.**

But I worked for ages trying to get the sound that Jack McDuff got on the *Rock Candy Live in the Front Room* album. It starts off with a very husky sort of black voice saying, "Presenting jazz organist Brother Jack McDuff!" with dubbed-in applause and then an amazing sort of tacky, spitty sounding organ. I think it must have been a freak of the recording. I found the sound by pure accident. You use a Marshall amplifier with the presence and treble turned full up. It exaggerates the contact sound. Lately, I've got a much cleaner sound, but I still like an element of click.

How do you orchestrate your keyboard parts?

You mean what music is to be played on what instrument? I don't know. I invariably start with the piano. From there on it'll go out either to the organ or to another instrument. It depends on how it sounds and on what the original intention is for the piece. If I'm pretty convinced it is going to be, say, a piano concerto, or it's going to be for ELP, then that will determine what instruments I'll use. Sometimes I've got that in mind before I start. I swap around for variety. I may have been playing one line on the organ for a long time and just by way of a change I'll play it on the Yamaha [GX-1].

Where did your interest in arranging other people's music come from?

Simple reason—I like the tunes. I want to play these tunes, but I want to play them in a way that's acceptable to our audience. And stimulate new interest in the original. You know I started doing this back in the Sixties, and that was my intention. But obviously since that time, audiences have become far more perceptive—intelligent. One doesn't really have to do that now. I think people are going for classical music as much as for any other form. You wouldn't have had your Chick Coreas five years ago. Chick Corea doesn't have to really dress up in blazer gear to get a wide following. It just goes to show you that it's not a question of image these days. It's more a question of the actual music. So I don't mean to be insulting the public's intelligence by saying the reason I'm playing "Fanfare for the Common Man" is because I want them to listen to the original. That may have been the case six years ago, but since then it's become part of what people expect of me. I still occasionally enjoy other people's music. If a piece comes out which lends itself to a particular situation, a particular meter, then I use it. If it doesn't, I don't force the issue. My music has been tagged with the label "classical rock," which I guess is okay. Broadly speaking, I guess that's true, but it's not a term that I want to really like.

Can you play just about anything you can hear?

No. I mean the "Fugue" on the *Trilogy* album was literally written out on paper before I ever played it. I couldn't work out a fugue any other way. Some people are very clever and can improvise them. It's great to be able to do that. But as for me, I have to write it down, look at it, and work it out. I don't write things that are easy for me. Everything that I write is a new step forward. Sometimes I hear it in the back of my mind and know the effect that I want, but I can't get it. I work at it for days and days and days.

How did you become fluent in playing so many different styles of music?

You get that way. You pick up different styles. I think my father was the chief influence there. He used to play in a dance band. He didn't read music, and his main wish when I started getting in touch with piano was that I be versatile. Versatility was his key word. They really had me taught some safeguards so that I'd always be able to make money someplace. Like as a sideline. That's as far as they wanted it to go. Versatility and being able to read were the two most important things as far as they were concerned. My background from my father's side was pretty musical, and his sister ran a dancing school. Ballet, jazz, everything. I started making money when I realized that versatility wasn't a game. It was an important thing. Because one second I'd be asked to play organ for a bingo session, during the intermission, and the next minute I'd be out playing a dinner and dance date or a club or a jazz date. I used to do all those sorts of things. All of this sort of went along with being taught music privately. I had a little old lady who was about 80 years old. In fact I had about three teachers altogether. They were all local. They taught as a sideline.

How much did classical music have to do with the development of your jazz style?

When I was about 14 I wanted to buy some books that would give me some insight on jazz piano. A piano player I knew told me he developed his style from playing Debussy. I tried it but really couldn't find anything of any value there that would influence a jazz style for me. I think what it came down to was playing a lot with a jazz orchestra. That exposed me to a lot of jazz improvisation. And you could buy arrangements sometimes for small combos or solo piano which had improvised solos in them. People like Brubeck and George Shearing very helpfully published books that had improvisations written out. I found that quite helpful. Until I bought those books, I was playing pseudo-jazz piano in the right hand and stride in the left.

Did you pick up things off of records?

I didn't have a record player, so I used to get it from the radio. I also used to go up to London to hear jazz. So my exposure to jazz was what was being played on the radio. When you do that, you have to wait and wonder, "Well, who was that?" And you might find out within a week. I remember one tune that was being played quite a lot. Floyd Cramer's "On the Rebound." That was a major influence on me throughout. And then there were various jazz players. [Musician/comedian] Dudley Moore was one of them. He had a TV show. At the time, I was playing stride piano because I'd bought some Art Tatum and Fats Waller sheet music. And suddenly I heard Dudley Moore. He played this style that sounded great. I couldn't figure out how he was doing it. When I tried to imitate him it came out like Fats Waller in the left hand and Dudley Moore in the right. That's when I realized what the advantages of having a bass player were. Before that I used to do concerts with just drums and piano, because I thought that bass players—well, you never really hear them anyway [laughs]. They only got in the way of my left hand.

When did you add the modular Moog to your setup? Did you consider it an extension of the organ?

It was. In those days I didn't really know what I was looking for. It was all trial and error. A lot of the sounds I was getting from the L-100 were completely accidental. With the Moog, I went into a record shop where they knew me. Wendy Carlos' *Switched-On Bach* had just been released. They played it for me in the shop. I didn't honestly like it. The guy played it for me because it had the Brandenburg thing in G, which I had done with the Nice [on *Ars Longa Vita Brevis*]. The guy asked me if I'd heard this version, played it for me, and asked me what I thought of it. I said it sounded horrible. It was too boggy, too laid down. But there was a picture of the thing it was played on, and I said, "So what's this?" And he said it was like a telephone switchboard. And I said, "Oh, that's interesting." So I bought the album. I got word through my office that a guy by the name of Mike Vickers had had a Moog shipped over to England, so I asked if I could have a look at it. We got together, and he set it up in his room. He explained to me the functioning of the instrument. I said, "Well, can it be used on stage?" And he said, "No way. You don't relize the complications in this. There's no

way you could do that." I thought there must be some way, and asked, "What if you hid down behind this thing and programmed it while I was playing it? You know, set up all these things and keep it in tune?" I was playing at the Festival Hall with the Royal Philharmonic and the Nice. I thought I'd use the synthesizer as an added touch. So Mike Vickers was hunched down backstage, but he'd pop up every now and then and put a plug in somewhere. It worked excellently. So I immediately sent off to Moog and got some literature back. At that time Bob [Moog] was developing his preset thing, so I said, "I want one."

What happened when you got it?

It arrived in a box, no instructions or anything. It was all in bits and pieces. I couldn't even get a sound out of it. I was at the point of throwing the damn thing out the window. I frantically rang up Mike Vickers and asked him, "How do I get some sound here?" He said, "Oh. You got it! I'd love to see it!" So he came around, and he couldn't figure it out either. He knew how to operate his unit, but it had taken him ages because he hadn't gotten any instructions either. He couldn't work out the presets. But he kept it for about three days and rang me up and said, "I think I've got it." He came over with diagrams to show which switches were the envelope generators, and which were the voltage-controlled amplifiers, and which were the mixers, and so on. He worked out a number of presets that were usable. I've been using that unit with the band ever since.

Do you find yourself using synthesizer mainly for effects?

Yeah. I think my use of synthesizer is basically all effects. It's just been a case of trying to get new sounds that you wouldn't hear on any other instrument. It's got to have a definite characteristic that's obviously a synthesizer. I think it's excellent what other people have done with, say, the Minimoog, where sometimes you can't tell whether it's a Minimoog or a guitar. They've found clever uses for the pitch and modulation controls. But I've never used the synthesizer to copy. There's no real point in it if you can't tell if that's a guitar playing or a Moog. With me, you say, "That is definitely a Moog." Otherwise you can get confused. It gets mixed in with that organ sound.

What about on "Abaddon's Bolero" from Trilogy? *Isn't that contrary to what you're saying?*

Yeah. That was an attempt to copy the Walter Carlos thing. That was one occasion where I tried to copy trumpet sounds and the like.

Emerson noodling on a blues in Montreal before rehearsing for ELP's disastrous orchestral tour in 1977. "Versatility and being able to read were the two most important things . . . ."

Was the solo at the end of "Lucky Man," from your first album, added as an afterthought?

As is usual on Greg's acoustic pieces, Greg [Lake] goes into the studio while the rest of us aren't around. I just happened to be in the studio with my synthesizer at the same time Greg was doing "Lucky Man." And Greg said, "Why don't you do something on the end?" So I improvised something. I didn't think much of the solo. Honestly, it's a lot of shit. But it was just what he wanted. I just did a rough setting on the synthesizer, went in, and played something off the top of my head.

Do you have any advice for kids who are getting started in music?

Well, get a good grounding from a good teacher. I think that's most important. The teacher has to be one who doesn't stunt your growth. The teacher has to give fresh ideas. There are so many different techniques, it's hard to choose the right one. I recently had a teacher who tried to get me to play in a relaxed fashion, but I'll never be a relaxed player. In England there's a school of teaching that came from a guy called James Shean. He's keen on technique, and his method makes a lot of sense to me. Try as many teachers as you can, and just collect information from as many teachers as possible. Don't stay with one all the time. Do this until you're satisfied that that is the way you want to play. People are all individuals and they're all going to end up playing in different ways, so it's a question of matching up a jigsaw puzzle. Finding the teacher that suits you can save a lot of time.

September 1980 — Many ELP fans were shocked by Love Beach *when it came out.*

I know—I was opposed to the whole thing. I even organized a survey to find out what people would think. We had people posted at O'Hare airport in Chicago with a little questionnaire, asking people first off, "Have you heard of this band?" and if they said yes, then, "Which of these album titles do you think would suit their next album?" They weren't told what the music would sound like, but they all indicated that *Love Beach* was at the bottom of the list. So I said to the people at Atlantic Records, "There you go. Doesn't that prove it?" But they were adamant about using that title. In the end I rang up Ahmet Ertegun [president of Atlantic Records] and said, "Look, man, it makes us appear like a bunch of beach boys, which we're not." And he said, "Oh, it doesn't really matter about album titles. What are titles, you know? Look at the name of the

Beatles. What does that mean? It doesn't make any difference." So I said, "It makes a lot of difference to me because it doesn't fit the image of this band." But they went ahead anyhow. It's a complete letdown.

It was hard to believe the album was done by the same band that did Brain Salad Surgery.

I know. It's a bit depressing. I feel there was a certain charm in "Canario." It had almost the same effect as "Hoedown" [from *Trilogy*] or something. And the second side had a kind of a concept about it. The lyrics are a bit gross, but it was all, as I said in the "Open Letter," because everybody but me wanted to get the hell out of Nassau. There were a lot of bad things going down. We'd go into the studio and just rap all day because we hadn't got any music down, and that was it. In the end I stuck the whole album together—nobody else showed up—and sent it off to Atlantic.

What kind of equipment are you using now?

Here in the Bahamas I've got a Korg 3300 and a Korg 3100 polyphonic synthesizer, a Minimoog, a Yamaha CP-30 electronic piano, a Yamaha upright, and a Korg vocoder. In England, I've got my Yamaha GX-1, which is still my favorite of all the synthesizer equipment. The engineer that we had on the road with us, Nick Rose, has built a system into it so that I can play a Minimoog from the lower manual, so I've got the Minimoog bass sound, which I've never been able to duplicate exactly on any other synthesizer. Nick also built a digital sequencer into it for me. At the moment it will remember about 100 notes, but Nick is going to expand the memory. I don't understand the technical side of it too well, but what Nick has done has thickened up the sound of the GX-1 quite a bit. It was always a bit too thin and lacking in guts for my taste. If you listen to records by Tomita, whom I admire very much, you'll hear the sort of wishy-washy sound I'm talking about. I hear that same sound coming out of the GX-1, but that doesn't stop me from using it. Stevie Wonder called it his dream machine, and it still remains that to me. A lot of people have said it doesn't replace the biting organ sound that I usually got, but I think when you lose a bit you gain a bit too. I've lost that biting quality by using the GX-1, but I've gained a lot of other possibilities. "Fanfare For The Common Man" [from *Works, Vol. 1*] should never have sounded right on the Hammond. The other day I heard someone at a local club playing it on a Hammond and it sounded ghastly. There are certain things that work better on the organ and certain things that

work better on the GX-1.

So you've given up playing the organ.

More or less. I've done a recording down here that uses a bit of Hammond, but it's not as wild as in my early days. It's controlled, and it's funky—I hate that word, but that's really the only way to describe it. I'm enjoying playing in a funky context, because it's such a change from the very technical approach ELP took. Carl [Palmer] heard it, and he said it was about time I painted my face black [*laughs*]. He said I'd been down in Nassau too long. Carl and I still correspond, which is nice. There's a possibility that we might work together again. We've spoken about it, but it's still a long way off. Quite honestly, I'm much happier now that I'm free of the pressure of going to the studio and wasting all that money arguing instead of playing music.

Your Hammond sound was so distinctive. I'd think it would be difficult to duplicate on anybody else's equipment.

You're right. Since my own Hammond is still in England, I've tried to get that sound myself on Hammonds that are available in Nassau, and it's difficult. A lot of my Hammond sound may have been due to the fact that it was running into very old beat-up Leslies and Hiwatt or Marshall amps that had been beefed up by a guy named Bill Haugh.

What about your Korg synthesizers? Any thoughts on them?

Well, I'm still using them. In fact, on the track on the *Inferno* album that has the choir ["Mater Tenebrarum"], the organ sound is actually the Korg, going through an MXR Stereo Chorus, plus a bit of echo. I think it gets quite an effective pipe organ sound. At the moment I really cannot feel confident enough in the Korgs to use them as a main solo instrument. They record too weakly. But I understand the Korg people are working on some changes. They keep telling me to just wait until I hear the new stuff.

What did you use for the bell-like sound on "Taxi Ride" from Inferno?

That was the Korg 3100.

What about the guitar-like solo line?

I think that was the Minimoog going through a flanger.

It's very different for you to play something like that. Does it reflect an interest in jazz-rock?

Well, I've been experimenting with reggae rhythms. Also, I'm hoping to get a junkanoo thing going down here. Junkanoo is a festival sound you'll hear in the Bahamas. It's the sound of percussion, whistles, boards—anything. I'd like to try to make something out of that. Some local guys have been experimenting with it, and it sounded very noisy, but I think if it's controlled it could be a very interesting sound. They have a junkanoo down here at Christmas and New Year's Eve, and if you stand on the street there's an incredible pulsing rhythm. It's different from the other Latin and Caribbean rhythms I've been working with. Usually I've just been going down to the studio without any prepared stuff and just jamming, because the guys I've been playing with are like—you know, a couple of bottles of wine, and it works wonders [laughs]. Oh, we've had some great times. The other thing I've been trying to get involved in is gospel music. I've been going around to the gospel churches here in Nassau with a tape recorder. One Sunday night I'd finished in the studio, and I took Mott and his assistant Dennis out and we scouted around looking for a church. Down here they really get going on Sunday night. So we were driving down the road, and we heard tambourines and shouting, so we stopped. I had my tape recorder, and I didn't want to disturb anyone, so I just stuck my microphone in the window and sort of observed. But one of the preachers who was standing in the back invited us in, so we kind of dubiously sat in the back with all this raving going on and continued recording. God, those services are incredible! People go into hysterics, and they're laying on hands and writhing around, and then they'll burst into another hallelujah chorus, with handclapping and tambourines, and I'm recording all this. At the end of it, everybody sits down in the pews, and the reverend gets up and speaks to the congregation, and he says, "Who are these visitors in the back of the church?" And I just said nothing. He said, "Do you have a spokesman?" I said, "Well, yeah, my name is Keith and this is my friend Mott and my friend Dennis." He said, "What is your purpose?" I said, "Well, I'm looking to record a gospel choir." He said, "What is your church?" I said, "Church of England," I think, so he said, "I'd like to see you often," and he hugged me hard. He said, "You come along on Wednesday evening. I have just the choir for you." So we went along on Wednesday, and it was no different than before—the raving was even worse! I'd like to write some gospel music.

What about your routine at home? Do you practice regularly any more?

When I'm up very late in the studio, like four o'clock in the morning, it doesn't always happen. But usually I get up in the morning and exercise, and then I come back and practice for two hours.

That practice could involve writing, or just practicing things that I feel I need to work on. It's difficult getting a piano I would like down here. I've still got my nine-foot Steinway grand in England. Down here I just have a little Yamaha upright, and if a string breaks or anything you have to wait months to get a new one. And of course it goes out of tune because of the heat and the air conditioning going on and off. I've been using the Yamaha CP-30, the electronic one, and that's fairly reliable.

Was "The Three Fates" [from the album Emerson, Lake & Palmer,] *an adaptation of something, or was it totally original?*

Totally original. Does it remind you of anything?

No, but so much of ELP's material involved quotes from other sources, and there were no credits for the Janacek or Bartok pieces on the same album. . . .

In the early days, I thought that "Knife Edge" was far enough removed from Janacek's *Sinfonietta* and "The Barbarian" from Bartok's *Allegro Barbaro* not to worry about crediting it. But I don't like to be thought of as stealing anything, and it gave me a guilty conscience not to have credited them. If the musician is alive, I always make a point of writing them personally or making sure that the record company contacts them and gets the royalty thing straight. Even though you still see no credits on that first ELP album, Janacek's and Bartok's heirs get their royalties. And ever since, we've made sure to list the credits properly. Those mistakes happened in the early days of ELP. I've gotten past making those same mistakes again.
Dominic Milano

Rick Wakeman
The Great Orchestrator

March/April, 1976 — *How did you become interested in playing piano?*

My father was a good piano player, and there were also some little girls living next door to us who were learning to play the instrument. I could hear them through the wall. So those two things put together got me wanting to play. When I was just over four years old I started taking lessons from the same teacher the girls had. I stayed with that teacher until I was eighteen, at which point I started going to the Royal College of Music in London. I stayed there until I was twenty.

Did you ever study anything besides piano?

I took clarinet lessons from the time I was eleven until I was twenty. I started church organ when I was fourteen, and I had separate training for theory and history.

What kind of music were you doing at that time?

I was playing in jazz and dance bands, rock and roll bands, that sort of thing. But what I really wanted to do was to be a concert pianist and teach.

When was it that you turned to studio work?

That's quite a funny story, because it was something that everyone dreams of getting into at first. The whole thing really came about through an amazing bit of luck. There are two sorts of sessions that you do in England. There are the sessions you do for friends, which are more or less favors, and there are the true sessions that are set up by a fixer. Those are the ones to really get into, because you can make a living at it. I knew a guy called Jimmy Thomas who used to be the lead singer for Ike and Tina Turner's band. He was the first person to take me into a studio.

Previous page: Wakeman onstage with Yes, playing a Polymoog and Hammond C-3. Below: A publicity shot for Wakeman's album "Criminal Record."

That's when I got lucky. During that session [producers] Tony Visconti and Gus Dudgeon were there. They started giving me sessions for other bands.

Was it through session work that you met [Strawbs guitarist] Dave Cousins?

Yeah. The first session I did for Dave happened when I was working at the Top Rank Bowl in Reading, and Tony Visconti phoned me up and asked me to come down to do what was called a BBC session at the Paris Studio. It was to play piano for a folk group called Strawbs. I did it and became quite good friends with Dave. I ended up doing all their stuff for them. Things just seemed to culminate and I fancied to join them. I had become disillusioned with session work. I was getting good bread, but I wasn't getting a chance to be part of the music: You're in there for three hours and then you're out again. So that was it. I joined Strawbs and stayed there for fifteen months.

What made you leave?

I suddenly got more and more on the outside of things, with Dave himself doing all the work. In the end, with the musicians that were in Strawbs at the time, things had gone as far as they could. There would have to be a complete change-around or it would have rotted away. Yes was having a change-around also, and asked me if I wanted to join. I said no, but went to one of their rehearsals anyway. I was only going to stay ten minutes, but I ended up staying about three years. In fact, I joined Strawbs on March 28, 1970, and left on July 31, 1971. I joined Yes August 1st that same year, and left May 18, 1974.

Could you tell us about your stay with Yes?

I had some great times and some lousy times. It was a band that was bonded together by music. There was little love lost. It wasn't bad until things got to a stage where I didn't know what direction the music was going in. I didn't enjoy *Tales From Topographic Oceans,* so I finished out the European tour we were doing and left.

And that's when you did your second solo album Journey To The Centre Of The Earth, *and began using an orchestra in your touring act?*

We had actually gone through that phase already. We had already done the Festival Hall concert, where *Journey* was recorded, and the problem was that there was nothing left to do. We wanted to go out and play, but had no material for a band. It was all material for orchestra. The only practical solution I had was to take the orchestra on the road with us. When we had done that, we came back and did *Arthur.* But present restrictions with recording and the orchestra pushed things about as far as they could go. It was time to say goodbye to that. That was when we got the English Rock Ensemble together. I already had a band, but we changed around some of the personnel to strengthen a few places and added a few things. The next album will be a band album. It all seems to be coming together.

When composing, is there a difference in the way you approach orchestral pieces and keyboard pieces?

The thing I always keep in mind is that you can't write for piano what you would write for harpsichord. The one problem I'd found with orchestra is that to listen to the way everybody else had used it, I always felt that they sort of got rock and roll parts together and then shoveled the orchestra over guitar, which doesn't work. An orchestra can't rock and roll. The musicians aren't taught to; they hold a whole different attitude that makes it absolutely impossible. So I thought the object would be not to integrate the group and orchestra, but to write the group parts to complement the orchestra parts. As for keyboards, that can be difficult because you're dealing with textures more than anything else. Instruments like Mellotrons and Moog synthesizers, the Moogs especially, are so thick. You have to be very very careful in your sound selections and spacings so you don't thicken things too badly, destroying any little colors or harmonies that you put in. Even though they have polyphonic Moogs, and I've got one, I think they should be monophonic instruments. They're better that way.

You've done a lot of work involving overdubbed keyboards. What should someone doing this kind of multi-track recording keep in mind?

It's important to record the instruments in the right order. You start with the acoustical instruments, the more rhythmic instruments. The Moogs and the Mellotrons come last, because it's harder to overdub rhythmically or percussively onto something that's melodic. As you're putting tracks down the thing takes shape. It's easy for it to go off in different directions, which makes it impossible to bring it back to where you want it. As it turns out, it's easier to shape a piece rhythmically, adding harmonies and such later. I don't work the same as I did in Yes, where we would have a guitar week that involved nothing but Steve [Howe] going into the studio with a guitar. This way you'd end up after six or seven weeks with a vocal week. I prefer to finish a track once

it's started, so that everybody is doing something all the time. Doing it Yes' way, taking six weeks for all the backing tracks and then coming back to do the vocals and overdubs, you've lost the original mood of the pieces by the time the album is finished.

How do you approach playing all these different instruments?

First you've got to know that no two keyboards are the same to play. The touch is dissimilar on all of them, and every instrument has its little idiosyncrasies. That's the thing you have to get used to. When you get your instrument, don't just take it on the road straight away. Take it home and practice on the thing until you know it inside out—until you know if it's going to do something silly and why it's doing it. One of the hardest instruments to adapt to is the straight harpsichord, because the keys are smaller. You really have to be on your toes, or else you will end up with 30,000 split notes.

What should people watch out for when switching from acoustic piano to electronic keyboards?

There are various things. You can always tell a piano player when he's playing electronic instruments because he'll still attack the keys according to the strength of sound. And you can always tell an organ player when he's playing piano, because organists invariably make dreadful piano players. They just play from their fingers instead of using the various other parts of the wrist and hand. Also, the piano player, when he first goes to the organ, tends to forget that he hasn't got any form of sustain, and the whole fingering technique is different. Which brings up another fault of organ players: They go to slide off notes on the piano, and it just doesn't work. It's basically down to having confidence on your instruments more than anything else. I can guarantee when I put a new instrument up there, even if I know it, for the first week in practice, something will go wrong. It will be my fault and not the instrument's. You just have to keep going until you iron out all the faults.

Do you do any warm-up exercises before you go on stage?

Yeah. About 36 cans of beer, and only about two bottles of wine. [*Chuckles.*] Really, I practice a lot. I try to put in three hours a day, otherwise my fingers stiffen up. And that practice can be anything. Sometimes I might have a day when I like to get out the old Bach 48 [*The Well-Tempered Clavier*] and bore myself to death. On another day I might leap through scales and

arpeggios. It just depends, you know. It's important to keep your technique up because you write according to it. That's the one fault with anybody who writes for themselves. They write what they know they can technically play. So if you keep working on your technique, constantly improving it, then that must help your writing, as it gives you a wider variety of things you can play. I think there's a lot of self-written crap going around because people are writing according to their technical ability. That's why we end up with these 3-chord rondos.

February, 1979 — What equipment did you use on Yes's Tormato *tour?*

This time around, the object was to cut down a bit. We've been noticing that for the last two or three years every band around has been taking more and more junk with them. It's getting to the point where there will be so much equipment onstage that you won't be able to see the band. So now we've gone full circle. Instead of seeing how much we can put onstage, we're seeing how little we can put onstage. That meant finding instruments that could do two jobs instead of one. So first of all, I hid all of my amplification under the stage. I used Moog Synamps. Then I only took the Hammond C-3, the Polymoog, the Sequential Circuits Prophet, two Birotrons, two Minimoogs, a Yamaha CP-30 electronic piano, an RMI Keyboard Computer, and a grand piano. That was it, besides the obvious little gadgets like some Sequential Circuits sequencers and things.

The object was to cut down and make the show a little more visible to the audience. If they can't see anything because there's three tons of junk onstage, they can't enjoy it. The Keyboard Computer took away the need to carry the Mander Pipe Organ this time. The new Keyboard Computer [the KC-II] is really very clever. It's far more advanced than the first one. The Prophet has taken away the need to have a lot of stuff onstage too. I can't begin to tell you how many instruments that replaces. The Yamaha CP-30 lets you do without a Rhodes, a Wurlitzer, the RMI Rockischord, The Hohner Clavinet, and the Hohner Pianet. The only problem comes up when you want to do something like play Clavinet and Rhodes at the same time, but then you just turn to the Prophet. Between the Prophet and the Yamaha you can almost do a whole show. But actually, when you start thinking about it, you can't. I need what I've got out there.

What kinds of things are you using the Polymoog for?

It's an interesting instrument. On the last tour and on the *Going For The One* album I used it mainly as a filler—a brightener. I used it as a coloring instrument, but for the *Tormato* album and also for my own album, *Criminal Record*, I used it more for soloing and filling. I think the first thing you tend to do when you buy the Polymoog is to look at it as a polyphonic instrument, and go flat out and play as many notes at once as you can on it. That's a mistake.

You get a lot of distortion that way.

Opposite: Wakeman onstage with Yes' Chris Squire and Jon Anderson, playing a Polymoog with a Minimoog in the background. Below: Tweaking a Clavinet and two Minimoogs at a sound check.

Right. And it's totally wrong. You can play lots of notes at once, so you do. But it's like if you had someone come out with a backwards car. You get it and drive it backwards for three weeks, but then you realize that you can still drive it forwards! You know what I mean? I've had lots of fun with it. Moog has come out with a new Polymoog that has a bunch of presets on it for the person who can't afford the big one with all the junk on it. I tried it out in New York. It's very good.

What about the Prophet?

The Prophet is a gold mine. I think it's a superb instrument. For the amateur or pro who wants a machine that's not super expensive but doesn't want to buy a piece of junk, and who wants something that he or she can be proud of, then the Prophet's the machine. It's just absolutely superb, and I'm not saying that as an advertisement for Sequential Circuits, because I don't endorse them. I wouldn't mind it though; they're that good at what they do.

What kinds of things have you done with the Prophet?

The first thing I did was to go through all their presets as they put them on and decide which ones I liked. Then I took one of my Prophets—I have two of them—and wiped of all the presets. Then, without looking at the sound charts that Sequential Circuits gives you, I tried to duplicate their presets on the blank machine. That way I got to know the instrument. It's the quickest way to learn an instrument. Then I reset the presets however I wanted them. I only kept about five of the original ones.

Do you remember which ones you kept?

They're mostly modulation sweep control things like numbers 25 and 35. I kept their harmonium-type sound, 31, because it was really a winner. I also kept the harpsichord sound, 16, but I moved it up an octave. Of those I kept, I didn't really alter them drastically. It was mostly little bits to suit what I was playing. Even that wasn't all that necessary, because you can go into edit mode and alter the preset. But when I get hold of a new instrument I like to play with it and play with it and play with it for a long time, so that when I'm onstage with it I know it inside and out.

Do you miss having a touch-sensitive keyboard on it?

No, because I don't really like touch-sensitive electric keyboards. It's always seemed phony to me. That's because of the fact that I'm a piano player. With the piano, the touch-sensitivity is a little more obvious. With electronic instruments you can alter the note after you've played it. I find it very confusing to do that with my fingers. I don't like it; I feel like it's cheating. But here's the strange thing: I'll do it with my feet. I feel like I've got more control if I do the effects with my feet.

You're using a Leslie now too. When we last talked, you didn't like Leslies.

I'm using the combination, yeah. I don't like Lelies very much, but I'm a stubborn old sort. I've never liked Leslies, because they've always taken away the basic sound of the Hammond. For certain things, the Leslie is important. But until last year I hadn't found the right combination. Now, with the Leslie-and-organ-fed-direct combination, I like it. I give the road crew a free hand and they surprise me a lot; 99 times out of 100 what they do is tremendous. The Leslie was one of those. I'd never heard a Leslie sound good at low volume, so they went away with little smiles on their faces and came back with a Leslie that sounded good at low volume.

What about drawbar setting on the Hammond? What do you use?

I've got two basics that I always work from: All the white drawbars are pulled full out and so is the 16' one, and the percussion is set to the second harmonic with soft decay. That's the one setting that I've used for years. It's the one that I use whenever I first sit down at a Hammond. It's very easy to work off of. I never keep the same setting from the beginning of a piece to the end of a piece. The other preset, the non-percussion one, is just the reverse. All the drawbars are pulled out full. Then I push various ones in, working backwards. I do that in the opening to "Into The Heart Of The Sunrise" [on *Fragile*]. That starts with all the drawbars out, and in between the runs I play an augmented fourth on the lower manual of the Hammond. The Hammond is also heavily phased and echoed, and you move the 8', 4', and 2' drawbars in alternately. The 16' stays out all the time. I think you have to keep playing with the drawbars constantly or it gets stale. It's like playing a Polymoog and just using one preset all night. It'd get boring and unimaginative.

Do you work out an arrangement on piano before you write it down for other instruments?

No, this is weird. I normally have the basic themes that I want to use. Then I hear in my head what instrument I want them on, so I write out my score paper. I don't touch the piano again after I've worked out the themes. Then I go in and fill out the accompaniment. Normally, I get

inspired by all this to do other little things. I do this against that, and so on. And I don't change anything until after I've heard it.

What about multiple keyboard parts?

Multiple keyboard parts. This is a strange one too. I normally have a good idea of what's going to go where. But you have to arrange them according to sound. You have to make sure nothing clashes. The parts are easy to do; it's finding the sound that's the difficult one. The hardest album to do that on was *Criminal Record*. I was putting down the third or fourth layer and not being quite happy with the sound, so I spent considerable time finding sounds that I wanted to use. There was an awful lot of replacement that had to keep going on until I was happy. I've never worked that way before. There were some combinations that theoretically shouldn't have worked, but did. Things like church organ and Polymoog. Really strange combinations. But I was happy with them. I'd like to do another album in a similar vein. I'd like to do an orchestral and keyboard album. Combine them both. I liked doing *Criminal Record*, but it didn't sell well over here, although it did in Europe. But sales don't worry me. I'd rather have an album out that I'm pleased with than one that's tongue-in-cheek and sells a million copies. I've gone past the gimmick stage. I like to let the keyboards speak for themselves.

Did you really record the pipe organ on Going For The One *over a phone line?*

That's right. Down a telephone line. That's true. We did it that way because that's the way things are done in Switzerland. On being together, they make the United States and England look like they're darkest Africa. Their telephone lines are the highest fidelity you can imagine. They said, "What do you need a mobile for? All you do is rent a phone line for a day." So we rented a phone line. I put on the can [headphones]; the guys put on their cans; and 1,2,3,4, away we went. It was great. The pipe organ was recorded direct into the studio. I listened back to it over the cans, drove back to the studio, cut a little overdub, and that was it. Finished! They were so together it was unbelievable. They did the choir like that as well. It's amazing, but it's normal to them. They do everything like that over there. The Swiss are clever. We could learn a lot from them. An awful lot. They take all the things the Americans, the Japanese, and the English have done with technology and they use them properly.

Dominic Milano

Wakeman surrounded by (clockwise from left) a
Mellotron, two Minimoogs, a Clavinet, an RMI
electronic piano, a Hammond C-3, a Steinway
piano, a Baldwin electric harpsichord, another
Minimoog, and a Rhodes electric piano.

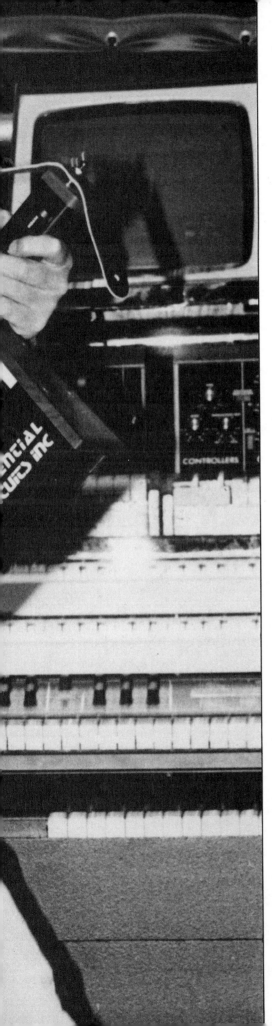

Geoff Downes
The Dream Survives

March, 1981; November, 1983 — Your keyboards are laid out in a straight line across the stage. Do you find it difficult to deal with a setup like that?

It's not the most conducive to good playing, really. I made a certain sacrifice for the sake of the visual show. I like to double up on certain keyboards, and with them all in a row, it tends to stretch me out a bit. I can't get the best angle on the keys. For the first Asia tour, I had the benefit of having the keyboards set in a semi-circle. I've obviously lost that now.

Do you think you'll change the setup?

For next year, yeah. This setup is definitely not the best thing for my playing, but I'll finish out the tour with it.

Does the straight line setup present any problem for you as far as monitoring the sound goes?

The monitors are set all across the keyboard setup. Actually, they're much nicer this way. They're set farther back, so they don't blast my ears out, and they're angled nicely so I get a really good stereo image from where I stand in the middle. The enhanced stereo image is the greatest benefit I get from having the keyboards all in a row like that.

Can you run down the keyboards you're using onstage?

Left to right, I've got a Yamaha CS-80, a Memorymoog, a Korg Mono/Poly, a Yamaha CP-70 electric grand, a Hammond J-122 organ, an SCI Prophet-5 with a poly-sequencer hooked to it, Moog Taurus bass pedals, the bass pedals to the Hammond J next to the Taurus pedals, a Nova-tron, a PPG, Fairlight CMI master and slave keyboards, two Minimoogs, a pedalboard, a Rhodes Stage 73, a Clavinet D-6, an ARP String Ensemble,

Previous page: Geoff Downes playing a Prophet remote keyboard. Below: Asia's first tour (l to r): guitarist Steve Howe, drummer Carl Palmer, Downes, and bassist John Wetton.

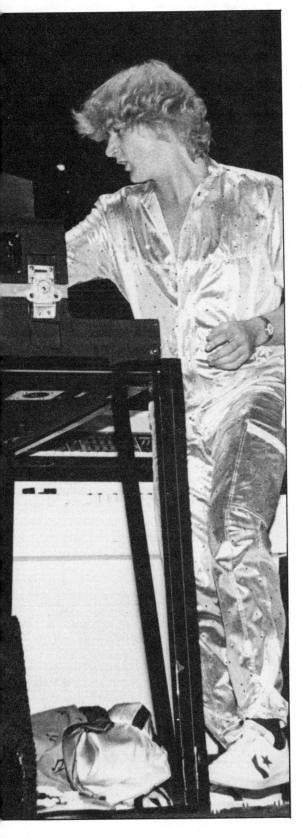

Below: Downes with Yes, playing a Yamaha CP-70B electric grand. As a member of the Buggles, Downes played on the first video MTV ever broadcast.

a Prophet-10, a Hammond B-3, a Linn drum computer [LM-1], a Korg Polysix, a Prophet-5 Remote, and a Moog Liberation.

Why two strap-on keyboards? Do you use them both during the set?

Yeah, I use them twice. In my solo, I've got everything going off on sequencers and I come down in front of the stage and play along on it.

What's the Linn for?

I use it in my solo, and that's all, really. Last year Carl used it for a tune called "Midnight Sun," where we all played keyboards. Carl sort of did finger drumming, except that it was all pre-programmed into the Linn anyway. It was all for show, really.

Has Asia tried recording with the Linn?

Yes, we did, but it was pretty unsuccessful. We did "Midnight Sun" that way, but the problem was that it didn't sound representative of the group. I think the Linn tends to promote music that can sound a bit anonymous. Anybody can go out and buy a Linn drum machine, but everyone cannot go out and buy a Carl Palmer.

Do you augment Palmer's drums with your keyboards, playing percussion effects?

Yeah. I use the CMI to do thunder crashes and timpani sounds, tambourines—just the odd bit of effects I do in addition to the instrumental work.

Are you still using a vocoder?

Yes, a Roland rack-mount unit that's tied into the String Ensemble with its chorus on. It sounds really sweet. I quite like the Solina [the European name for the ARP String Ensemble]. It gives me a little icing. Its sound is nothing like any other synthesizer. It's got a little sharp edge on top. It's really a horrible sound when you think about it, all distortion and intermodulation, but with the right balance with the other keyboards, it's very effective.

Why did you add the PPG? What will it do that you can't get the Fairlight to do?

I fell in love with the sound of the PPG. It has such a rich original sound. You can't compare its digital sound-generating facilities to that of the CMI, because the CMI is more of a sample-to-disk machine. Its waveform drawing is quite different. But the PPG has a very up-front sound. And I like the fact that it has some analog controls in it [filtering].

It sits where your Polymoog used to be. What happened to it?

I replaced it with the PPG. I mean, if you look at the sorts of polyphonic instruments available today, it should be apparent that the Polymoog is

out-classed. I just didn't need it.

But you're still using a Novatron.

Yeah, it's there to hold up my PPG, CMI, and Minimoogs [*laughs*].I used it for the opening pipe organ in "Daylight." It's double-tracked, and you get this wonderful up-front sound with it. It does get a bit dodgey at times. I get a few crackles and stuff out of it, but it's still operating. You just have to take care of it, and it will be good to you. It has a sound that I quite like which you can't really duplicate on other keyboards, exactly. You know, the tapes really sound crude, but even the Fairlight won't duplicate that effect. And there have been times when all the other keyboards have gone down, and the Novatron still kept going.

What tapes are you using with it live?

I've got strings, choir, and pipe organ in it now. I've got a few other sets which I use in the studio every now and then. One of them is of a Hammond with a Leslie speaker on it.

Why do you use the Novatron for that when you have two Hammonds already?

I don't use it live now, but I remember once when my Hammond broke down, I had this Hammond sound on Novatron tape which I sampled into the Fairlight. It sounded better once

I got it in the Fairlight, and I got the added bonus of having the velocity sensitivity of the Fairlight applied to the Hammond sound. So I used my CMI as a Hammond to fill in for the broken-down Hammond. A lot of my friends thought it sounded better than the Hammond, but I don't believe it.

There's a Hammond solo on "The Heat Goes On." Are you focusing on playing more Hammond?

Yeah, I've dragged the old Hammond into action. Our second album is more dense than the first. You'll find more subtle keyboard work in the open sections, like intros, but when you're competing with all the other instruments bashing away, it's nice to have an instrument that you can really grab hold of and almost take over with it. I think the B-3 has sufficient frequency to be able to get through there and be heard. A lot of people have forgotten that Hammonds exist, but I haven't. I've got two of them.

Do you find that each has its own sound?

Quite naturally. The J is a spinet that doesn't have drawbars, where the B-3 is a tone-wheel organ. The J tends to be a bit reedy-sounding, and the B-3 has a much thicker texture. It has a much broader sound.

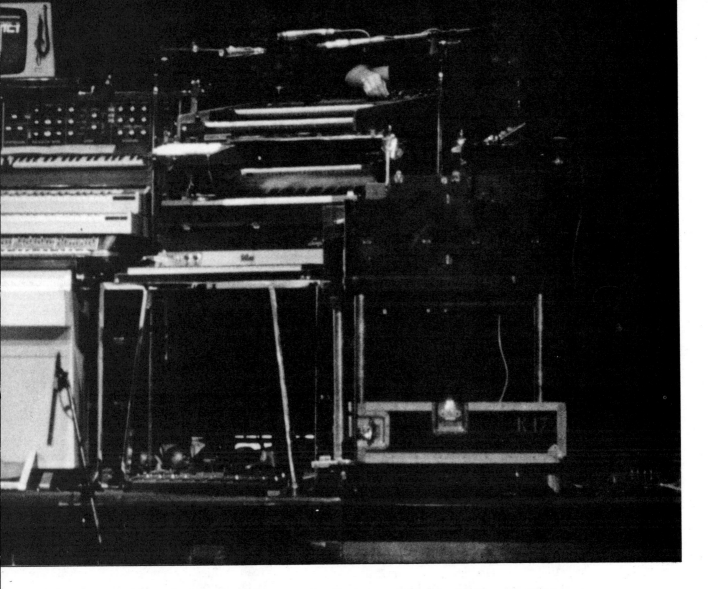

The Downes system: (l. to r.) A Yamaha CS-80, a Prophet-5, a Hammond J-122 organ, a Yamaha CP-70B electric grand, two Minimoogs, Fairlight master and slave keyboards, a Polymoog, a Mellotron, a Prophet-10, a Solina string ensemble, a Clavinet, a Rhodes electric piano, a Hammond B-3, and a Moog Liberation.

How are you amplifying the Hammonds?

I run them both through a Leslie. A Leslie 700 or something. I've tried going direct, but I found the direct signal a bit boring. I know Keith Emerson used to split the signal and go into a Leslie and run the straight signal into something like a phase shifter, and I used to do that onstage, too. I've still got space in my pedal board for a direct feed which you run to phasers and stuff, but I've abandoned it. I've just got a splitter box so I can run the two Hammonds into one Leslie. And I've got the Leslie built into a special case with mikes positioned all around it. It's a pretty good sound.

Do you remember any of the drawbar settings you use?

I remember that a friend of mine told me that somebody asked Booker T. what he used, and he said he used them all flat out—take a ruler across the drawbars. So I had a go at it, and that's basically the sound I use, with the Leslie wound up and almost to the point of distorting. Mike Stone, our producer, has a trick of putting four microphones on it, two close in and two distance ambience mikes. You get a stereo swirling effect that way, provided you've got the right room acoustics, a stone chamber or something.

You write most of the material with John Wet-

ton. Is it composed on piano initially?

For the most part, yes. John plays a bit of piano, so he does half of his writing on piano and half on guitar. We really connect our ideas over a period of time. Sometimes we go to my house or somebody's place for a couple of weeks, play each other what we've got, and maybe put a couple of ideas together. Then we'll do a rough demo on a Fostex 4-track cassette, and play it for the others to see what they think.

How far do you go with the production of the demos?

Only as far as putting a Linn drum part down over a basic track of piano, a couple of synthesizer overdubs, and vocals. For the synthesizer, I'll use a Moog or Prophet. It's just a demo, so there's nothing too serious about it. It's just enough to give anyone a general idea of the song's direction.

Does any material ever get rejected?

Yes. We had a couple of tracks in the show that didn't make it on the album. We have to sit down and decide what we think are going to be the best tunes for a particular album. That's the criterion we go for. If someone brings a tune in we always have a go at it. I think you have to keep that in a group. You have to have a sense of collaboration. We'll do the backing tracks and then things will start to fall away from there. We must have recorded 14 tracks for this album, but only 11 got on. As you work on them more and more, time starts to get tight and you realize which are the ones that seem most likely to make the album. It would take a hell of a long time to do 14 songs for one album.

How long do you spend on recording?

It probably takes us a year from the songwriting, which takes about two months, to rehearsal, which takes about three, to recording and mixing, which takes another six or so months. So you're looking at a year.

How do you hack out arrangements?

They usually come out in the rehearsal period. It's such a slow process. You get one idea and that will stay through the following day. You'll start to build on it, get into it, and then maybe throw it away. I think the main thing is to make sure everyone has a part to play that's constructive to the arrangement. I think the drum part is probably the most important.

Do the other guys ever trade ideas—don't play this, play that?

Yeah, they'll say, "I don't think you should play that," and I'll say the same to them on occasion. It's only fair. I mean, I obviously wouldn't

have played it if I didn't think it was really good, but then if a couple of people turn around and say maybe it shouldn't be there, I respect them enough to know they're probably right. The thing about having a group is that you've got to be prepared to take criticism, and you'd better be prepared to accept that you can be wrong. Each person has got to like what he's doing, but there can't be a lot of interference. There are times when you run into conflict of concept. I think that if everyone put down what they thought, you'd either end up with a very unimaginative record or a very weird record.

What did you do on the second Asia album that you hadn't done on the first?

I think I got into more layering effects. We thought the first album was a bit open, which wasn't bad, but we had a different collection of songs that seemed to lend themselves to textures that were much more harmonic. So I got into this layering, where you can't necessarily hear the layers but they give a subliminal effect. In some places there are incredible amounts of things happening, but you aren't actually aware of them.

That wall of sound effect.

Yeah. It doesn't come easily. A typical layer might consist of Prophet-10, Memorymoog, acoustic piano, and a Hammond. All that is just to build up movement within the chords. That'll serve as the basic pad. Then on top of that go the lines and CMI stuff. I used a lot of Hammond coupled with acoustic piano for that thick texture. Prophet-10 played a large role, too.

Do you think you're leaning towards staying with that wall of sound texture? Or do you think you might go back to a more separated sound in the future?

I think I'll probably move into much more open musical directions after this album. I think that we all thought that what we did for this record was the right way to approach it, but I think that we did limit ourselves in a musical way as well. You can build up all these textures with layers and layers of instruments, but it's not the most fulfilling thing at the end of the day. I could probably say that we'll be moving into a slightly different direction, not even like the first album. The important thing for Asia as a group is that it doesn't remain static. Carl's been getting into his Simmons [electronic drums], Steve's been changing his guitars, and John is using different basses. I'm going to be experimenting with more digital keyboards.

Do you foresee cutting your setup down?

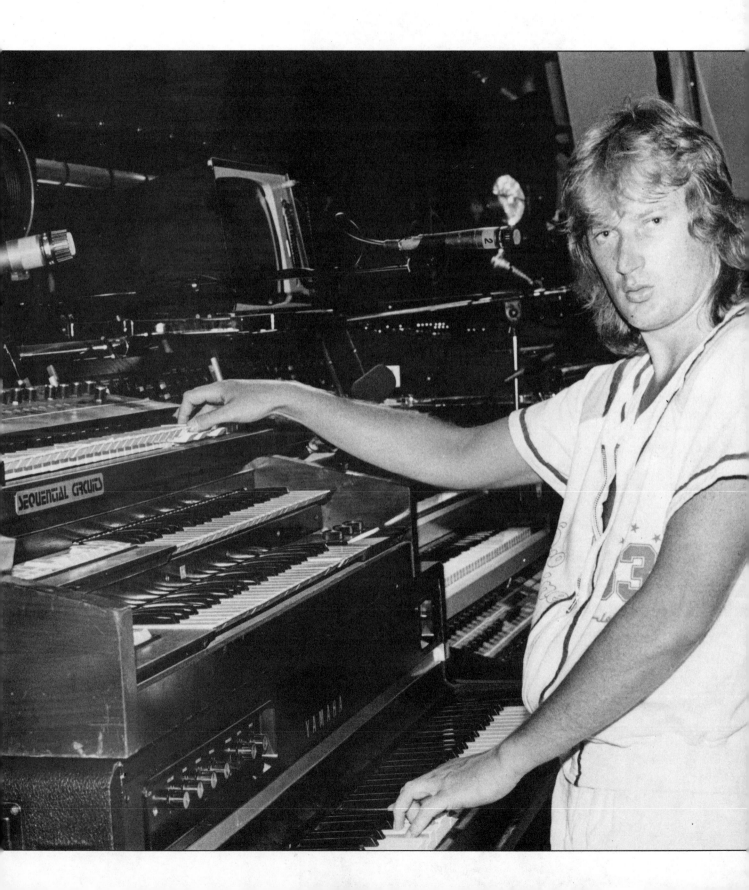

Downes live: "There's a lot of work that goes into recreating the subtle textures . . . I'll do whatever seems best at the time, so I don't actually make everything identical to what's on the record."

Well, yeah. I think I'm done with this one now. The tour we're doing now will be the last one with this particular configuration of gear. I know that your friendly readers will be happy to see me cut down. I've been following the letters you've received about my setup. It's really quite amazing, but I think it's a matter of taking what you need. One of the reasons I have so many is because it's not possible to play everything I want to play at the same time. It's not just gross indulgence. I would like to work out a setup that is a completely self-contained CMI system.

No other keyboards but a CMI?
Oh, a few CMIs. Four or five.
Four or five?
Yeah, I'd need that many because the actual polyphony of the instrument is not sufficient to allow me to get everything I'd want out of one machine. You can't hold a five-note chord in one hand and play a handful of notes with the other, either. I'd be able to with two instruments, but then I'd be limited to the number of sounds which could be programmed. With four of them, I could be playing two at the same time while the others are being reloaded with sounds.

Do you try to reproduce what's on record live as well as possible, then?
Not absolutely note-for-note. It's not possible. I just try to have the essential ingredients. I know that when I go through a part, there are certain landmark parts in the music. They're what are important to reproduce as best as possible; otherwise the song won't sound the way it did on record. There's a lot of work that goes into recreating the subtle textures, and there's more room for variation in the solos and stuff. I do a lot of transferring of lines to other synthesizers which weren't used on the album. I'll do whatever seems best at the time, so I don't actually make everything identical to what's on the record.

It's surprising that you don't have an acoustic piano onstage.
It seems a bit of a hassle. I've thought about it, but it's hard enough with all the keyboards I've got now. The CP-70 does well enough for live performance.

It's very hard to tell who's doing what in the wall of sound. Do you do a lot of doubling with the guitar?
Yes. It is quite difficult to tell what's going on. Sometimes we've got as many as 40 different tracks of that kind of thing, and it's not always the easiest thing in the world to feature everything.

The keyboards seem more prominent on side two of Alpha. *Was that conscious?*
Yes, they are more prominent. I think it was because Mike [Stone, producer] was pretty conscious about having singles on the first side, where the second side was to be a bit more esoteric and thoughtful. On the second side it didn't matter to him that things popped out at you, whereas on the first side you want to play it a bit conservatively. You don't want too much keyboards in the sound. On the whole, I think he's done a very good job. You know, there were things on the first album I didn't like.

Such as?
Some of the mixes were too simple. But like I say, you gain on the swings and you lose on the roundabouts. I think that you can really get selfish about the whole question. The important thing is that at the end of the day the whole thing sounds like a composite of parts rather than too many individual parts just jammed together. That was one of the main problems with Yes. There were too many producers. Too many people getting involved with wanting to hear what they wanted to hear rather than being happy with the group sound. The *Drama* album is an example of that. I remember when we mixed that album, there were actually five pairs of hands on the faders at any given time. That's not the way to do it. Group production is rarely a good thing. I think that you get too much featuring of things here and there and the whole becomes contrived. You have to learn to settle for a good overall sound.
Dominic Milano

IV. Laid-Back
Rock Piano

A midst all the excitement of progressive rock, and the almost daily strides being made in keyboard design, something funny was happening. Bit by bit, tune by tune, a new sound—or rather, an old one—was edging its way into the charts. Gently, with a new maturity and a hint of nostalgia, the piano was returning to the heart of rock. It wasn't the maniacal piano of Little Richard and Jerry Lee Lewis, though. The times had changed, and a generation that had been dancing nonstop for over a decade was ready for a break. People still wanted to hear the beat and drink in the spirit of the music they'd been raised on, but they were also ready to listen to the words and musical nuances that had been drowned in the psychedelic welter for several years. They had begun to mellow out, and they would soon discover that there is no better instrument to mellow out to than the piano.

Although it had never entirely disappeared from rock, the piano had lost popularity by the late '60s. To some extent, it was a victim of technology. As musicians pushed after ever escalating thresholds of volume, amplifying the acoustic piano became more and more of a hassle, especially since you could plug an organ or electric keyboard into a P.A. system and blast away with no trouble. Instrument designers were more interested in pouring their expertise into a "hot" field like electronic instruments than in devising more sophisticated piano pickups. After all, kids were more likely to buy nifty little organs that they could tote from gig to gig than to rely on clubowners to supply them with playable grands. Besides, there was a slight cultural stigma attached to the piano. Everybody's parents listened to people like Ferrante & Teicher and Roger Wil-

The Circle Completed

liams, whose dainty filigrees repelled a young generation more enticed by the tribal gleam of Jimi Hendrix's immolated guitar. For the moment, the piano was a suspect intruder in the rock fan's consciousness.

Few rock musicians were concerned about it either. The piano's unique timbre, a rich and resonant pastiche of overtones, could not be duplicated on any other instrument, but acoustic timbre was not a major concern to the typical rock keyboardist of the day. The drone of the organ, the metallic bite of the electric piano, and the first sonic stirrings of the synthesizer preoccupied him more. When someone like Keith Emerson sat down at a piano, it was almost a novelty diversion, an interlude between electronic extravaganzas.

But a piano revival was nonetheless underway as far back as 1964, when the Beatles began giving it an occasional prominence on their records. As in so many other musical areas, they were ahead of their time in using it for its tonal rather than percussive qualities. No one in the band was a keyboard whiz, but they knew that they could give songs like "Not A Second Time" a depth with the piano that would have eluded them on guitar. The piano was important to them because, unlike practically everyone else performing rock, they were true songwriters. They worried over their material, looking for novel twists in the melody line or unexpected chord sequences. Great songs were a negligible commodity in those days because the major groups—Led Zeppelin, the Cream, the Who—were caught up in the virtuoso game. Tunes with too many complexities tended to distract listener and player alike from the glories of marathon solos. Clapton, Hendrix, Page, Beck, and the other killer guitarists sounded most impressive when working against simple repeated riffs, so songwriting suffered as long as audiences could be transfixed by twenty minutes of high-watt blues blowing on "Spoonful," "Red House," "Whole Lotta Love," and similar bare-bones material.

Eventually, other rock artists began to follow the Beatles' lead. People like Paul Simon, Joni Mitchell, James Taylor—new-folkies with a sensitivity to lyrics and melodies—started composing more for posterity, less for the immediate thrill of solo vamping. As they sculpted their repertoire, they discovered what the Beatles had known all along, and what people like Cole Porter and George Gershwin had known long before: Pianos and songs were made for each other. The piano could handle any voicing, underscore any lyric, and span the range of human emotion.

Under Laura Nyro's hands, it could slap out "Save The Country" with gospel urgency, then breathe a gossamer sheen over "New York Tendaberry." Carole King would use it to brew up "You've Got A Friend," "It's Too Late," and other pop masterpieces like tea on a country stove. Through pearly arpeggios the classically-trained Judy Collins would evoke images of a lost childhood in "My Father," and after composing a number of haunting introspective guitar ballads, Joni Mitchell would cultivate new ways of expressing her message by teaching herself to play the piano as well.

None of these composer/performers could truthfully be said to represent the rock tradition, but they did help set the stage for others who would bring the art of quality songwriting into rock and roll. Like their folk-oriented counterparts, these rock composers used the piano mainly to accompany their own vocals. Technical demands were therefore fairly light when it came to the keyboard parts, allowing self-taught players like Tom Waits to stumble into the business without having to undergo extensive piano study; in fact, Waits, known for his low-life vignettes, explained in the April '77 Keyboard that he sought refuge in music composition because it "beat the hell out of putting aluminum siding on recreational vehicles, or fixing radios—or writing for a magazine." Others were more thoroughly trained, like Randy Newman, the mastermind behind "Short People," "Sail Away," and other ironic numbers. His piano parts were always spare, but deliberately so; Newman, in fact, put more care into his playing than most of his peers, because of his formal study as a pianist and as a composer: "I know I'm a pianist," he stated in the June '78 issue of Keyboard, "and the piano is integral to what I'm doing. I never thought I had any technique. I've never been particularly knocked out by it. But one thing I can do is play softly, steadily, which isn't easy."

The first rock piano superstar since the days of Jerry Lee Lewis had been a colleague of Newman's for a brief while at Metric Music, a publishing firm that contracted promising songwriters to spew forth marketable pop tunes. Newman was a full-fledged member of the Metric staff, but Leon Russell was somehow never officially signed. Given the list of memorable pieces that Russell has since authored, including "This Masquerade" and "A Song For You," we can assume that a few publishing ex-bigwigs may yet be kicking themselves for letting him go. Still, it is as a piano player—for a few years, as *the* rock and roll piano player—that Leon plays his most crucial role in our story.

The old fire that smoldered in Jerry Lee Lewis' records erupted again when Leon took the stage. His one-way shades glinting in the spotlight and his long silvery hair and beard gave him an otherworldly air. When he tore into rollicking renditions of "Give Peace A Chance," "Roll Away The Stone," "Delta Lady," and his other foot-stomping classics, he left an even more vivid picture in sound. Where Newman's playing was sparse and meticulous, Russell scattered tremolos, holy roller punchy chords, and his trademark alternating left- and right-hand octaves across all 88 keys beneath his snarling ecstatic vocals. He was a facile player; long years of session work with the Byrds ("Mr. Tamborine Man"), Bob Lind ("Elusive Butterfly"), Herb Alpert ("A Taste Of Honey"), and on dozens of records with Bobby Darin, Frank Sinatra, the Phil Spector artists, and countless others, had fine-tuned his technique and turned him into a thorough professional long before he had headlined his first show. None of his studio polish obstructed his passion once he was putting his own act together, though. Few performers could match him on his good days.

Russell's roots were in the rural South, where tent show revivals shaped his piano and vocal stylings. Born in Lawton, Oklahoma on April 2, 1941, he was brought up in Tulsa, where he began taking piano lessons at age three. His father, a clerk, and his mother both played the piano and had hopes that Leon would become a "serious" musician someday. But their son's sympathies were with popular music. He curtailed his keyboard studies at 13, learned to play the trumpet, and at 14 he organized his first band. Despite being underage, Leon finagled a string of local club dates, which led in turn to some early sessions with Ronnie Hawkins And The Hawks, later known to the world as the Band, and a six-month tour with Jerry Lee Lewis.

Still below legal working age, Russell settled in Los Angeles in 1958 and began hustling a successful career in the studios there as a freelance arranger and player. He recorded one single under his own name for A&M in 1966, watched it drop from sight, played a few times with the *Shindig* television show's house band (the Shindogs, then featuring Billy Preston on organ), then withdrew to build his own home studio. For a while he worked with a group of future rock all-stars in an outfit called the New Electric Horn Band, but it was in 1968 that Leon began making an impression on the music world through his first LP with the Asylum Choir, a rough but rousing group he co-led with guitarist Marc Benno. Though album sales were low, he was at last start-

ing to win notice from the public as well as music business insiders. The big break came when he played on singer Joe Cocker's second album in 1969. During the following year Russell founded Shelter Records with English producer Denny Cordell, cut a debut album in London with Eric Clapton, Steve Winwood, a couple of Beatles, and other heavyweights sitting in, and organized the now legendary Mad Dogs And Englishmen tour for Cocker. Russell assembled and directed a roistering gaggle of over 40 musicians, singers, babies, animals, and hangers-on as a last-minute favor to Cocker, and their inspired performances behind the singer left rafters ringing and Leon Russell a star.

For a few years Russell shared an honored position within the rock aristocracy. The Beatles, the Rolling Stones, and Bob Dylan—the Holy Trinity in the late '60s—all clamored for his ivory-tickling services. By the mid-'70s, however, Leon had shifted his attention from rock to country music. He created a "cosmic cowboy" persona for himself, using the name Hank Wilson, and played extensively as accompanist to his fellow Southwesterner Willie Nelson. But in leaving rock and roll behind, he propped the door open for others who hoped to follow his footsteps from the piano bench into history. The three artists profiled in this chapter are the only ones so far who have been able to carve out reputations at least equal to Russell's as singers, performers, songwriters, and masters of the reborn discipline of rock piano.

Like Leon Russell, Malcolm John Rebennack was born in the American South. His home was New Orleans, a melting pot of ethnic music and early rock and roll. Mac, as his friends called him, started young in show business—he was featured in Ivory Soap advertisements as an infant—but soon found his true calling in music. Through his father's record store he was exposed to "hillbilly" music and the blues, and an aunt taught him the rudiments of boogie-woogie piano. A member of the musicians union at 15, Rebennack worked mostly as a guitarist at first, but he continued to pick up pointers on his first love, piano playing, from James Booker, Huey Smith, Professor Longhair—the living legends of New Orleans R&B.

By the mid-'60s Mac was a big name in his city's studio scene. He had been recording for ten years, producing other artists for nearly that long, and laying down piano tracks for singers like Frankie "Sea Cruise" Ford and Joe Tex. But the greener pastures of Los Angeles drew him to the West Coast where, like Russell, he played studio dates for Phil Spector, as well as Sam

Cooke, Sonny & Cher, and Kate "God Bless America" Smith. More important, he came up with the idea of adapting the voodoo character of Dr. John to a stage act. A familiar name in Louisiana backwoods legend, Dr. John cut an exotic figure, resplendent in feathers and bedecked with mysterious beads and good-luck charms. Originally Rebennack believed that his friend Ronnie Baron, with whom he had recorded as a keyboard duo named Drits & Dravy, would best benefit from this alter ego. "But somehow as I began to make the demos for him to pick up on," Mac told *Keyboard,* "it just worked out that I did it."

As Dr. John, Rebennack released the album *Gris-Gris* in 1968. His prowess at the piano didn't become apparent until his 1973 release, *In The Right Place,* however. Since then, he has shed his voodoo trappings, preferring now to don a dark suit and fedora and rumble out familiar tunes at the keyboard with the distinctive rolling left-hand syncopations of the New Orleans school. Rebennack, equally strong as a soloist and as a sectional player, projects an obvious vocal and pianistic kinship with Leon Russell. In fact, the Dr. John album *Gumbo* was partly inspired by a jam session involving Rebennack, Russell, and producer Jerry Wexler.

Leon also played an inspirational role in the career of another landmark figure in the rock piano saga—the first true piano superstar, in fact, since Jerry Lee Lewis himself. Yet it would be hard to find a less likely heir to the Killer's crown than Elton John. Born Reginald Kenneth Dwight at Pinner, Middlesex, England on March 25, 1947, Elton was no Ivory Soap baby. Nothing in young Reggie's chunky appearance foretold the amazing successes that lay ahead, though he was musically precocious. He eagerly accepted piano lessons, dreamed of playing on the concert stage, practiced diligently, gained admission to London's Royal Academy Of Music at age 11. Then one day his mother brought home two pop singles—Bill Haley's "ABC Boogie" and Elvis Presley's "Heartbreak Hotel." Out went the lessons, on went the radio, and to the chagrin of his father, a former RAF squadron leader, Reggie was playing R&B with a band of budding rockers called Bluesology by the time he had turned 14.

The piledriver style of Jerry Lee Lewis dazzled the young musician, and soon he was whaling away on mothballed uprights behind the many American R&B stars whom Bluesology backed on British tours. After dropping out of school two weeks before final exams to concentrate completely on his music, he bought himself a Hohner electric piano, but spiritually he was still wedded to the rich sonorities of the acoustic piano. For two years Bluesology worked as English blues singer Long John Baldry's group. Through his stint with Baldry, Dwight picked up a lot of performance savvy and a stronger technique; and through matching up Baldry's and Bluesology saxophonist Elton Dean's first names, he came up with a stage monicker as well.

That was just about all he was left with when Baldry opted for a solo career and Bluesology broke up in 1967. Desperate for work, Elton answered a newspaper ad announcing a talent hunt sponsored by Liberty Records. Despite an unsuccessful audition, at which Elton tried for the first time to present himself as a singer, a perceptive executive recognized the young man's songwriting talent, and arranged a correspondence between him and an out-of-work lyricist named Bernie Taupin. Musically and personally they hit it off, and in 1969 Elton recorded one of their collaborations, "Lady Samantha," as his first single. A debut album, *Empty Sky,* followed, and in 1970 his first big sellers, *Elton John* and *Tumbleweed Connection,* scaled the record listings.

The Elton John that would shortly become an international celebrity—phenomenon may be a better word—was a much more balanced artist than Reggie Dwight had been. Few pop composers could match his knack for fusing melody with lyric, his ear for catchy "hooks" or themes, and his efficiency; often he could turn a sheet of Taupin verses into a potential hit tune within half an hour. Thanks to his sense of the outrageous, Elton became a spellbinding performer too. In years to come he would delight in singing "Your Song" onstage at Disneyland dressed in shorts and Mickey Mouse ears, and in performing an adaptation of Tchaikovsky's *First Piano Concerto* in Leningrad before swooning devotees and perplexed bureaucrats. The man had cheek as well as chops, and his fans loved him for it.

As a pianist, he also grew. He polished up his wrist action for old-time rave-ups like "Saturday Night's Alright For Fighting" and "Crocodile Rock," but he also brought the art of rock ballad accompaniment to perfection. Elton combined the elegant Judy Collins style, which was basically patterned after fingerpicked folk guitar figures, with the hard tone and syncopations of rock in "Rocket Man," "Goodbye Yellow Brick Road," "Don't Let The Sun Go Down On Me," and many of his other slow tunes. Ballad pianists before Elton had to some degree been trapped in the Ferrante & Teicher mold, obligated by popular convention to inject rippling arpeggios into practically everything they played, no matter how the song might be structured. Elton ignored that practice, concentrating instead on playing propulsive off-beat accented chords that invigorated even his most romantic material by bringing its rhythmic vitality to the surface.

And visually, he made the piano a part of his act in a way that no one, not even his early hero Leon Russell, had done since the golden days of Jerry Lee Lewis. Elton's gleaming white grands were spectacular even in repose, but when he began doing his keyboard handstands, or kicking his bench dramatically across the stage, or falling to his knees for a more subterranean perspective on a particular passage, they became reference points for the audience, highlighting Elton's mad exertions by their very stolidity. Others had played the piano in rock before this diminutive giant had splintered his first piano stool, but none can claim more credit for bringing the king of the keyboards back to center stage.

Although Billy Joel must be considered much more than an American counterpart to Elton John, the similarities between the two artists are unmistakable. Both are pop songwriters with years of journeyman rock piano tucked into their fingers. Both are equally comfortable on ballads and up-tempo tunes, and both feature the piano prominently onstage and on records. But Joel's background includes lounge and limited jazz work that lends his piano voicings an "uptown" quality missing in John's more straightforward gospel style. Some of his best numbers, like "Just The Way You are," "Honesty," "She's Always A Woman," and "New York State Of Mind," settle on the blurred border between rock and contemporary cocktail piano, though Joel—like Elton—tends to play with a harder touch and more punchy rhythm than most Holiday Inn Horowitzes deign to display.

Born on May 9, 1949 in Hicksville, New York, Joel was shuttled off to his first piano lesson at age four, when his parents observed his delighted reaction to a Mozart piano piece. His studies ended in 1964, when the Beatles record "A Hard Day's Night" jolted him out of his exercises and into his first band. Suddenly he was gigging several times a week with teenage intensity, and catching up on his sleep in school.

After years of performing and fruitless recording with a succession of Long Island bands, Joel finished his first solo album, Cold Spring Harbor, in 1972. Following a six-month promotional tour, he fell into a financial dispute with the record company, which he resolved by disappearing into the cocktail piano circuit of Los Angeles for some anonymous lounge gigs and lots of serious songwriting. Columbia Records tracked him down and signed him in 1973, and Piano Man followed a year later, the title cut cynically recounting his experiences as a barroom entertainer.

Success was late coming to Joel; it wasn't until 1978, when his LP The Stranger went platinum, that he was really established as a major worldwide concert attraction. But truly the scene had been set for him years before by Elton John, the man who had reintroduced the piano to big-time rock and roll. Perhaps it had taken Joel a little longer because his approach to the piano, and to music in general, fit the temper of the late '70s as snugly as John's circus-like act matched the more lighthearted mood of the early years of the decade. Elton was basically a kid-cult figure. He dressed like a wild-eyed youngster set loose in a costume shop, while Joel wore nondescript jackets and ties onstage. With his acrobatic assaults on piano keys, lids, and benches, Elton sustained a symbiotic relationship with the instrument; his high-flying handstands implied a frustration with the piano's bulk and immobility in a music that demanded movement, action, even the threat or promise of destruction. In this sense, it was adolescent in character, perhaps anti-authoritarian in its image.

But Joel was in harmony with the piano. It had helped him keep his bearings through bleary nights at the Executive Cocktail Lounge in L.A., and it gave him a connection with the Gershwins, Porters, and other creative spectres who haunt the musical boulevards of his New York home town. Joel's amicable feeling for the piano was similar to the attitudes that jazz and cocktail players fostered, and it offered one of the first clues that some elements of the rock audience were ready to water down the rebellious spirit in their music, enjoy only an occasional return to the old hammer-handed piano style (as in Joel's "Angry Young Man"), and settle into a more sedate listening posture.

Rock and roll was born on the battered keys of the roadhouse uprights where ancient mystics conjured the blues and boogie-woogie long ago. Thanks to the performers whose interviews comprise this chapter, the piano is still with rock as it eases into respectability, a familiar friend even to the end.

Bob Doerschuk

Elton John

Poetry with a Beat

February 1981 — *You said that you had always considered yourself primarily a pianist. Is that still your view of yourself?*

Well, I consider myself a much better singer now than I used to be. It's gradually coming together, but I suppose I consider myself mostly a pianist. I mean, when you're onstage you try to sing the right notes, but you also have to hit the right chords. When I first recorded as a singer it was because no one was recording Bernie's and my songs, and somebody just suddenly pushed me into a studio and said, "You can do it." "Lady Samantha" [a single released in 1969] was the first really decent record I ever made as a singer. When I was in a semi-professional band I hardly used to sing at all. I knew I could sing—I always used to sing in the bath and things like that—but I had to be pushed into doing it on *Empty Sky*, and then I was pushed into getting a band together to go out on the road and sell the record. Everything was sort of an accident, a falling into place. So right now I'm probably fifty-fifty as a pianist and singer, although there was a time when I would concentrate on my playing rather than my singing.

Is that one reason why you did a solo piano tour back in 1979, accompanied only by percussionist Ray Cooper—to even out that fifty-fifty balance?

That was done mainly to get me back into playing live. I never really thought I'd go back on the road after having come off of it in 1976. I had enjoyed everything we did in that tour. I had really good bands and very rarely played bad concerts, but I felt a little stale both singing-wise and piano-wise because the last thing I was thinking about onstage was singing and playing. I

"When you first sit down at a piano, within a minute you can tell whether you're going to like it . . .
The piano I have now has been doctored so muc[h]
that the action is ridiculous."

was thinking instead, "Can they hear the band?
Are the monitors right? Is the lighting right? Is the
audience getting beaten up?" Everything was
becoming a little mechanical, so I decided to try a
little tour of Europe, doing a couple of solo
concerts in England and another one with Ray
Cooper. Of course when you go out alone you
have to play and sing the right bloody notes, so I
concentrated real hard and I actually enjoyed the
discipline, every single minute of it. Throughout
the 125 gigs I did in 1979 I never got fed up, not
with one of them, because without a band you're
free to extemporize whenever you want, within
certain limits when you've got Ray onstage with
you. But there was no real framework, and it was
quite exciting. It also gave me my confidence
back as a musician. I had become lazy, and after
'76 I didn't want to see another piano. The solo
tour gave me a good time, though, and it was the
only thing that could have gotten me back into
touring.

Did you carry your own piano on the road?

I always do, yes. It was the old nine-foot
Steinway, the same one I've had for five or six
years now.

Are you a Steinway artist?

No. They've been most unhelpful in placing
ads and things like that. They don't really need to
have anybody advertising them; they're like Rolls
Royce in that respect. I play Steinway because
I've gotten used to the piano, but I've also played
great Yamahas, and the best piano I've ever
played on is a Bosendorfer Imperial. That's my
favorite. It's incredible. That's what I used on
Tumbleweed.

*How long does it take you to decide whether
you like a certain piano?*

I think that when you first sit down at a piano,
within a minute you can tell whether you're
going to like it because of the tone quality, but
the action is really even more important to me.
The piano I have now has been doctored so
much that the action is ridiculous; it's just like an
electric piano.

How so?

It's real fast. The action on it now is absolutely
incredible. But when you buy a Steinway I think
you have to live with it a couple of years to let it
settle down. I knew it was a great piano to start
with, but it's a question of easing into them when
they're brand new. Like any instrument, they can
be temperamental sometimes. If you're a guitarist
you've got to have your one guitar, but for pianists I think it's even more important to have your
one piano. If you're going to be doing concerts
all around the world it's important to know

exactly what you're going to get. I mean, I playe[d]
on the worst pianos in the world back in the ea[rly]
days, from '70 to '74. We used to have a separate
piano every gig. It was potluck. You're there to
play and you should be able to play on anything,
but it's a sound man's nightmare. My piano is
also completely miked and wired inside—not th[at]
I'm electrically minded, because I'm not, but the[y]
don't have to set up any mikes when they get
there. It's all on the inside already. Eleven years
ago, when I first came to the States, miking a
piano was a real problem. I remember when I g[ot]
my first Helpinstill. And in the early '70s I used t[o]
play on uprights with two mikes hanging down
the back.

*This was after your first albums had become
successful?*

Oh, yeah. Yes indeed. I've played on many
one-legged grands in England. I've played on
some dreadful pianos here as well. In fact, when [I]
came over in '70 for my first American tour, I
played with Tracy Nelson and Mother Earth at th[e]
Electric Factory in Philadelphia, where the piano
was held up by orange crates! Having your own
piano is a real luxury, especially when you can
travel with someone who knows it inside out an[d]
takes care of it for you, like it was his Rolls Royc[e.]
My piano has gotten to the point now where
there's really nothing much wrong with it. [*Ed.
Note: Elton's equipment man, Adrian Collee,
reports that the piano is miked by a Helpinstill
pickup, two PZM, or pressure zone sensitive,
mikes, and one capacitator mike, with a modifie[d]
Clair Brothers pickup box containing an active
mixer. The action has been lightened, and the
hammers have been hardened. The piano signa[l]
is modified at the Clair Super Board by a Lexico[n]
224 digital reverb unit.*]

*You said a while back that you were involve[d]
in one of the only piano trio acts in rock back in
the early '70s. Did you see yourself then as a har[-]
binger of a keyboard renaissance in the decade
to come?*

Well, I sort of arrived at the same time as the
Carole King album *Tapestry,* which probably ha[d]
more to do with it than I did. I was trying to thin[k]
of other piano, bass, and drum acts, and there
weren't any then. There was Emerson, Lake &
Palmer, which was mainly organ, and there was
Lee Michaels, which was just organ and drums.

Not much piano, though.

No, and that probably had something to do
with our popularity. When we came to the
Troubador the first time, people honestly thoug[ht]
that because of the *Elton John* album I was goin[g]
to come out with an orchestra! Then when we

came out and played rock and roll, everyone just went, "Huh?" And afterwards they said, "We didn't expect that!", even though I've always been a rock and roll player. But I don't know how much of a new thing I was, because back in '70 I'd been influenced by Leon Russell, the Band, and people like that.

Have you played many other keyboard instruments in recent years?

That's one side of the keyboards that I really don't understand too well. I'm not the most technical person. There are only two records I've used them on that I'm really proud of: "This Song Has No Title"[from *Yellow Brick Road*], on which I played all the electric things, and "Song For Guy" [from *Single Man*]. I could do it if I had more patience, but usually I don't because I don't understand programming and computers.

Do you still play sessions occasionally for other artists?

Yeah, if they ask me. If I have the time, I love to play sessions. I think people are afraid now that I will say no, but I've played a lot of dates. I played piano on the Hollies record "He Ain't Heavy (He's My Brother)" [from *The Hollies' Greatest Hits*]. *At that time I was just a struggling new artist in England. Then when it was a hit they said it was their bass player playing! I was so mortified [laughs]*! And I played on the follow-up, "Can't Tell The Bottom From The Top" [out of print]. I used to sing on a lot of records. I played or sang on a lot of records by English groups— the Scaffold, the Baron Knights. I sang on [singer] Tom Jones sessions. I've done the whole works, from crazy people down to Tom Jones.

When you play a session now, do people ask for Elton John-type piano, or do they ask you to adapt to some other style they're working toward?

I usually go in and play the way I feel on the track. The only problem is that I sometimes overplay when I should underplay, so they might ask me not to play so much. But most of the time it works. I usually tend to take over a session when I get in there. With studio musicians there's usually no problem, but when you get a bunch of musicians from groups coming in to play for an artist, and they've never played together before, someone's got to take the lead, you know? Someone's got to say, "Come on, let's do it." Otherwise it's going to be a disaster for the producer.

Do you ever get insights as a composer from playing other people's material?

Oh, yeah. It's all just good fun. I mean, I'm not one of those people who'll stay up 'till four in the morning playing "Twelve O'Clock Blues," but I do like to play with other musicians. You have to take risks. You can't play safe all the time. There are things I'd love to do in the future, like just go to the studio and do a mini-Keith Jarrett— extemporizing and using the best of it—because I can sit at the piano and play for hours and hours. Even with Taupin, when I was working off of lyrics, I'd just play around till I found a chord structure I liked. I know I could do a really good album that way. There's something within me that would love to do an album solo, just absolutely raw, with maybe some singing as well. It's a matter of finding the time and place to do it.

Do you ever record the piano and voice simultaneously?

No, hardly ever. The only time we did that was on "Ticking," which was on the *Caribou* album.

That sounded like a pretty complicated piano part too.

It was, but playing the piano without the voice was harder. I would think so much about the voice that I wouldn't play the piano right. Gus [Dudgeon, producer] was always a stickler for separation, but I had to tell him, "Look, the only way we're ever going to get this thing done is by doing the voice and piano together, and forget about the leakage." It would only be the voice leaking anyway, so why care? When we're doing the instrumental track, though, I usually whisper a rough vocal into the headphones, because it's helpful for other people to play if they can hear a guide vocal. That can be frustrating, though, because you have to whisper it to avoid leakage into the piano. But we've also done things like "Saturday Night's Alright For Fighting," which was recorded without the piano, but we put it on later because we couldn't get the right feeling.

When you're playing alone for your own enjoyment, do you often extemporize freely?

Oh, yeah, all the time. I very rarely sit down and play—I don't just get up every morning and play the piano—but when I'm in the mood to do it, I can play for hours. Just playing "Stand By Me" for hours is wonderful; those chord changes are so fabulous. But I mess around all the time, and then out of something like that comes a song. My songs aren't planned; they just come out of the blue.

Do you have any warm-up exercises or preparations before going onstage?

The only thing I do is, when I haven't played for a long time, I usually put Nu-Skin on my fingers, because my nails crack and sort of go into the skin. It's a horrible yellow plastic film that bowlers use that really does help your fingers a lot if they split easily. You just take it off with some kind of solution afterwards.

You've had some trouble with bleeding fingers, haven't you?

Oh, yeah. Once at the LA Forum I was in absolute agony. This was before the days of Nu-Skin. And I remember once at a session I did with [singer] Jackson Browne I had to do a piano part with a lot of glissandos. I hadn't played for a while, so when I came away from Sunset Sound studios my hands were bleeding and they felt terrible. If you've been away from the piano and your nails have grown, you really have to take care of them before you start banging away.

How did that uninhibited performing style evolve? You weren't leaping around in your days as a pub pianist, were you?

Well, I was always physically held back from wearing what I wanted to as a teenager, so being able to put on any clothes I liked helped to evolve that style, I suppose. People used to say that it detracts from the music, and I can understand their point of view, but I was just having a good time. I enjoyed it, and I think people did too, because I didn't take myself too seriously. When the singer/songwriter thing did evolve in the early '70s, a lot of musicians were starting to get very intense about what they were doing, and people did take them maybe a little seriously. I mean, look at the cover to the *Elton John* album. It was so confusing, all dark and mean and mysterious, yet there I was onstage, popping along with Mickey Mouse ears. I've always been a rock and roller, so maybe if that album had had a different cover it wouldn't have been so confusing.

So there was never a moment when you kicked over your first piano bench and decided to change your style.

Not really. I used to do that in England before we came over to the States. Pete Townshend [of the Who] used to smash his guitar and amplifier on some nights. I can't remember how it evolved. I think maybe one night I just kicked the piano stool over, and it got to be a regular part of the act. But I haven't had too many scenes like that lately. You can't really argue with a piano stool too much.

As a piano player in a world suddenly filled with synthesizer players, do you ever feel lost in a sea of electronic keyboard players?

Sometimes. I mean, I love to play electronic keyboards, but I'd like to play guitar more than anything, because you can write different songs; there are guitar songs and there are piano songs, and you can write better four-chord songs on guitar. They're hard to write on piano because if you're a trained piano player, four chords sometimes aren't enough. Sometimes I do get frustrated. I wish pianos were that small [indicates toy piano size]. Someone should invent a mini-chip piano. The trouble is though, that once you get a great sound on the Steinway, you don't want another one. The Yamaha electric grand was great, a revolution, but even so it's not exactly portable. Like I say, when I'm onstage, I feel like I've got to move. The thing with being a piano player is that it sticks you in one position, which for me is the most frustrating thing of all time. But I really am quite happy just playing piano.
Bob Doerschuk

Elton John posing at the Minimoog (l.) and the Freeman string synthesizer. "I love to play electronic keyboards, but I'd like to play the guitar more than anything."

Billy Joel
Keeping the Spirit Alive

December 1981 — *Are you playing less piano now than before?*

No, I'm playing as much, but it's not featured. I use the piano to write more than I use it to play. I'm not a virtuoso pianist: I'm a piano player. A lot of times I write on the piano, but I mean for it to be translated to the guitar. On the *52nd Street* album we had a really good guitar player named David Brown, so there was a little less piano because I wanted to feature him.

Has your stage show come to reflect this change?

Yeah, it's changed, I think, since *52nd Street.* Because we were doing the bigger rooms, the guys who do my sound and lights wanted me to get up front more often. I've always been chained to the piano, but it's very static in a big room to just see some guy sitting there. So they gave me a wireless microphone, because I'm pretty clunky, tripping over cables and stuff, and I kind of ran around doing this big shot number and saying, "Hey, this isn't bad!" It was sort of fun to get away from the piano. It started building up my confidence to not have to use the piano as a crutch.

Did you have any other problems with playing piano all throughout your show?

Yeah. The "piano man" thing became too piano-heavy for me. I didn't want to base my sound entirely on the piano. I never really did, but I figured I would get away from it someday. That doesn't mean I won't go back to it or that I won't write any songs that do feature a piano, but I always wanted to have a lot of guitar power, and now that I do it gives me a chance to do other types of things.

Are you keeping your piano chops up even when not playing a lot in concert?

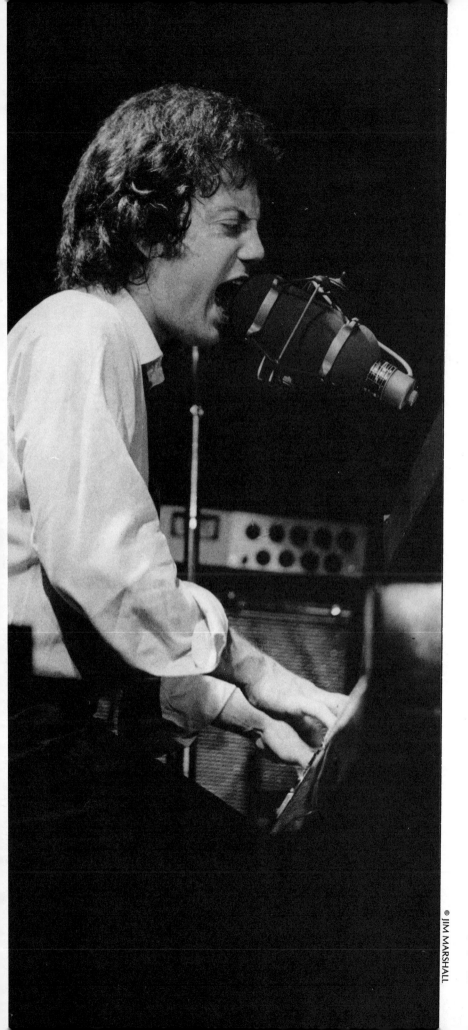

© JIM MARSHALL

Joel on large audiences: "You feel like you have to pound the hell out of the piano. I break bass strings constantly, at just about every show."

Yeah, I still play a lot. As a matter of fact, it's almost harder now to play in a miniature style inside of an arrangement than outside of it, because you set a signature for a song on the piano. You can fool around and make mistakes when you're playing solo, but that's part of it; that can be chalked up to improvisation. When you're playing inside an arrangement there's not a whole lot of room to step out of a rhythm section because you screw up the whole song.

Has your piano style changed a lot since the days you were working alone in little clubs?

No, my style hasn't really changed at all. That probably the one thing that's stayed pretty much the same. If I do a song that's just me and the piano, I do it now just like I would have ten year ago.

Don't you play differently in front of thousands of people than you do in smaller surroundings?

I think I just play harder. It doesn't really make any sense, because hitting the piano harder doesn't mean you're gonna get all the way to the back of the room any more than if you play softer, since you've got all this amplification. But you want to reach those people in the back row at someplace like Madison Square Garden, and for some reason this makes you feel like you have to pound the hell out of the piano. I break bass strings constantly, at just about every show.

How would you characterize your keyboard style?

A lot of it is actually based on ideas I have for the guitar. I've always wanted to play the guitar, so what I do in a lot of my writing is to compose the guitar part on the piano, then come into the studio and say, "This is what I want. I'd like to hear this on the guitar." The producer or somebody will say, "Why don't you play that on the piano?" And I'll say, "But it's not supposed to be for the piano!" See, I've never really thought of myself as a stylist. I think I'm a lousy piano player.

Many of our readers would disagree.

Well, I took classical piano when I was growing up, and I know how good a really good pianist can be. My left hand pretty much plays octaves all the time. My right hand can play some flashy stuff, and I can play choppy chord things pretty well, but I don't really ever step out of a certain number of keys. Like B , to me, is really adventurous. And E ? Wow!

Why, then, have you always played the keyboard parts on your records? Why not hire a more accomplished session player?

I found that extremely accomplished keyboard players tend to get outside of the original conception of a song. We're going for a simple band sound most of the time, like the Beatles. Everybody looks at the Beatles individually and goes, "Ringo wasn't so hot." Well, I think he was fantastic, because he didn't try to play like Ginger Baker. Paul McCartney is a great bass player because he doesn't try to play like Stanley Clarke. I never really felt the need for fancy instrumentation, except for once in a while like on "Zanzibar" [from *52nd Street*], which was begging for [trumpeter] Freddie Hubbard, or with [saxophonist] Phil Woods on "Just The Way You Are" [from *The Stranger*]. Maybe that's another admission of defeat.

Were you ever influenced by jazz piano players?

I've always been fascinated by great jazz keyboard players: Bill Evans, Art Tatum, Oscar Peterson. I'm in awe of those guys. When I fool around I can boogie-woogie or fake it, but I don't have the talent to play like that. It's a whole other art form. I kind of touch on it every once in a while, but then I back off because it's scary when I realize the tempo I'm entering into.

But again, is that what you really want to do?

Well, it's not something I feel bad about. I realize I can't play the piano like Bill Evans did, but I'm not gonna beat my head against the wall the rest of my life because of that. With the jazz player it's almost always pure instrumental expression with variations on a theme, but without the songwriters the jazz guys wouldn't have a whole lot to do variations on, so it's kind of a symbiotic relationship. To me, it's not the singer or the instrument; it's the song. And that attitude seems to get in the way of a lot of people: "Gee, I didn't hear enough piano on the last album." But sometimes I think it's effective to underplay the piano. Like in the midsection of the song "Don't Ask Me Why" [from *Glass Houses*], there are 15 pianos overdubbed on top of each other, which I thought was especially effective because you didn't hear that much piano before then.

You also seem to go out of your way to cover lots of different styles, from bluegrass to jazz to whatever, and you probably can't adapt the piano to every single format.

Right. I think it should be held in reserve for when it's meaningful and when it's going to have some impact. A whole album of piano-based songs can get real tiresome. I think Elton pulled it off pretty well because his style was novel. He was playing a lot of arpeggio-type stuff with a lot of rhythmic things too.

Is there any solo you've recorded that you're especially proud of?

Let me think. There's a pattern I like a lot, in a song called "Summer, Highland Falls," on the *Turnstiles* album. It's a series of bits, starting on *F*, with the left hand playing riffs. It goes up to a *C*, drops back a fourth, goes up a fifth, back down a fourth, up another fifth, and somehow or other it resolves itself. I didn't know what I was doing when I wrote it. I didn't set out to do anything particularly clever, but after I finished the song and saw the symmetry of it, I said, "Hey, that's really neat!" Then there's a piano part in a song called "Cold Spring Harbor," which is on *Songs In The Attic*. It's a solo, but the piano is doing a rhythm guitar part that's really hard to play. It always makes my hand ache, but I get a kick out of the fact that I can do it. It goes back and forth from *C* to *F* in real fast arpeggios. Then when it comes to the bridge I start banging with both hands like I'm playing bongo drums. I call that particular style "lucky fingers," where you should be hitting every wrong note in the world, but somehow or other your fingers are trained to go to the right ones.

When you started using synthesizers in your records, how did you familiarize yourself with them?

I had a guy come in who knew how to program it, and then I would explain what I wanted in these nebulous terms: "Well, I'm looking for this sort of Jupiter's moon, *Star Trek* . . ." And he'd go, "Is this it? How about this?" We'd go through all these combinations before I finally found what I was looking for. But I really wanted to play synthesizer.

How'd you get interested in it?

I started playing the Minimoog because it seemed to be an easy way to get different colors without having to go outside the orchestration. I could get a flute sound, or use it as an organ, or whatever. I'm limited, but in a way that ended up being a style in itself in not knowing how to get all these crazy effects. I'm a believer in simplicity.

Maybe that wasn't such a big jump, since you used to play organ in rock and roll bands.

I'm a better organist than I am a piano player. I can *scream* when I'm playing an organ! When I got my first Hammond organ—I think I was 17—I bought every Jimmy Smith album there was, every Jimmy McGriff album there was. I got all the Groove Holmes records. I'd play that stuff with my eyes closed. Actually, I have more fun playing organ than playing piano.

Why did you move over to the piano, then?

For writing, it's a better instrument. I went back to piano to write because organ was too much fun. I'd get carried away playing it and forget about the writing part. That doesn't mean I'm not gonna go back and write on the organ again, though.

How do the songs you write on organ differ from the ones you write on piano?

When I write on the organ, the organ is usually pretty locked into the arrangement of the song. The sound of the organ kind of makes the song what it is. When I write on the piano I can leave the piano out or put it in.

Is there any conflict between your classical training and the way you play rock nowadays?

Yeah. My fingering has suffered with rock piano. I suppose I have a Mongoloid style. I played a lot of the classical stuff by ear anyway. I got tired of reading the music, so I'd go out and buy the record. I had to learn the Beethoven *Sonata In D Minor* [Op. 31], so I went out, got the record, and learned it pretty much by ear. I'm sure I missed a lot of notes; the teacher looked at me and said, "What arrangement is this? That's not on the music!"

How long did it take to learn it that way?

About two or three days, I suppose, if I sat down and listened for an hour and a half each day.

That's incredible.

Well, it was really laziness. When you're lazy you become very ingenious in certain ways. I just got tired of reading those black dots. To this day I can't sit down and sight-read. When I was about 12, I was able to sight-read great, but I just can't do it no more. It's too slow. My ear's a lot quicker.

What kind of piano do you use? Do you carry one with you on the road?

We carry two acoustic pianos, both Baldwins: a 5'8" and a 7'.

Why two pianos?

The 7' grand is stage right in the setup, and this points my back to a certain section of the audience. I was always uncomfortable with that: You can't carry a piano around like a guitar, you can't make the moves, so I said, "Why don't we put a smaller piano stage left and higher up so I can run up to it and face the other side of the room?" I turn around to the people in back of me when I'm at the second piano and say, "Now you've got the lousy seats." That makes me feel better, because you want the audience to get its money's worth when they come to see you. That still amazes me. I mean, they want to see this face!

What other keyboards are you using?

We also carry a Yamaha CP-80, a Rhodes, an OB-X, and a Minimoog. Richie [Cannata], who doubles on Hammond organ, also uses a Crumar synthesizer.

Since you've already got an acoustic piano onstage, how do you use the CP-80?

I look at it like sort of a Rhodes. It's got its own sound, even though a lot of people use it to replace an acoustic piano. This funky thing happens with it when the strings bottom out, especially in the bass, and it's also a lot more adaptable than the acoustic piano to being used with effects. With an acoustic piano you have to use Helpinstill pickups and microphones, where you can go direct through some kind of effect with the Yamaha.

What effects do you use on it?

Mainly the Lexicon digital phaser/flanger.

How do you use the OB-X?

I use it for solos. A lot of times I use it with the guitar; it'll play along, and I'll be a third above, like on "Sometimes A Fantasy" [from *Glass Houses*]. Or I'll use it to sound like a Farfisa organ, which I did in "Sleeping With The Television On" [from *Glass Houses*].

That really sounded like a Farfisa organ.

It sounded more like a Farfisa than a Farfisa, but it was a preset on the OB-X. I was thinking of hauling out an old Farfisa for that cut, but I thought I'd see if I could get it on the OB-X. I kind of stumbled on it by accident, and everybody in the band cringed and said, "Ooooh, I remember that." It was just what I wanted, a junior high school band sound.

Do you anticipate exploring synthesis to a greater extent in the future?

I don't know. I lump synthesizers into this mathematical machine that I don't understand, which is why I have an affection for the piano. I can always go back to the piano. It's also tied to my singing. I sing a certain way when I play the piano that's different from how I sing when I'm standing up or playing a different keyboard. I really sing to, or with, the piano.

In between your days with Long Island bands in local clubs and your emergence as a major concert attraction, you spent some time working a piano bar in Los Angeles. Did you learn anything in that gig that you can apply to your music today, as a rock performer?

I suppose I learned how to develop attention-grabbing stuff. What you're doing in a piano bar basically is playing for tips, so you try to pick out what will get bread out of the audience. Is this guy Italian? You play the *Godfather* theme or something like that. Is this guy Irish? You play "Danny Boy." You try to get those five-dollar bills in the brandy glass. For years after that we were the opening act for the Beach Boys, the Doobie Brothers, and a lot of big groups, and as most people know, nobody wants to see the opening act. They want to see the headliner, so it was like, well, what should we do? You just couldn't go up there and do "Piano Man," because the crowd came to hear "Help Me Rhonda," so I would say something outrageous, or do my Joe Cocker imitation—anything to get attention—and then we'd do "Jumpin' Jack Flash." If it was a rock and roll crowd, we'd say, "Throw out all the sweet stuff! Let's do the barbarian set!" So I guess I picked up a certain amount of smarts. The main thing I learned from working in the piano bar was that I didn't want to do that any more. Now I know what I don't like.

What exactly didn't you like about the piano bar?

It was just . . . depressing. I suppose "Piano Man" says it: drunken people sitting around asking for requests. I had to do standards, and I actually learned how to fake a lot of standards that I didn't know. You just play a lot of major seventh chords in a stock kind of progression, and you can play any standard in the world. There was always somebody trying to grab the microphone and sing, and drinks were pouring all over you.

Many of our readers have the kind of piano bar gig that you used to have. Maybe you could share your thoughts with them on how to survive that kind of a job.

Let me think. Tips for guys at the Holiday Inn. This is going to require some thought.

[*At this point, Joel asked for the tape recorder to be turned off, and for some time to ponder his answer. He left the room, poured a cup of coffee, stared off into space, and five minutes later returned. The tape began spinning again.*]

Okay. If you're working in those places, number one, you know you wanna get out of there and on to something better, so you might as well have fun while you're doing it. It's actually a good place to develop original material. Try out original stuff, but don't lay too much of it on people, because they're gonna mainly want to hear familiar things. What I used to do is, I used to goof, like if somebody asked for a Sinatra song I would get into doing a whole put-on Sinatra thing. I'd be having a blast, and they would think I was really into it. So I suppose a certain amount of sarcasm helps in those situations. You'll end up doing some things you really don't want to do, but I would stay away from songs like "Feelings" or "Jeremiah Was A Bullfrog (Joy To The World)." If you want people to come back and see you, if

you want an agent to get interested in booking you, try to do something different from what everybody else is doing. Like, don't be in a wedding band.

You mean, don't play wedding gigs?

Well, actually, I'm talking to wedding bands too. I mean, don't play the stock repertoire that wedding bands do. Don't just go to the fake book; "Okay, let's do number 14, three beats. . . ." You've got people listening to you, you've got an instrument, hopefully, you've got some kind of PA system, so it's a good time to see how your material hits people. That's an advantage that I don't have anymore. Sombody in my position doesn't have the opportunity to test new material out. I just put it out, and if it bombs it fails big, whereas you have a better chance to develop your own stuff slowly.

How can creative musicians keep their heads together in essentially uncreative situations like that? There are lots of good piano players who are stuck in unrewarding bar gigs.

Well, one thing I know about working in those places is that outstanding musicianship usually goes right over the heads of people who go to those places. They want to be entertained, not overwhelmed with riffs, so you develop some kind of stage rap that does get people's attention. I'd just say, take all the things you can get out of it and turn it into something positive. Keep in mind, though, that you really want to get the hell out of this place! Jeez, hopefully you're getting free drinks.

Bob Doerschuk

Advent of the New Romantics

The Seventies were belt-tightening years in many areas of life, including the music business. As record executives helplessly watched the economy wither, they began taking fewer risks, signing less stylistically daring groups, and putting their money on proven winners. Excellent, but commercially safe, acts like the Rolling Stones, the Who, and Bruce Springsteen flourished during these lean times, while new artists clamored for a piece of the diminishing action.

For those musicians who were lucky enough to have a lucrative income and a following to spend it on, this was a boom decade. The superstars of the Seventies were not too musically adventurous, but neither were they content to churn out dispirited shows in whistle-stop tours. Most of them had been bred in the Romantic climate of mid-Sixties rock, yet they were also open to the new spectrum of sounds being opened up by the dawning revolution in sound technology. These two interests combined with the common wisdom that albums sold best when backed with appearances to kindle a dramatic expansion of the rock concert experience. Gone were the days when Elvis Presley could guffaw at his hysterical fans on *The Ed Sullivan Show*, or when the Beatles could weather the frenzy of their admirers and soundlessly mouth the words to a handful of songs for thirty minutes, then call it a night. The fans expected more in the Seventies, and they got it.

Stadium shows became more frequent, enlivened by intricate laser displays, split-second theatrics, and song arrangements that were structured not so much for musical sophistication as

V. Multi-Keyboard and Mega Rock

for powerful audience impact and involvement. Performances were crafted with the fans' collective reactions in mind; at appropriate points at a typical rock concert, one might see a performer unaccountably elevate on invisible wings above the stage, get the audience swept up in a call-and-answer or clap-along episode punctuated by sudden teasing silences, spit flames, get his head chopped off, and even disappear into a flying saucer amidst a cold white forest of laser beams.

Musical hardware kept pace with these visual distractions. As dazzling as all this was to the eye, the ear was just as frequently stunned by shimmering synthetic string lines, unbelievably quick sequencer riffs, and previously impossible levels of amplification that wafted the softest acoustic piano nuances to the most distant corners of large arenas and stadiums. As handmaiden, in a sense, to the goal of eliciting a tribal response from huge crowds through multi-sensual assault, music became less a matter of notes, less a display of grafting complex classical themes onto the body of rock, and more a question of presenting the basic elements of texture and rhythm in a high-tech milieu.

All this added up to a revival of mid-Sixties romanticism in the mid-Seventies. The new romantics owed much to the progressive rock of the early Seventies, particularly with respect to their use of the synthesizer for rich tone shadings, but these young players, most of them Americans, preferred to apply their mastery of keyboard technology to the fundamental groove elements of rock, rather than to exotic explorations of extended classical forms. Emerson's upfront virtuosity fell out of fashion because rock musicians no longer needed to prove that they had the chops and the vision to handle esoteric material. Once the lessons of ELP, Yes, and the other progressives had been absorbed, the time came for a return to more traditional and essential structures, though with greater resource than had been available in the keyboard instruments of the Sixties.

Progressive rock, for all its contributions, ultimately served as a bridge from Billy Preston and Felix Cavaliere to Gary Wright and Journey. The new romantics, like Cavaliere, could happily hold down a simple C chord for two or three minutes, finding their challenge in manipulating the tone colors of that chord and integrating the effect into the overall musical effect. Few actually took that simplistic an approach, but to one degree or another all the artists presented in this section subscribed to the belief that synthesizers could best be used not as building blocks in complicated arrangements of Bartok or Bach themes, but as tools to raise the romantic banner to its highest ascent.

This philosophy was clearly expressed by Edgar Winter, one of the first to use synthesizers within the new romantic formula. In describing his keyboard work with White Trash, his successful band of the early and mid Seventies, Winter told *Keyboard*, "I didn't want things to be over-powered by synthesizer. There are already people doing that, Keith Emerson being the most obvious example. I wanted to take a different approach. I didn't want to compete with those other people. I just wanted the synthesizer to be another voice in the group's texture."

Years later, Jonathan Cain of Journey offered

Previous page: Gary Wright onstage, with custom remote Oberheim keyboard. Right: Wright's gear, including a Polymoog sandwiched between two Minimoogs with keyboards removed.

Keyboard a similar perspective. "I am not really interested in taking long synthesizer solos," he explained. "I think lead playing on synthesizer has really sort of peaked out. Everybody has heard it, and there are only so many things that can be done. Melodies, themes, and ways of supporting a song are more important than playing a bunch of psychedelic licks. I don't think that keyboards are really the best kind of instrument for that anyway. Keyboard solos are sometimes very one-dimensional. They just take away from the basic fundamentals of rock and roll."

Is this post-progressive revisionism? Were younger keyboard players backing away from the prominence offered to them by the examples of Emerson and Wakeman? Not at all. Cain, like Winter, was seeking a balance for his work within his band's arrangements, so that he and his fellow musicians could create a unified emotional impact together, rather than struggle over individual moments in the spotlight. One of the youngest of the new romantics, Johnnie Fingers of England's Boomtown Rats, moved even further from the progressive preoccupation with form, and harked back to the priorities of Cavaliere, Preston, Price, and the other Sixties pioneers in placing feeling above all else in his music: "Rock has really very little to do with music," he insisted to *Keyboard.* "It's not a musician's thing. It goes further than that; it has another sphere. It has more to do with feel, like blues. It doesn't have very much to do with how good you are technically."

Between Winter and Fingers, new romanticism flourished. Fans flocked to hear Kerry Livgren and Steve Walsh of Kansas, Richard Tandy of the Electric Light Orchestra, Gregg Rolie of Santana and Journey, Al Greenwood of Foreigner, and Michael Cotten and Vince Welnick of the Tubes adorn the hard-hitting music their groups produced with synthesized embellishments. None of these artists, however, reflected the impact of keyboard technology on the spirit of Sixties romanticism as vividly as Seth Justman of the J. Geils Band.

When his group released its debut LP and drew *Rolling Stone*'s vote as Most Promising New Band of 1970, Justman was an old-style romantic from feet to fingertips. The Hammond was his main axe, and he played it with the spiritual intensity of a Cavaliere or Preston. Throughout most of the Seventies he stuck with the B-3, reflecting the band's stubborn allegiance to a fire-breathing R&B-based sound that grew more nostalgic with each passing year. Yet as the

decade drew to a close, Justman suddenly picked up two popular synthesizers—a Sequential Circuits Prophet-5 and a Yamaha CS-80—and began working them into the J. Geils sound. Immediately the group's record sales, always respectable, exploded; "Love Stinks," "Angel In The Centerfold," and "Freeze Frame," each crackling with a new electronic texture, became sizeable hits in the early Eighties. The important lesson of these records is that the band's high-energy romantic approach was updated and enhanced, not diluted or diverted, by a tasteful dose of Justman's rock-steady synthesis.

During his peak years in the mid Seventies, Gary Wright was the most visible of the new romantic keyboardists. His hit records—Dream Weaver," Love Is Alive"—reverberated with layer upon layer of synthesizer. And in his concerts Wright fronted a band that boasted three back-up keyboard players, with no guitarists or bass guitarists in sight. To further bring the message home, Wright performed in center stage on a portable custom-built controller, allowing him to play several different synthesizers from one lightweight remote-control keyboard slung around his neck. Others had pioneered this idea—notably Billy Preston and Edgar Winter—but Wright took it to new peaks of sophistication in his carefully-crafted arrangements. Like Justman, Gary Wright had strong ties to the rock romantics of the Sixties; born in 1943, he dropped out of a postgraduate psychology program in the University of Berlin to gig around Europe, and eventually achieved coniderable success behind a Hammond organ with the English group Spooky Tooth. But his greatest contribution came in the Seventies, when his guitarless bands heralded the arrival of the keyboard revolution within the romantic revival.

Perhaps Michael McDonald is best known as a singer/songwriter. Blessed with one of the most distinctive voices in pop music and a facility for writing infectious melodic tunes, McDonald was the guiding light behind the Doobie Brothers' second-wind successes of the late Seventies. But he also brought a solid, rhythmic keyboard style to the Doobies when he joined them in 1975 as a last-minute replacement for the ailing guitarist and singer Tom Johnston. In truth, it was McDonald's keyboard playing that most dramatically altered their sound. Prior to his arrival, the Doobie Brothers were exclusively a guitar band, indicative of their roots in the folk music boom of the early and mid Sixties. McDonald single-handedly yanked them into the keyboard era. The

chart-topping Doobie hits during the McDonald year—"What A Fool Believes, " "Takin' It To The Streets," "It Keeps You Runnin'," "Minute By Minute," and "Real Love"—all drew their flavor and rhythmic emphasis from McDonald's hands. Few keyboardists so decisively affected the direction of a major group, or so clearly signalled the world that the age of guitar suzerainty over keyboards in rock was over.

With the possible exception of Kansas, no new romantic ensemble showed the influence of progressive rock as strongly as Styx, a Chicago-based quintet that enjoyed phenomenal popularity among teenage listeners in the late Seventies and early Eighties. Much of the credit for this goes to Dennis De Young, whose aggressive multi-keyboard style echoed Emerson's and Wakeman's earlier fireworks. De Young, who holds a music education degree from Chicago State University, even delighted in such progressive diversions as recording on church pipe organs ("I'm Okay") and quoting classical themes (the trace of *Clair de lune* in the intro to "Ballerina"). But these were fine touches to the band's simple, punchy songs, never integral elements in the structure of these tunes; for this reason, De Young stands with the new romantics. "Lady," "Babe," Why Me," "Come Sail Away," and the other Styx blockbusters were all tightly-written pieces, with no non-commercial excess baggage. What often made them notable was De Young's sparkling organ or synthesizer licks, which in turn established him as one of the most prominent new romantic keyboard soloists.

But in terms of finesse and polish, the evolution of the new romantic keyboard style reached its high-water mark with Toto. By the time that band broke into the album charts in 1978, all six members, including keyboardists David Paich and Steve Porcaro, had logged long hours as studio musicians in Los Angeles. In fact, Paich and Porcaro were both sons of seasoned session players, so they were raised in the tradition of professionalism, technical competence, and musical teamwork. In addition to their many album credits as sidemen, Paich had written charts and songs for the Doobie Brothers, Boz Scaggs, and other rock luminaries, while Porcaro had performed with Scaggs, Leo Sayer, and Gary Wright's synthesizer-saturated band. They had also studied progressive rock, focussing on the definitive Keith Emerson records with fanlike ardor, and, especially in Porcaro's case, investigated the art of modular synthesis to exacting detail.

By the time Toto made its trial debut under a false name in Hawaii, Paich and Porcaro had developed a precision unmatched by any other duo keyboardists in rock. Though both players had manual dexterity to burn, they avoided ostentatious solos and concentrated on more subtle forms of interplay. Their fine-tuned ears for tone colors was most evident on *Toto IV*, released in the summer of '82. They marshalled their massive collection of synthesizers not for sonic overkill, but for unprecedentedly subtle timbral blends that helped make "Rosanna," "Africa," and other cuts on that album masterpieces of tasteful restraint and pace-setters for the new romantics of the future.

And there's no mistaking the fact that the new romantic movement is here to stay. As synthesizers continue to offer greater features at plummeting cost, younger players will keep finding new applications for them that will even further broaden the range of rock romanticism. Their innovations, their search for fresh angles and approaches to the gospel feel of this style, may ultimately measure the resiliency and endurance of rock and roll as a musical art form.
Bob Doerschuk

Seth Justman

House Rocker Extraordinaire

October 1979 — How did you first encounter the J. Geils Band?

I went to school at Boston University, and on my first day up there I was real green. I had just gotten housed, but I wanted to get away from school to see what was going on, so my roommate and I looked in the paper to see what music was around, and we saw this ad that said "J.Geils Band." He had heard of them, so we got out early and went to this club, the Catacombs. It was a basement club, a real seedy-looking place, underneath a pizza parlor which was below a pool hall. I didn't know what was going on, but I went down there and I ran into this guy with slicked-back hair—just like I had at the time—and it happened to be J., so I said, "Hey, man, we're coming down tonight. We're really interested in checking out your band. We hear you do a lot of rhythm and blues; maybe if there's time we could talk about what's happening." So that night I heard them, and it blew my mind. It was the exact type of band I had always wanted to be in—the right personnel, the right sound, everything. So after the gig, my mind blown totally, I went up to Peter Wolf and said, "Man, I've really got to get together with you. If I could jam with you, I think I could really get into what you're doing and maybe help the band out. I'm right on the same wavelength as you guys." He thought I was a speed freak at first, so he totally discounted me, but I got a phone number, and I followed them from gig to gig after that.

They were working without a keyboard player?

No keyboard. And I became obsessed. This was exactly what I wanted, so I'd call them every

107

"Now I don't get crazy with the settings, but I'm into the subtleties of certain drawbars. I really like those screaming distorted organ sounds."

day, find out where they were playing, and go there. After I had been doing this for about four or five months, they got to know me by name, so I'd show up and say, "Hey, man, this and that, and blah blah blah, I'm into the blues and all this stuff, so Jesus Christ, give me a break! Let me jam with you guys!" It went on and on until I finally semi-gave up. I joined this other group, a horn-type band that was fairly big in Boston, and worked with them until I got kicked out.

Why was that?

I don't know; it just kind of fell apart. I got real depressed. I mean, I got down so low that I was thinking about getting back into school, so one day my roommate said, "You've got to call Geils again. That's the band you're made for." Well, I called them, and amazingly enough, they said, "Why don't you come over Tuesday? Bring your organ." I went over, we all played and jammed, they made a tape of it and they said, "We'd like you to join the band." I think once they saw the organ it kind of impressed them.

The Farfisa Mini-Compact?

No, it was a Hammond L-100, with Leslie speakers. I had already gone up the Farfisa steps to the Duo-Compact, and then I got the L-100 after I had gone back to D.C. in my latter high school days. I put it to the test, running it through the Leslies and miking it, that kind of thing. They hadn't ever even seen a Hammond in person

before. Actually, Wolf didn't love it; he said, "It looks like it belongs in my mother's living room." But the rest of the group was truly impressed. There was definitely a connection between them and me.

When did you get your white B-3?

After I joined the Geils band. It definitely opened some new things up for me, because it has so much more variety than the L-100 in the things you can do with it. It has more drawbars, better percussion, cooler vibrato stuff, and bigger keyboards.

Do you have any favorite settings for the Hammond?

Well, I don't work off the presets. I don't think I ever really used them. I checked them out, but I didn't find them advantageous at all. The first thing I did when I got the B-3 was to try out the Jimmy Smith settings. I guess everybody does that. You've got to be influenced by Jimmy Smith. Now I don't get crazy with the settings, but I'm into the subtleties of certain drawbars. I enjoy a lot of the different sounds people can get with the Hammond. I like Dave "Baby" Cortez and Jimmy Smith, and there's a wide range between them. Usually, though, I pull the first three or four drawbars out, and I use the percussion on the third and second, to get the breath effect happening. I turn the Leslie up a lot so that it distorts too. I really like those screaming dis-

torted organ sounds, with a lot of bite.

How do you get that effect in the studio?

Well, I still use the L-100 for certain things, because it's real nasty-sounding. Also, the L-100 has a particular kind of vibrato that's a little weirder than what you have on the B-3, and sometimes I use it for that reason.

It's an unusually small setup, though. You have no synthesizers onstage, for instance.

Well, I have two of them at home—a Prophet and a CS-80—but I haven't used them that much, because I've just been learning how to play them. I haven't used them live yet. I'm into the new sounds, but I'm real impatient when it comes to getting all that technical stuff down. You've got to work at it and be persistent, and I find that real exciting. I like to see where it takes me as I learn on it. I'm really into the Yamaha CS-80. For some reason I have an affinity for it.

Do you think using more synthesizers might dilute the basic roadhouse rock feeling of the J. Geils Band?

I really don't know what they'll do, but I'm anxious to find out. I'd just like to see what the possibilities are. I'm not at all afraid of changing the sound anyway, as long as it maintains credibility, emotion, and soul, and sounds good and pleasing. Other than that, I'm not too worried about it. I'm trying not to have preconceived notions on what's going to happen.

So when will we be hearing the synthesizers in the band?

Well, it depends. When the right song comes along, or when I feel that I have it together enough to make sense musically on them, I'll start playing the synthesizers. I've already used Minimoogs a little bit for bass stuff on records, but for a while I really felt intimidated by synthesizers. The main thing, though, is to find an area where I can use them. You see, the way I view my function in the band is to find the best way to back up what is going on. What can I do to help the sound of the group come out as one thing? I do a lot of the arranging, and I'm sensitive to playing behind lead singers and soloists.

Do you ever wish you had more of a soloist's role yourself?

Sometimes. A lot of times Peter will say, "Hey, man, why don't you take a solo here?" Well, that's cool with me, and I'll try it out. We're loose about all that stuff. It just evolves as we try this or that. Often we'll decide to have a solo on the spot. When we do some old blues thing like "Serves You Right To Suffer," a John Lee Hooker song [from *J. Geils Band and Full House*], we'll let it all hang out. "Southside Johnny" [from *Bloodshot*] is loose, and we wing it. "Getting Out" [from *Nightmares*] has a fairly tight structure, but there's a jazzy piano solo in there sometimes, where I rumble and go for a low-end bang style.

The intro pattern to "Wild Man" [from *Sanctuary*] also has kind of a jazz feel.

Which keyboards do you most enjoy soloing on?

I really like the piano a lot, but it changes. For a while I'll be into the piano more than the organ, and then I'll start to get into the organ more. A lot depends on what I'm listening to at the time, or how I'm feeling. In any event, I don't often think of myself as a soloist as much as a complementary player working toward creating sheets of sound.

You seem to use the organ to accent the upbeat, while relying on the piano to do fills more frequently.

That's true a lot of the time. But then again, often I like to stab with the piano too, like on the vamp to "Give It To Me" [from *Bloodshot*]. That turned out really well, with a lot of staccato punches, keyboards jumping in and out, and everything working together like a machine, but real emotional, not sterile. I used the piano there to make an impact, not just to play fills.

When you play the piano that way, you frequently do octave passages and jackhammer triplets. Did you have to build up your wrists and practice for that kind of playing?

I have to practice to do everything [*laughs*]. When a record comes out and you just have to know how to play something on it, that means practicing until you get it. As soon as I discovered Jerry Lee Lewis, that style became like an addiction for me. I still practice that kind of stuff—Meade Lux Lewis, Albert Ammons, or Otis Spann things—and left-hand bass figures at home. I don't have too much trouble with the wrist. I'm a real pounder, though. Sometimes I play with my elbows, shoulders and back.

You do a lot of keyboard slides too. How do you handle them?

On the organ, I slide down the keys with the base of the thumb, and sometimes on the piano I use the base of the hand. I really like that kind of thing. Billy Preston does that a lot, and I'm a sucker for it. I've got callouses from all that Jerry Lee Lewis stuff [*laughs*].

You use kind of a windmill motion onstage when doing those slides.

It's the show. I've always been into the idea of doing a good show. When you see a James Brown-type singer, with real quality music and a tight show as well, the overall effect is just that much better. I remember when the Sam And Dave Soul Review came to town; it was dazzling! Or the early Ohio Players. We used to go to this club and see them before they were big. They used to come out in their hot pants and high leather boots, doing their precision movements, and the music was so hot and loud and sweaty and evil, it blew me away.

What kind of piano do you prefer using?

Well, I've always used Steinways a lot. It may be an illusion to me, but they seem to be brighter and I really dig them. It depends on the piano. If it sounds good, I'll use it. I've used Yamahas and Baldwins and various other things too. I like a piano that really responds fast. It's hard to describe how, but I more or less know by touch what I like. I'm a percussive player to a great degree, and the precision with which I can play has to do with how fast the instrument is. I sometimes do repeating octaves here and there, just to have the piano jump out, like in the intro to "Detroit Breakdown" [from *Nightmares*] or certain blues tunes we do. For live gigs I always used to use my 7' Baldwin with a Countryman pick up. It sounded real good, but it wasn't as consistent as I wanted, so when the CP-70 came out, I thought I'd give it a try, and it seems to be working out pretty well.

How do you set the tone controls on the electric grand?

It varies from tune to tune. On "Teresa" [from *Sanctuary*], let's say, I'd go for more bottom to fill the whole thing out. I'm still experimenting quite a bit, but for something funky, like "Southside Shuffle," I'm going to go for an attack kind of feel on the piano. I can get some pretty bright sounds, I have a mixer and pot, and some EQ.

What kind of mixer do you use?

This is another thing that varies. Today I used a Biamp. But we've gone through many a mixer, preamp, and all that, and I've never been supersatisfied. I'm loose about it, though. I'm willing to try just about anything to see how cool it'll be.

What effects do you run your piano through? It sounds like you often put a touch of digital delay on it in your records.

We've experimented with it. There are some people on the board out front who put a few things on the piano. In the studio, we're definitely into using different effects on it. We've used the DDL [digital delay line] stuff, and sometimes we've put some phasers on the piano. I don't have a lot of pedals onstage, though. Sometimes I use a Morley wah-wah pedal, but that goes on the Clavinet. I love the Clavinet.

Do you ever take solos on it?

I never have, other than while jamming. I haven't recorded one, but it's certainly not out of

he question. Sometimes I use it to double the bass guitar line, although it's nothing conscious; I just use it for what I think might sound good at the time.

How do you set the tone?

It depends on what's going on in the rest of the band. We make use of a lot of extremities in range, in terms of treble, mid, and bass, but the harmonica makes it tricky sometimes. If you hear our songs without the harmonica, you'd see how much it changes the texture. You have to be real sensitive to that, and to what's going on between the harp and the guitar. It's an unexplored area, to a great degree, in rock and roll. In the blues area, of course, you've always had piano, harmonica, and guitar, but when you start adding organs, Clavinets, and synthesizers to the harmonica, you're getting into an area where everything is open to experimentation.

What about the Rhodes? You've used that on some of the albums.

Yeah, and I've used it on and off live too, but not to a great extent, because we never did enough tunes that used it. It's got a mellower tone, which doesn't always work in an outdoor show, like we did today, because we don't always do a lot of the slower stuff there. But in an indoor show we sometimes do, and the Rhodes might fit in there. We'll do things like "I'm Falling" [from *Monkey Island*], or Start All Over" [from *Bloodshot*], or "Monkey Island," which is a jazz-type feeling, except for the beginning.

Didn't "Monkey Island" begin with some kind of a rhythm box?

Yeah, it was a Roland Rhythm Machine. We use the machine onstage for that too.

To round off your keyboard setup, you have a large mirror on top of your Clavinet. Do you use that to pick up cues onstage?

Yeah. I like to leave enough space for Peter to work out, and it's necessary sometimes that I face

the other way while he's doing that. This helps me see what's going on behind me without having to crane my neck and look around. We all like to have a good time up there, and if you're feeling a little isolated, you can lose touch with what the feel is.

What kind of impact has new wave rock had on your sound?

I don't know if it has had an impact on us, but we feel very close to it. I find a lot of the young bands with energy really exciting, and sometimes very interesting musically. Elvis Costello is great, but I hate to mention just a few names and leave some others out. I just like a lot of the stuff that's coming out.

When you record, is the entire band always there throughout the session, or do you come in at separate times and do your parts individually?

When we do tracks, everyone is in the studio, pumping away. There are times when some people aren't around, like when there's going to be an extended session of, say, the guitar, but J. is usually hanging in there. It's hard to be there all the time, but the main thing is to try to keep it exciting for us, since we hope that it'll then be exciting for other people. We try to have no preconceived notion about what people want to hear, while hoping that our tastes will coincide with what audiences will like. So far it's worked out. It's an exciting experience for me to write the tunes with Peter; working with Wolf is stimulating, to say the least. And in the studio I have a very active role. I think that intuitively this comes across in the way we play. I'm just really consumed with this band.

Bob Doerschuk

Gary Wright

The View from Center Stage

May 1978 — Are people frightened by the idea of there being no guitars in the band?

It's a threat to musicians. Bass players especially, I've noticed. They come up to me and say, "How do you get that incredible sound? It's so full and so round." There are certain things that you can't play on a Moog that you can play on a guitar, like the Stanley Clarke pulled-string effects, but you can't bend notes over two octaves on a bass either. The threat comes in when people start thinking, "Well, if someone else can do it on a keyboard, what's going to happen to me?" I'm not saying that the synthesizer is going to outmode the guitar or the bass. I'm just saying that it's going to emerge as an entity that has equal importance.

Have people given you grief about using string synthesizers instead of real strings?

No. It's a head trip to get into a stupid argument about that. I use string synthesizers because I like the sound of synthesized strings. If I wanted to use live strings I would use live strings. I think that synthesized strings sound better in an all-synthesizer band. There's more of a total melding of sound that you create.

What type of effects devices are you using on the keyboards?

I use a Roland Space Echo on mine. We do have some Echoplexes and an English echo device made by H&H Electronics. We have a Mu-Tron Bi-Phase, and some of the keyboards are fed through Leslies. We also have two rhythm boxes. One's made by Univox and the other by Roland. There are two Moog drums that are fed through two Micromoogs. All of it is there to help recreate the orchestrations from the albums. We

Previous page: Gary Wright on a chopped and portabilized Minimoog keyboard. Right: "My own style of playing is more like singing, really."

have digital delays and Eventide Harmonizers, too.

You mentioned that everything was run direct into the PA. Where do the Leslies fit into the setup?

They're offstage, being miked. We don't run everything through them. Just the Crumar organ, my Polymoog, and my Minimoog. Sometimes the String Ensemble is fed through one. There aren't any particular sounds that I prefer to use the Leslie on, but I use it mainly for solo work. I run it at fast speed, so most of the sounds sound pretty. You can't use a very soft sound to get the right effect. It has to be harsh and aggressive to get the sound to really come out.

How would you set the Polymoog to get that harsh sound?

Sometimes the harpsichord is a neat sound to put through a Leslie. The brass is also good if you use the pulse and sawtooth waves together. Then you just have to work with the resonator to get it right. Polymoogs are very, very sensitive. With those sliders for the resonator you have to be very careful, because it's very easy to distort. I also use the mixing section of the Poly so that the filter and the resonator are the most prominent, and maybe sometimes I'll add just a touch of the direct, but not very much of it. Usually I use a combination of the resonators and the filter.

How is the Clavinet treated within the band?

Basically as a rhythm instrument. I'll put it through an Echoplex and treat it like . . . I guess it really functions as my guitar. My rhythm guitar.

When you record, do you use the Clavinet on the basic rhythm track?

Usually the first thing I put down is a keyboard track with the Clavinet. But it depends on the tune. Sometimes I'll record something playing Moog bass with one hand and Clavinet in the other with a Rhythm Ace going just to get the general feel. Then I'll go back and overdub the Clavinet and the Moog bass part again, adding organ, Oberheim, or whatever on top of that.

So you try to do all of the keyboard work on your albums yourself?

Mostly. Again it depends on the track. On the new album, *Touch And Gone, I played most of the things except the drums. On "Night Ride," I played everything but the drums and the Clavinet. On "Loss Of My Emotion," I played it all except the organ.*

How do you decide that you're not going to do a particular part and call in a studio player?

If I think that the particular style I want on a track is something that may be a little bit outside of my own field, and more within the realm of another player's specialty, I'll just ask them to do it. I've got a good feel of the players around me, so if I think that I can't play something particularly well, I'll ask someone else to do it.

When did you first start playing music?

When I was about 12 or 13, I taught myself how to play the piano. I took a couple of months of classical lessons, but I've forgotten it all. Basically what I play comes from having worked things out myself. I can't really say that anything else that I did in my past bears any conscious relationship to my playing. I'm sure that all the things I studied in college and all the other kinds of things I've experienced in one way or another helped my approach to playing and life in general. It's hard to say in a conscious way what things have had this and that effect on the music, though. In fact, I left school, where I was studying psychology, in order to get more into music. I guess it was to get more in touch with what I really wanted to do. It was music above academics.

Do you think of yourself as an orchestrator?

I see myself as a singer, a writer, a producer, a keyboardist, all of those things, which are all interfaced into one personality. I don't see one as being more important than another. I do use the keyboards as my orchestra. I think I've demonstrated in my live concerts that you can create a whole rich environment of music without needing a guitar or stringed instruments at all. It's all done on keyboards. I think it's created a lot of fear in people's minds, saying, "Oh, well, he should have guitars!" But I don't think so. I've made hit records and I've made good-sounding records without having any guitars. The guitar fits into most people's formula, but I want to use other things—other things that I feel fit into my music better than the guitar.

Have you ever used modular synthesizers?

No, but I've heard about them. I think on my next album I might use one. I think I want to get into a big Moog or something. I'd like to have something that you could do some nice sequencing events on—events that go on for three minutes. More complex stuff. I'm interested in getting into different kinds of modulations, like on *Dream Weaver* where I got those tinkling bell sounds. I'd like to extend that type of effect and get into things that are more sophisticated.

Do you have any interest in computer interfacing with synthesizers?

We have a programmer in the Oberheim for storing up patches. But other than that, no.

How do you feel about the ARP String Ensemble?

They're okay. I use them mostly for the high string sound. The Polymoog and the Oberheim have better sounds for that rich, thick lower string sound. I like to doctor the String Ensemble's sound by feeding it into a Leslie for that fuller vibrato sound.

Have you ever used anything else made by ARP?

The first synthesizer I ever used was when I was in England working with Spooky Tooth. It was a 2600. There are some nice things you can do with it. I guess I'm drawn more to the Moog sound, though. I like the oscillators better. I like the Oberheim for its brass sound, too. On the four-voice, you can program a lot of nice orchestral things. You can get nice things on the bigger ARP stuff, but it's not there for me really.

What happened to the B-3 in your setup?

We didn't bring one with us because the Crumar Organizer-B actually sounds better than the Hammond when you put it through a Leslie. It's not as heavy, either.

What do you think about the Yamaha electric grand?

It's good for the road. It doesn't get the same kind of acoustic piano sound you'd get on a Steinway or a Bechstein, but it's certainly good and easy to work with. I haven't worked with it in the studio yet, but I am going to on the next album.

What kind of action do you prefer on keyboards?

I like a quick action—something like a Minimoog.

How did you adapt yourself to all the different actions?

Just by playing them over and over again. You realize just what the limitations are with each keyboard. Like on the Oberheim you don't have the versatility that you do with a Minimoog. On a Minimoog you can do things like sustain a high note and play lower notes with some space

between those lower notes, so you can get the higher note triggering in between the lower notes. With the Oberheim there are other things you can do. Like set it up for random assign, so that you might get one module on the top note of a chord one time and another on top the next time. That really makes the horn sounds realistic.

What gave you the idea to hang the Minimoog keyboard around your neck?

I just wanted to get away from standing still. I'd seen it before with the Univox pianos—like what Edgar Winter and Billy Preston did. So I knew something like that could be done. I'd also seen Winter use the 2600 keyboard around his neck. The Minimoog was my instrument, so I looked into doing the same thing with it.

Who would you name as your strongest influence musically?

That's really hard. My own style of playing is more like singing, really. I try to play like I would sing. If anything, Indian music has had the strongest influence on my music, because I like to play against strong rhythms. But my style of soloing is really my own. I'm more or less unique when it comes to that. It may not be technically perfect, but I just try and get the best *feeling* possible.

Some of your songs are coordinated with films, aren't they?

We have four different songs with corresponding films. I did them with two friends of mine in Los Angeles. Their company is called Homer. We have a click track that's piped through headphones so everyone can stay in sync

with the films, which are combinations of laser photography, still photography, surrealistic art, NASA space photography, and things like that. My music is conceived with visual images in mind. It's very visually oriented, and I think the future will see me doing video albums. That's the direction I'm going in.
Dominic Milano

Michael McDonald

From the Streets to the Stadiums

August 1979 — What kind of musical training did you receive as a child?

Well, in short, I really had very little formal study in my background. I took piano lessons when I was a little kid from a guy in St. Louis who was a friend of my father's. He played piano, and my father was a singer, an Irish tenor. Dad never sang professionally, but he sang in every bar all over the city of St. Louis. In all the years I knew him my father never took a drink, but he was in more bars than any drunk, because he loved to sing. My whole family is like that. They're music freaks. They're brought together by music, and they love it. I learned about it at that level, as a kind of basic human habit from just being in the family. They're thrilled to death at what I'm doing now.

Do you remember your performing debut?

Oh, I remember it explicitly. I was real little, four years old, and it was a typical Saturday. My father was a bus driver, so on Saturdays he would go by the bus station, then he'd go by the bars, and I would hang out with him. Like I say, he never drank; he just met his friends, and he liked to socialize. Anyway, on this particular Saturday, they got me up on the bar, and I sang "Around The World In Eighty Days." I couldn't even hold a tune, but I loved it. More than anything, I think I enjoyed the recognition from him and all the people. It was a very young age to be hit with such a positive reaction to something, so I was hooked. From that moment on I wanted to be a musician for the rest of my life, truly because of that experience.

Did you primarily want to be a singer?

I pretty much always wanted to be a singer. I

**Previous page: Michael McDonald with his Ober-
heim 8-Voice. "Some of my better songs are written out of ignorance."**

really don't consider myself much of a piano
player. I played to write songs, more than anything else. I have a certain knowledge of harmony and chord progressions, but I wouldn't call
myself a pianist, really. I mainly decided to pursue
it so that I could sing and play at the same time,
but studying the technical part of it just didn't
appeal to me as a kid, so I let it go and I didn't
really pick it up again until I got into rock and
roll.

*Did you do any more formal studying after
that?*

Yeah. I took lessons recently from a guy
named Fletcher Peck, a teacher who was living in
LA. He's such a great teacher. First of all, the guy
is an excellent pianist, but he taught me more
about the piano than I'd ever known before. I
was much worse at the keyboard before he got
to me than I am now [*laughs*]. During the year I
knew him, he expanded my horizons as far as my
writing was concerned, too. What he did mainly
was to give me harmonic exercises and things
that got me better acquainted with the piano—
scales and stuff I never knew I was doing before.
Not that I know now about everything I play, but
I just took a huge leap forward by knowing that
guy. A lot of the inspiration for the writing and
playing I did on our last album [*Minute By Minute*] sprang from working with him.

*Is it true that you mainly played banjo for a
while when you were a kid?*

I played some banjo, but in my first rock and
roll band I played guitar. I went from that to just
working as a singer, and that was a disaster. I
never made it performing as a stand-up singer, so
I started playing the piano and writing then.

*So you took up the piano largely to have
something to do onstage?*

Well, that was one reason, plus it just slipped
back in there when I started writing. It felt more
natural for me to compose at the piano than at
the guitar.

*You can often tell with the Doobie Brothers
whether a song was written by Pat, for example,
on guitar, or by you at a keyboard.*

That's true. What I notice about that is that
piano songs don't travel in such a straight line all
the time, because with the piano the relation-
ships of the tones are all laid out in front of you. I
think more ideas come to your mind when you
can look at it like that, whereas with the guitar
you tend to write more abstractly; more of the
music is square or geometric, somehow. With me
and the piano, though, the main thing I've always
noticed is that some of my better songs are writ-

ten out of ignorance, based on what I didn't
know. Chord changes that I really enjoy and like
now I have no basic reason for coming up with,
other than pure accident.

*Are you saying that your creativity has at times
been inhibited by what training you've had?*

No, never by what I did have, but miracu-
lously I've been taken in another direction by my
lack of it sometimes. If I knew more about what I
was doing, I don't honestly think I would have
written some of the songs I've done. I shouldn't
really say that, because the more I learn about
the piano the better are the songs I write, there's
no doubt about that. But as I look back on a lot
of the earlier stuff, I find a certain charm and I
realize I wouldn't have written things that way if I
had known what I was doing. It's not a question
of being musical; it's just the spirit and the simplicity of these songs. I would hate to lose those
qualities in trying to incorporate all my chops into
songwriting.

*How did you write your first hit with the
Doobies, "Takin' It To The Streets"* [*from* Takin' It
To The Streets]?

The chords came first on that one. I heard the
chord changes as I was driving in my car. I wasn't
sure if I could play what I was hearing when I got
to a piano; I didn't know if it was one of those
ideas that sound great in your head, but once
you sit down and try it out it doesn't sound right.
I guess it worked all right, though.

*How about your collaboration with Kenny
Loggins on "What A Fool Believes"* [*from* Minute
By Minute]?

Kenny called me out of the clear blue sky one
day. I'd never met him in my life, but he said that
he enjoyed our records and would love to write
something with me. So I said, "I'd love to write
together with you too. Why don't you come over
this week or something?" We made a date for
the next night. I knew that I wanted to work with
him on this song, which I'd been trying to finish
but had kind of reached a dead end with. To
make a long story short, he came over and we
worked on it until around five in the morning for
a couple of nights, and on nights we didn't get
together we talked on the phone about it. In
about five days we managed to write the song.

*Did you have the keyboard arrangement in
your mind as you wrote the tune?*

No, it was hashed out later. Billy Payne [for-
merly of Little Feat] and I just did it by head. I'd
already cut the track with either electric or acoustic piano, I don't really remember which, and I
just had Billy bring in his synthesizers. It was

mainly a matter of us sitting around going, "Well, you do this and I'll do that." I'd start to show him the part I wanted, and I'd wind up playing it myself on his synthesizer. Then he just sat around and came up with the string part on the Oberheim Eight-Voice. During the course of the session he was working with sort of a half horn and half steel drum program on the Yamaha CS-80. Patrick came up with his guitar parts later.

How do you evolve your own keyboard parts?

The tune kind of dictates them itself. By the time I've just about finished writing a song, I find that I'm trying to compensate for the lack of bass and other instruments in the room at the time with what I play on the keyboard. Pretty soon I'm playing every conceivable movement that could be played in a piano part, so a lot of times I'll have to go back later to force myself to play a lot less and let the band start playing the song.

Often there is a lot of left-hand work in your piano playing.

Yeah, and sometimes there's even a lot more before I get through doing it with the band. I have to let go of some of that and let them come up with their own parts.

Since you used the piano a lot to accompany your own singing, did you learn to play easily in whatever odd keys your voice happened to fit?

Mainly I started out in C, because for some reason it seemed to me like the easiest key for playing. I always felt I could sing wherever I had to, which I think is a good philosophy for singers, because it lets you stretch your capacity beyond where you would think your limits were if you thought you were straining your voice all the time. You either have to have a throat that can take your sitting there and screaming, or you really have to build yourself up to it. When I'm off for a while I don't try to kill myself during the first couple of days of rehearsal. I might sound like a dying dog, but I'll let myself go through that, and if it doesn't feel right I won't sing the whole song. After a few more days I'll be ready to sing again. I work my way up to it gradually that way, but usually I keep my voice in enough shape to at least be able to get up and yell.

Did you absorb a lot in your sessions with MOR artists like Jack Jones that has helped you in your current career?

Oh, yeah, I picked up a lot. I worked with some great musicians there. I really had no business doing those gigs, as far as that goes, but nevertheless I learned so much, primarily about how to make records. I made the most of the opportunity I had in those situations.

Were they helpful in learning how to adjust your playing to other styles of music as well?

Yeah, although I learned a lot about that in playing piano at various club dates. Playing clubs is a whole other aspect of growing musically, and it deals with things like how to build your endurance, how to play with an ensemble, how to keep up your energy, and other elements that don't really come into play all the time when you're doing sessions. You can do a lot of sessions and still not experience the kind of playing you go through live onstage with five other musicians in terms of being inspired or playing behind somebody's solo, just using your creative mind spontaneously to build dynamics together with the soloist, and trying to relate to other players so you can guess where they're going and figure out how to meet them there.

Did you ever record on keyboard with Steely Dan?

Oh, no, I've never played keyboard with them, except onstage. I sang on *Katy Lied*, and on every one of their albums since then they've just used me for background. Those guys are the all-time greatest for me. I think they're the best songwriters I've ever heard in any category. I just enjoy working for them, and I always look forward to the next session.

Do you feel that your arrival signified a change in direction for the Doobies?

Things did change, but kind of naturally. It's not that I just showed up and changed everything. The band has changed me a lot too. I really started out just filling in for Tom Johnston, who was kind of ill, by doing some singing. I think Pat had originally intended to do all of Tom's vocals, but then we wound up splitting them between us. When "Takin' It To The Streets" came about and it was time to do another album, things got kind of chaotic. Tom was still ill, so anybody who could write a song came up with something.

Now that Jeff Baxter has left the group and a second keyboardist, Cornelius Bumpus, has been added, do you feel that the Doobies will have even a stronger keyboard orientation than before?

No, I don't think so, really. I think that John McFee, the guy who's playing lead guitar with us now, is a pretty formidable guitarist. He's not the same as Jeff, but in his own way I think he's just as much of a personality. He's a little more rock and roll than Jeff was. But just off the top of my head, I can hear some changes he and Corny are bringing in with the way the group sounds. It's a funny kind of effect, actually. I see Corny kind of

yanking the band more in the direction I might have yanked it, and I see John yanking it probably more in the direction that Patrick would have yanked it. I think this all makes it more interesting. Hopefully it'll just continue with the kind of diversity we've had for the past few years.

How has your onstage keyboard setup changed through the years with the Doobies?

I've gotten it down to a pretty simple arrangement now. I used to get up there with an Oberheim Eight-Voice synthesizer, which was silly because I never got the chance to use it too much, since I'm always singing leads. I was using a Yamaha 6-foot grand piano until I switched over to the Yamaha CP-70 electric grand. Now I've got a Rhodes, a Clavinet, and a 5-voice Sequential Circuits Prophet synthesizer.

How do you like the Prophet?

It's a good little instrument. There are a lot of things you can do with it, even though I'm not really into synthesizers in a very fanatical way. My use of it is really very limited by my knowledge of it. I just kind of arrange it for parts that would otherwise be orchestrated like I'll use it for horns and strings. Usually I modify the attack for what I need, but basically I stick to simple horn patches. A lot of times I'll use some kind of envelope that isn't either a string or horn sound particularly but I'll play it in that register to serve that purpose anyway. I find myself using generally mellow sounds to blend in with everything else.

Where was your first contact with synthesizers?

It was with this band, actually. I did a demo with a Minimoog on "Losin' End" [from *Takin' It To The Streets*] in Tiran's [Porter, bass guitarist] basement.

Did you ever use the Minimoog onstage?

I never really played it live. I never soloed on it or anything. I don't take many solos now but when I do it's usually on piano. I'm still not really comfortable with any of the synthesizers. I go from song to song and learn what to do in each case to get what I need. I haven't really spent any time sitting around trying to figure them out. When I first joined this band all I had as a setup was a small Wurlitzer electric piano going through a Twin Reverb or something, and that was it. That's all I used. I'd just throw it in the back of my car, haul it from club to club, set it up, and play.

What interested you in the Oberheim?

I was mainly turned onto it by our road crew. I just liked the sound of it. It was also very adaptable to pretty much anything you wanted to do. You could do a lot with it as far as programming each VCO module separately, and with all the switching mechanisms, it just seemed like the state-of-the-art synthesizer at the time to me. Mainly, though, I went with it because it was one of the first polyphonic synthesizers I even knew of at the time.

Why did you switch to the Prophet?

Mainly because I found myself not getting into synthesizers so much. It just wasn't me to be that involved with them. Most of my preoccupation was with writing. The Prophet was just the easiest of all the polyphonic synthesizers to play. A lot of things attracted me to it: I liked the tuning mechanism live, I thought it sounded great, and I thought it would just be easier for me to deal with on the road.

On which of your keyboards do you feel most comfortable?

I'd say the piano—the electric grand and the Rhodes.

"I'm not that quick-minded with synthesizers . . . I like to sit down and sing in front of people. I like to rock and roll."

Do you play the 88-key stage model Rhodes?

Yes. It's been modified somewhat. Dixie Swanson, our stage manager, got inside and rewired it, and put a little preamp right behind the input to give it more of that suitcase model Rhodes sound; the high end has a sparkling kind of sound now.

Do you have any trouble with the Rhodes action?

Yeah, although I've adjusted it a couple of times. It can be worked with, so now it's not too bad. I have a terrible technique, though. From learning by ear I play like a hoofed animal, slopping around the keys, so the Rhodes is still particularly hard for me to play. Sometimes I hit the thing too hard, so I'm breaking tines all the time.

Have you ever gone back to the Wurlitzer?

I've used it lately when I'm looking specifically for that kind of effect, the Wurlitzer sound, but I haven't done anything that's really called for that with the band.

Do you run the Rhodes through any effects?

I like to use the Vox Chorale on the Rhodes; that's a nice pedal. I don't use much else. For a long time I'd just take the Rhodes direct, and Grey Ingram, our engineer, had an Eventide Harmonizer. Now I use my Rhodes with a Leslie in a small wooden cabinet, like a 147. We put it inside a road box when we're on tour and just mike it through the board from offstage. It really sounds neat, and I've found that that's the best sound we can get with it so far.

Do you change Leslie speeds often?

No, I usually don't. Sometimes I might if I'm using a B-3 kind of sound on the Prophet; in that case I'll kick the speeds in and out just like I would on an organ. There are other ways of doing that with the Prophet. You can simulate a Leslie with the modulation section, but it sounds better with a real Leslie.

You mentioned that you used to play a Yamaha grand piano with the Doobies. What did you like about the Yamaha?

Well, it was a good piano; still is. In my house I have a Yamaha C-7B, and it's the greatest instrument I think I've ever played, as far as producing a really beautiful sound goes. I've don't think I've ever played a Steinway I've liked any better than my piano, although I recorded a lot on 6 and 7-foot Steinways. In fact, I guess every acoustic piano I've ever used in the studio has been a Steinway; we just took the Yamaha grand on the road.

Are there any other keyboards you're interested in using onstage?

I don't know. I might add something later on, but what we're doing now is developing ourselves instrumentally with what we've got. We're pressed to just learn the vocal parts and get the songs down at the moment, what with the new guys in the band.

With the recent changes in your lineup, did you have to redo the vocal arrangements a lot?

No, we're pretty much left with the guys who sang. I think we may start developing our songs again later as far as instrumental breaks and arrangements are concerned, though, and at that time I'll probably want to incorporate a lot more synthesizers than what I'm using now. I'd like to learn more about keyboards as I go along; it seems like I can't help but incorporate them into what we do. I've tried to develop that, so the kind of stuff I'll be writing may be less vocal and more instrumental. The recordings may change a lot with the new members; there might not be quite so much singing and we might even do instrumentals on the next studio album. Some of the guys are real good instrumentalists and they also write music, so I'm anxious to explore their material.

How will you and Cornelius Bumpus, your other keyboard player, interact on your instruments?

Corny and I may develop some kind of exchange of solos or coordinate our synthesizer playing, but I don't know; it's tough sometimes to add that much synthesizer stuff into a live show. I'm just not that quick-minded with synthesizers, and I think that's the main thing that keeps me away from being a real expert with them. I mean, my style is a whole different bag. I like to sit down and sing in front of people. I like to rock and roll, and I like to just relax and perform, as opposed to having too much going on at once that distracts me from simply enjoying the song and doing it the best I can. We play rock and roll as good and better than most, and sometimes it's even better-sounding live than it was on record. But it's tight, you know, and we try to keep the band as solid, tight, and impressive as we can. None of us are virtuoso players or anything, but as a band we have a certain talent. We're entertainers in the sense that we have a good time when we play in front of people, and that's always a very relaxed situation for us. I enjoy live performing very much. It's a chance for me to sing out all night long, and it's a big release. I don't think I could live without it.

Bob Doerschuk

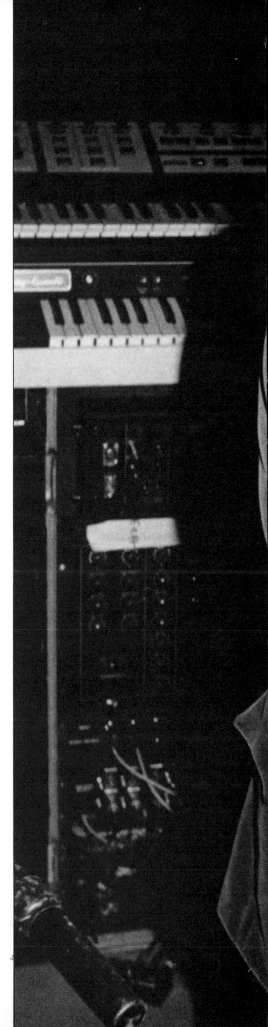

Dennis De Young

Teeny Bop Grows Up

January 1981 — *Judging from your work with Styx, you seem to have had some keyboard training. When did you begin playing?*

I started playing accordion when I was seven years old. It was a fashionable instrument at that time, very much in vogue. There were not a lot of electric guitar players in those days, and besides, I had an Italian mother, so I took accordion lessons for about seven years. I became old enough to make my own decisions when I was about 14, so I quit music altogether and started playing football. I was in high school then. At that point the accordion was beginning to become passe, so for about a year and a half I never touched the instrument.

What got you back into playing again?

One day during summer vacation, when I think I was 14 or 15, I was walking down the street where I lived, and I heard music coming from one of the houses on the block. It was the Panozzo brothers. I knew their sister, because she was closer to my age than John and Chuck; they were 12, and when you're 14 those 12-year-old kids seem really young. So I walked up on the porch and went into the house, and there was this little three-piece combo playing, with John on drums, Chuck on guitar, and this accordion player. It was the first music in a small ensemble I'd heard in my life, because when I played accordion it was always in these giant accordion bands that were big in those days—you know, two thousand guys. So I'd never really played with anything other than accordion, and I was fascinated. The minute I heard them I said, "Jeez, I would really like to play again." So I went home and got out my accordion, which had been hid-

Previous page: Dennis De Young surrounded by (clockwise from left) an Oberheim OB-X, an ARP string ensemble, an Oberheim 8-Voice, a Hammond B-3, and another Oberheim OB-X. Left: Playing the 8-Voice and B-3.

den away for a year and a half, to see if I could still play. Then the next day I called the Panozzos and said, "Why don't you come over to my basement tonight, and bring your equipment. I'll help you carry it over. I can play accordion a lot better than the guy you've got in your combo!"

This was after you'd made sure that . . .

. . . That I could still play! But the other guy was only a beginner, and when I had quit I was really good as an accordionist. So they came over, and that's how the nucleus of Styx was formed. We're still together, John and Chuck are now our bass player and drummer. So actually my training was on accordion, and then I bought my first combo organs, a Vox Continental and a Vox Jaguar. Those were the first two I owned, because the Beatles had Vox equipment. That's when I started teaching myself to play this way [on a horizontal keyboard].

Had you ever played piano up to that point?

No. I'd never touched one in my life. In fact, I only bought my first piano, a console, in 1975, and literally the only time I had ever played acoustic piano before that was when we recorded "Lady" in 1972. I had to walk in cold to that session; that was my first real attempt at playing acoustic piano.

Have you had trouble developing your left hand as a result of your learning exclusively on accordion?

Yeah, sure. My right hand is probably as good as any right hand anywhere, because it was developed on the keys themselves. But for so many years the left hand only played a little bass, and you don't use your thumb on the accordion, so the hardest thing to do is to start getting used to using the thumb. I just had to teach myself how to play piano and organ.

Did your accordion background affect the way you phrase on other keyboards?

That's a good question. I don't know. Nobody ever asks me these questions—they always ask me about songs and singing—but I was thinking about it today, and I'm not saying this to be pompous or egotistical, but when I listen to my synthesizer and keyboard playing, stylistically I don't ever hear anybody else who plays like me. Maybe that has something to do with the accordion, although I never thought about it in those terms.

Was it hard to get your accordion chops back?

Yeah. It took me, I'd say, about ten days, because it had been a long time since I'd last played it, and the keys were so small and so close together.

How about your arm muscles?

To tell you the truth, that was the hardest part. In the old days I used to play four-hour gigs with the accordion on my back and not think anything of it, but one song now and my whole left shoulder hurts because all those muscles were not being used for such a long time. The hardest part of all is the left wrist; that's really the strain on an accordion player. When I was playing all the time, all the hair on the underside of that wrist would be worn off from all the pulling.

Did you jump onto the synthesizer band-wagon during its early days?

I *hated* synthesizers! I hated them with a passion for the longest time. You have to remember that I started playing synthesizers when they first came out. It was in 1971 or '72, and the Moog 10 was the big deal; they didn't even have the Mini-moog then. The first time I saw it was when I went in the studio. I didn't even know what a synthesizer was. I knew there was some neat-sounding instrument on *Abbey Road,* but I didn't know what it was. Then Emerson's first album with ELP came out [*Emerson, Lake & Palmer*], right about the time that we were making our first record. I said, "Goddamn, what is that?"

The synthesizer solo on "Lucky Man"?

Right. So I went in, and there was the Moog 10 in the studio. It looked like the switchboard for Bell Telephone. I said, "What is this?" Some guy who was there said, "Don't worry, I'll program it for you. All you have to do is play." Well, he sat there with those stupid patch cords around his neck plugging them in for hours. The guy didn't know his ass from a hole in the ground. If anything destroys creativity and spontaneity, it's waiting for an hour and a half for somebody to patch something. So on our first album I used the Moog 10, but I hated it because I had no idea of what the hell it was. All I knew was that it took forever to get it in tune, and then you were lucky if it stayed in tune. So right after that we went and bought two ARP 2600s. J.C. [John Curu-lewski], who played guitar for us then, used one of them and I played the other.

Did you ever interface them?

We kept them separate. J.C. was big on sound effects. That's probably the only thing the 2600 is good for—the champ of white noise. He wasn't a good technician on the keyboard, but he was interested in the electronic end of the instrument, so he was able to program it for all the sounds. So what we would do in those days was, I would play the melodic theme on my 2600, and he would do the sound effects, or sometimes we would do sound effects together. But the 2600

was a pain in the ass. It drifted out of tune all the time. It was difficult to play in a live situation because it took so long to get in pitch, and you had to have the headsets on to get it right, and then it would just [*snaps fingers*] again.

Well, no doubt it was good for teaching you the ins and outs of working with a synthesizer.

That it did. In other words, you had to understand about the filters and the envelopes and all that. It was an electronics lesson. But let me tell you something: I don't care. I don't give a damn about it. I never have and I never will. The only important thing is the music. I don't care about the electronics. The only important thing to me about the synthesizer is the music you draw from it, not necessarily the way in which the sounds are created. To me, that is of no importance. In other words, to me a musician is someone who hears the French horn or the flute or the guitar, and he knows how those instruments should be applied to music. That's the main thing.

But in order to realize that sound you have to know how to do the correct patching.

Not any more. You did in those days, and consequently I became very negative toward synthesizers in the beginning. I bought an ARP Pro-Soloist after getting rid of the 2600, and I used the Minimoog in the studio. This was before a lot of the other models came along. The thing that disturbed me most about all the early synthesizers was their inability to stay in tune. The organ and the piano, if it was tuned before I went on, I could count on for being in tune when I played them, so I got away from the synthesizers that would not stay in tune. I went to the Pro-Soloist, which I hated because it was nothing, but at least I knew when I played the damn thing that it was going to be in tune

What do you mean when you say it was "nothing"?

One oscillator. Monophonic. It was what I would call the sound of the American TV commercial.

Did you do a lot of monophonic synthesizer overdubs back then?

Yeah. We did a thing on *The Serpent Is Rising* that was really a steal from Beaver and Krause in many ways, with all the oscillators sweeping in different directions and finally ending up on a chord. That took many many hours, because we had to get the timing right for when the notes sweep up to that chord. That took hours and hours to do. I would say it was worthwhile for us, except for the fact that the studio we recorded at had incredible technical difficulties with their EQ and their monitor playback. That's why the album

sounds as bad as any album I've heard in the history of recorded music.

What was the first album on which you used a polyphonic synthesizer?

Grand Illusion.

What are you using in concert nowadays?

Onstage now I play an Oberheim, two OB-Xs, a Rhodes, a Hammond B-3, and a Yamaha C grand piano. I don't use any ARPs anymore, except for their String Ensemble. I want to say one thing about ARP, because I've been bad-rapping them a little bit. The ARP String Ensemble, the one I have, which is six or seven years old, is the best electronic string instrument made, and you can tell ARP that I said so. The newer ones are crappy, but those original ones, magnificent.

What do you like about it? The attack?

No, the attack is terrible. String Ensembles are hard to play, because all you have to do is barely touch a note and it sounds, so it's a very delicate kind of instrument. But what I like is the tonal quality, the ability to, in the right application, recreate the sounds of a violin, like the sound of 55 violin players holding a note. It has that ability.

How did your organ setup change after you moved on from the Vox gear?

I went to a Farfisa Professional, which I played through a Leslie preamp and speaker, so it really had a pretty nice Hammond sound. Nothing is a Hammond but a Hammond, of course, but for a guy who didn't have any money and didn't have

the wherewithal to carry around a big organ, it did the job. After that I bought a Hammond M-3, played it for a number of years, and then I went to the B-3.

What led you to move from one model Hammond to another?

The low notes, that extra octave or so on a B-3 that's not on an M. The first B I owned was a piece of crap. It had sat in somebody's basement forever and it was really beat up, but that was all I could afford, so I bought it and had it reworked. But the one I play now, the blond one, is a beauty. I got it from this woman who had just kept it in her home—it sounds like one of those advertisements out in California—and it was perfect, rich-sounding and all clean inside. Of course it's been reworked so that I can run it straight into a Leslie preamp and then into the Leslie, depending on what power amp is working—I've used a BGW, a Crown, an Acoustic. Other than that, there are no other modifications on the organ.

What about the Leslie cabinet?

The Leslie is a 122, the same one I've used for ten years, with a JBL driver. I just used the one Leslie, but the real key to my organ sound is in my Wilder speaker cabinet. Wilder was based out of Chicago, but they went out of business eight or ten years ago. This guy sold them to me because he had them sitting around the place. These cabinets are for a bass guitar, with three 15s, Wilder speakers, and they have a sound

**"I've always like Mozart, so all my things are kind
of Mozartian; they have that same metered feel,
and that just has to be done on a real piano."**

unlike anything else. They give my organ that rich
and powerful quality. If I unplug them the organ
sounds terrible, because you really don't hear the
bottom rotor in the Leslie.

You don't mike the bottom of the Leslie?

No, just the top, and we also mike the Wilder
speakers. Basically what you hear onstage is the
high rotor and the Wilders for the bottom. Every
roadie I've ever had has tried to convince me that
I should buy this cabinet with JBLs or that cabinet
with something else, and every time they bring it
in and I play through it, I say, "Tell me which
sounds better." And they say, "You're right, it
doesn't sound as good as the Wilder."

Do you use the fast mode often on the Leslie?

Almost never. Almost always I leave it on
chorale. There are a couple of effects that
obviously call for it, the old Booker T. things, but
I don't like the sound of the fast spin. It's reminiscent of roller skating rinks to me. It's also a great
place to hide, like the fuzz tone for your guitar.
That fast speed makes everything you play sound
more special than it might be, by throwing out
sound in all directions. When I do use it, though,
I trigger it with a vibrato pedal that my old keyboard roadie built for me. It's right on the
volume pedal of the B-3, so I don't have to lose
one hand or one foot from what I'm doing when
I want to turn it on or off. It took a little practice
to be able to do that without swelling the volume
up and down at the same time, but it's no problem now.

*How about the percussion and the vibrato
dial on the B-3?*

I keep the vibrato dial on C-1 on mine, but on
other Hammonds I've played it at another position. I keep the percussion on soft, fast decay,
and pitched to the third.

*How did you get that rough-edged organ
sound in the intro to "Blue Collar Man" [from
Pieces Of Eight] ? Did you just overdrive the Leslie in the studio?*

No. That sound is actually done with a digital
delay. I wish I could tell you the exact settings on
the DDL, but it's a combination of the miked
organ sound and its own delayed signal. "Blue
Collar Man" is about blue collar workers, factory
workers, and I wanted something that sounded
like machinery starting up. So we tried it. The first
mixdown we had was the organ straight, just as it
was recorded, with just a little chamber, a little
reverberation. It sounded absolutely wrong.
When it was finished I had an argument with the
engineer because he liked the sound, but I said,
"It sounds churchy." Whenever you put any kind

of reverberation on an organ it sounds churchier
because it sounds like it's something big in a big
room. I said, "I want that sound to be up front,
right in your face. The first thing you hear has to
be this angry sound." So we fooled with the digital delay until we figured out how much of it
should be used with the original signal to give
that quality I wanted.

*When you began getting into progressive
rock and multi-keyboard setups, did people like
Rick Wakeman have an effect on you?*

Never Wakeman. I know people have said
many times in the early days that they felt my
style was like his, but if I'm gonna claim that
somebody in that style influenced me, I'd have to
say it was Keith Emerson.

*What do you see as the main difference
between the ways he and Wakeman play?*

Emerson's a lot better. If he has a fault, it
would never be considered his technique,
because his technique is impeccable. From my
point of view, it would be that he doesn't concentrate enough on the melody. As a soloist,
Wakeman is more melody-oriented than Emerson, but he is also more interested in the ensemble, kind of like me: How do these instruments work with each other? But I'll tell you
what's wrong with Wakeman, for me. You know
how when the Beatles first came along and you
really liked them, that meant when the Rolling
Stones came out you couldn't like them? Well,
Emerson was first, and I was so much in love with
what he had done for keyboard players by making it possible for us to be somebodies in our
bands, that I just couldn't get that much into
Wakeman. Besides, I was listening to Yes records
when they first came out, when Tony Kay was
their keyboardist. I liked him too, so when
Wakeman replaced him it was like, who is this
guy?

*Like Emerson and Wakeman, you've been
recorded on pipe organ, in the song "I'm O.K."
How was it recorded, and how did you reproduce that sound in concert?*

We had two mikes when we cut the record.
There was one in the middle of the church [the
Cathedral of St. James, Chicago] and one by the
pipes. When we did it onstage I pushed in all
four high settings and both low setting on the
String Ensemble, with the sustain all the way off.
This gave a kind of pipe organ sound—a very
crappy pipe organ sound. In addition, our bass
player had some Moog bass pedals, which he
used to play the bottom notes, and J.Y. [guitarist
James Young] doubled little parts in between on

synthesizer—it was probably an OB-1—and when we did all that together, it really had a pipe organ sound. It was very impressive.

Several times during your show your roadies wheeled a Rhodes and an OB-X on and offstageon a dolly. Is the Rhodes your favorite electric piano?

I had a Wurlitzer for year. I used the Rhodes on *Cornerstone* because I wanted to do something I'd never done before. It's a beautiful-sounding instrument, so I used it a lot, but it's also absolutely the most difficult keyboard instrument to play, and I hate it. I wish Rhodes would get their act together and make a piano that sounds as good as theirs does while making the life of the keyboard player a little easier. The Rhodes is positively the most tedious, time-consuming keyboard instrument I've ever played in my life.

Well, often you play it in a somewhat unusual format. Where many keyboardists use the Rhodes in more legato passages, you seem to enjoy playing it almost like the Clavinet is usually played—as a staccato rhythm instrument, like on the song "Love In The Midnight" [from Cornerstone*].*

You like that? You're pretty sharp if you hear that in the mix. Good for you [*laughs*]! Here's what happened. About three years ago in December I went in to my friend's studio to do a demo for a song I'd written—it was called "Babe." I played his acoustic piano, but it was out of tune, so my friend said, "I have this Rhodes." I'd only played on them a few times and I'd always hated 'em, but I said, "Okay, I'll play the Rhodes for the demo." Well, he had a really nice one, so I tried something; I played the introduction. That was all ad libbed; I just did it on the spot in the demo, and the demo became the record. What I did in the studio that day is what you hear on the single, because it sounded so good. In fact, it was so good that we wound up recording the whole *Cornerstone* album there.

Did other people share your enthusiasm for the Rhodes as part of a new Styx instrumentation?

Oh, yeah. I'd play it for people and when they heard the introduction to "Babe," where I was just fooling around a little, they were surprised because they'd never heard that sound out of us before: "What is that? Is that a marimba? Is that a xylophone?" So I went out and bought a Rhodes because of that demo, and when I got it in the studio I started experimenting to find out what this instrument could do and how it could be applied. I realized that by using an Eventide

Harmonizer on it, splitting the sound, rolling all the low end off and boosting the high end, I could make it almost sound like a Clavinet, but better, because it has that richer tone.

How long have you been carrying an acoustic piano on the road?

Since about 1975. We used to rent them out before then, but we couldn't demand the right stuff in those days because we weren't anybody important. The pianos that would show up were so bad that we ended up doing an arrangement of "Lady" that was just for guitar. So we went out and bought our own. I played a Baldwin for a while.

What steered you toward the Yamaha?

I think the Yamahas sound more like Steinways than any other pianos, and they're very reliable and roadworthy, although the low strings on my Yamaha are starting to go. They're two years old now, and they've seen a lot of miles.

One might ask, then, why not a Steinway?

They're so hard to find. The better Steinways are always older. If I went out and bought a new one it wouldn't be what I wanted. I'd probably want a Steinway B from about ten years ago, and that's a seven-foot piano. It's just that much more room taken up onstage. The reason we have the piano come up behind the band on a pneumatic riser is that when it sits on the stage with the other keyboards it takes up so much room.

How do you amplify your piano in concert?

We use a Countryman.

Have you considered using something like the Yamaha electric grand instead of an acoustic piano live?

I don't like that piano. Electric pianos sound like electric pianos. There's no substitute. My style of piano playing is reminiscent of maybe classical music. There's always a hint of the classics in it. I've always liked Mozart, so all my things are kind of Mozartian; they have that same metered feel, and that just has to be done on a real piano. Maybe it's not fashionable for me to say this, because I know you deal a lot with all these modern instrument, but I'm a romantic. The closer it is to the real thing, the more I like it.

Do you find that the way you write songs is affected by what instruments are at your disposal?

Yeah. I've often said that if you have a piano in your house, you tend to write a lot of piano songs. That's the way it is. And if you have an electric piano or an organ, you'll write for them. I got the Oberheim Four-Voice in 1977, and as soon as I heard it I said, "This thing is incredible! I'll use it!" I went into the store, the guy showed it to me and brought it to the studio, and I just bought it. I went wild. I used it in every song. So when I get something new, it's not because I went out to get something that fit a particular preconception of mine. But if I hear something new and it makes me think, "Yes, I can utilize this," *then* I'll get it, so in that sense I am affected in my writing by my keyboards.

Did you use the Four-Voice to get the harpsichord sound in "Castle Walls" [from Grand Illusion]?

Yeah, that's an Oberheim program with a B-3 mixed in. It's hard to play that particular setting because if your fingers bump the wrong note when there's too much decay on a program, it rings forever. So it was good on the record, but for live performance I can do better with the OB-X.

Have you ever owned any other Oberheim equipment?

I had an Eight-Voice. I used it on the *Pieces Of Eight* album, but I got rid of it because it had a lot of technical problems. When I first got it I spent about two months around Christmas programming it, but then on my first day in the studio with it the battery that controls the programmer went dead. I didn't have a cassette interface, so all my programs went down the drain. I also decided to get rid of it because I started hearing about the OB-X. I use it to duplicate sounds I've done on the Four-Voice, but it will be used more in the future, because it has a marvelous capacity I really want to tap. But for now the Four-Voice is primo; it's absolutely my favorite solo synthesizer.

Frequently in concert you leave the keyboards and run out to sing in front of the band. Do you drop certain recorded parts at those points, or do you only take the spotlight where there are no keyboard lines on the record?

There are a few places where we had to drop some keyboard stuff out, but mostly when I'm out front I'm doing songs I've written for myself to sing when there are not keyboards playing. I've tried to think in those terms. Many times when we're working a song out I think in terms of how it will be performed, and I try to avoid the kind of catastrophe where I might have two seconds to run from the synthesizers back to the piano or something like that. We've made our career from live performance. That's very important to us. I don't like going to hear a band that doesn't play its songs the way they sound on their records. That disappoints me. You certainly can't accomplish that with every one, but you try.

During one part of the show, you keep one note sustaining on the Four-Voice, then run over to another keyboard to play something else. The audience seems to dig that.

Know what I do? I tape the key down with a piece of black duct [industrial] tape, I hold my hand up, and I go play another keyboard, because it's a common note that gets sustained through all the chord changes. See, I had to figure out a way to deal with the fact that I needed two hands on one keyboard and one hand on another one, and this is how I did it.

Are there any volume pedals on the synthesizers?

I've got two volume pedals, but they interchange. I have a neat little system. I can run one OB-X and one String Ensemble through the same channel. They're never played together, so I have a switch that kills one and allows me to use the same volume pedal for both instruments. I also have a patch panel with ten different channels, and an AB box built into the two pianos. Each channel has two separately-isolated outputs, although I'm only using five of them in concert.

How do you warm up before going onstage?

I go out onto the stage and play just before the curtains go up. I sit at the grand piano and play a couple of scales and arpeggios. Some nights the fingers feel good, and some nights they feel like lead no matter how much you play before you go on. I also go out and tune my own synthesizers every night just before I play, because I don't trust anybody else with that job.

Given your many-faceted role with Styx, do you see yourself primarily as a keyboardist, a singer, a songwriter . . . ?

I think I'm a singer/songwriter who plays keyboard. To me the most important thing is the human voice. That's the best communicator. They haven't made an instrument yet that could communicate like that. The voice can sing words, and to me that's number one. Songwriting is second, because that's also a great form of communication. And the keyboards come in third. Probably I shouldn't be saying this to *Keyboard* but that's the way it is for me.

Bob Doerschuk

Toto
State of the Art

May 1979 — Steve, since your father is a drummer, did you learn to play drums before you started out on keyboards?

Porcaro: Not really. I started playing piano as soon as we got one, which was when I was four years old, and at around five I started taking lessons, but for a long time I only studied piano on and off. My parents never forced it down my throat, so consequently I had a lot of friends and played a lot of baseball instead. Now I wish they had forced me to practice more.

Paich: I started tinkering around on piano when I was five years old, but then I got interested in drums, and I wanted to be a drummer. I used to sit next to Louis Bellson, Shelley Manne, and all these guys, and they gave me drums, cymbals, and that kind of stuff. I started taking formal piano training when I was eight, and I kept it up until I was sixteen, but probably the best thing I ever did was to play drums before playing piano, just because I do rhythm for the concerts.

What is there specifically about knowing how to play drums that has affected your development on the keyboard?

Paich: Well, for me, first of all there's the standpoint of learning to play real steady, in real symmetrical time. Then from a rock standpoint, your left hand learns to correspond a lot with the bass drum beat. If you play drums, I guess you just start laying down the time in a more direct manner; all kinds of paradiddles and drum rudiments translate into rock rhythms on the piano.

What kind of music were you originally exposed to as a child?

Porcaro: All I knew about before the Beatles was Miles Davis and everything else my father lis-

Previous page: David Paich surrounded by (clockwise from left) a Roland JP-8, a Yamaha piano, a Yamaha CS-70M, a Roland organ, a Yamaha CS-80, and a Yamaha GS1. Right: Steve Porcaro dwarfed by Damius, his massive polyfusion modular system. Also shown: an E-mu Emulator, a Trident mixing board, a Roland JP-4, and a Roland MicroComposer.

tened to, including classical music, which has always been a big influence. But although that was all I was listening to at first, I never got the chance to get good enough at the keyboard to be able to really play any kind of jazz. The piano I knew up until the time the Beatles came out was really basic. Your John Thompson books have very little to them as far as jazz goes.

Paich: Up until I met Jeff [Porcaro], I'd been in a lot of jazz-oriented combos. We weren't necessarily working gigs, although we did work parties, but mainly we just got together and jammed. I was into certain Oscar Peterson tunes, trying to emulate him. I had pretty decent chops, enough to be playing eighth-notes.

When did you start picking up on rock keyboard styles? Did the Beatles affect your approach to keyboard playing?

Porcaro: Not really. When I mentioned the Beatles, that was from the standpoint of, "Hey, look what these guys are doing with music!" They were playing in stadiums, people were screaming, and stuff like that. What got me into playing rock keyboards was when David and I went to see Emerson, Lake & Palmer in their first headlining concert in LA, at the Hollywood Bowl. Their hit song on the radio was "Lucky Man," and no one knew what to expect from them; we were there to see Edgar Winter. But when they came on, I saw this guy [Emerson] just sit down at a piano and really play. I mean, what was there before that? There was the Lee Michaels type of stuff that I never had much interest in, but now here was this guy with real classical chops, and at the end of the show he was stabbing his Hammond. It was that combination that got me the legit stuff and the ability to put on a show and enjoy yourself.

Did that experience lead you to change your style immediately?

Porcaro: That's just about it. That's the way we were at the time. It was like, "Don't worry about the Hammond; let's go down to the hardware store and get ourselves a good set of knives [*laughs*]!"

Paich: But the bottom line is to get something musically valid happening, and then you can do anything you want. You can sit down and wail some Barber or Bartok pieces, like Emerson does, and no one's going to be laughing at you, because you've got the chops.

Porcaro: Keith just showed everybody. There are very few people who can sit there in the middle of a stadium full of people and really keep the crowd entertained by playing a piano.

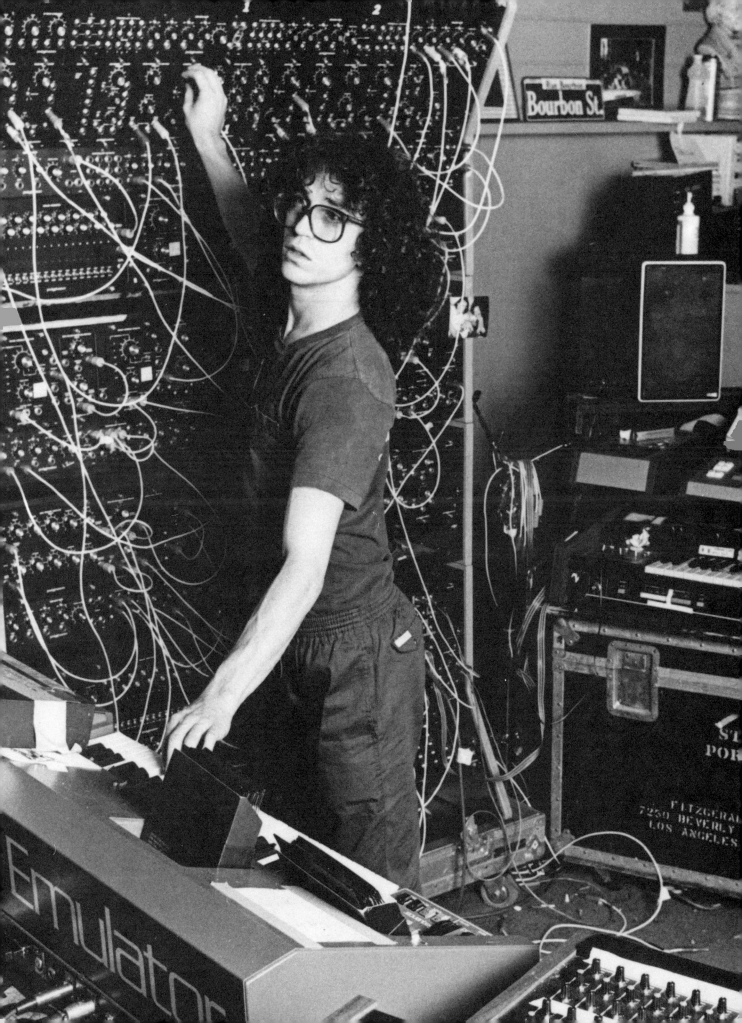

It's easier for a crowd to get off on some guitar player, but Keith was able to do that.

You both got into studio work pretty soon after leaving high school, didn't you?

Paich: Yeah. I had just started playing with [singers] Seals and Crofts around the time I got out of high school; on my first couple of dates I did their *Diamond Girl* album. I was doing string arranging, too. This was at the same time I entered USC, so I was studying composition by day and doing those dates at night.

How important to your career were your studies at USC?

Paich: Well, I don't want to put it down. I mean, I recommend that everybody go and get their musical training. I definitely benefited by it; I learned a lot about modulation and stuff like that, but they got too far into contemporary music and avant-garde music for my taste. I wanted to go there and learn about Beethoven, but it was so *progressive*. You'd get into composition class, and people would put their hands on the the bottom notes of the piano, and the teacher would go, "Yeah, that's happening!" But I'd be saying, "Where's the melody? Where's the prettiness of it?" My father has a master's degree in composition, so I've been kind of his private pupil, studying scores since I was a kid. I got educated by him outside of school, so that was a different situation than most people have.

When was the first time you actually worked together?

Porcaro: That was with Boz [Scaggs, guitarist], although I'd known David for years. He and my brother Jeff had this group in high school that played all the dances. I'm three years younger than David, so I used to hang around the bandstand watching him. David was my idol, and he was doing what I wanted to do. When I got to high school, they had moved on, so our guitarist, Steve Lukather, and I kind of took over that band. We did a lot of the same material. I left high school a month before graduating to go out on the road with Gary Wright—Kenny Lupper, who used to play with Billy Preston, and I were both playing keyboards with Gary. Meanwhile, David, after being in the studios, had started working with Boz on his *Silk Degrees* album.

Paich: We went out to tour after doing that album, and we needed another keyboardist, so we got Steve. He and I did a year of touring.

Porcaro: I'd been with Gary for about a year and a half, but Boz mainly needed a second keyboard player to cover all the synthesizers.

What first got you interested in synthesizers?

Porcaro: That was when we heard Emerson, Lake & Palmer at the Hollywood Bowl. He had a modular Moog, and I'd never heard sounds like that. I really wanted a Moog, but it was always like, "Man, those things cost over a thousand dollars!" At that time, a thousand dollars was like a million dollars to me. But I had a friend in high school named Jay Cernik who was always in ELP groups, so he had a digital sequencer, an Oberheim DS-2—it was like the fifth DS-2 ever made—a Minimoog, a Hammond C-3, and something like the fifteenth Expander Module from Oberheim. I was always hanging out at his house, and I'd go hang out at the Guitar Center in LA because they'd let me play the synthesizers there, so after a while I started being able to know my way around them. I auditioned for Gary Wright playing Minimoog bass; I was able to handle it halfway decently, so I got the gig, and as soon as I had it, my brothers loaned me a couple of grand to buy the Minimoog, DS-2, and Expander Module.

How long did it take you to feel comfortable with them?

Porcaro: Not too long, once I bought my own stuff and sat down with it. I learned just through the necessity of being familiar with the instruments people ask you to record with. The first time someone called me down for a session and asked if I could play Minimoog, I said, "Yeah," but when I got down there it was like, "Give me a couple of hours, guys, and let me get my sound together [*laughs*]."

Did you have any trouble integrating pitch-bending into your solo style?

Porcaro: No, I was totally into it from the start, because I've always been kind of a frustrated guitar player. I was more into Hendrix-type guitar licks than into keyboard licks. I still don't feel comfortable when it comes to working with patch cords on the [ARP] 2600, though. I'd much rather deal with tone knobs than wires.

David, what turned you on to synthesizers?

Paich: This guy right here. I'd been in studios watching Paul Beaver with his banks and sequencers, but then Steve brought home this little unit, set up his bass pattern, and instead of repeating, he was playing against it. It flipped me out, so I started getting really interested in the possibilities of digital sequencers. Now we're using not only our two hands during a show, but our two feet and all these foot pedals as well. I'm still in my infancy as far as my knowledge of it all is concerned.

What keyboards are you using onstage?

Paich: I have a Hammond A-100 organ, a Yamaha electric grand, a Minimoog, and a Yamaha CS-80 polyphonic synthesizer. That's the bare minimum for me to get by with. I'm going to get some other stuff later—a Rhodes, Pianet, Clavinet. . . .

Porcaro: I'm using a CS-80, and I have an ARP 2600, which is mainly used with a Sequential Circuits sequencer. I also have a Minimoog, which I use a Sequential Circuits programmer on and which is also hooked up to a unit built for me by Wayne Yentis, who does lots of modification work in L.A.; it's a design which consists of an Oberheim DS-2 and two Oberheim Expander Modules. But there is a lack of keyboards. I'm going to add some other keyboards to get a greater variety of sound.

Do you have any particular ones in mind?

Porcaro: We were about to buy a Prophet. We wanted to get another polyphonic thing happening for the live gigs, but we heard all these stories from other guys who use them. It was like I had my checkbook out, then all of a sudden three stories came in about three different Prophets that were messing up on the road, so I started to think about it. We're just waiting to see how roadworthy it actually is. But by the time this story comes out, we're probably both going to have a Prophet. We're thinking of having some stands made that will serve as a console for both the CS-80 and the Prophet.

Anything else?

Porcaro: We want to get some Birotrons, definitely. When I was with Gary Wright we did a bunch of gigs opening the show for Rick Wakeman when he had his English Rock Ensemble, and he always had Mellotrons. Well, we had just left that tour and we were doing some gigs in Connecticut when some guy came up to me and gave me his card, which said, "Birotronics, A Division Of Rick Wakeman, Ltd." It was Dave Biro, the head of Birotronics, and he was saying, "Wakeman's given me all this money to build these instruments for him," but I had just been doing gigs with Wakeman, and all I saw him play was Mellotron. This was right after *Keyboard* ran its first Wakeman cover story [March/April '76]. I thought this guy was full of it, so I totally blew him off, but sure enough, the last time I saw Yes, Wakeman had those two Birotrons, and they sounded incredible, like someone had perfected the idea of using tapes.

Paich: It's important to get the best stuff we can for the road, because the road is so happening. That's why I'm into the CS-80, the Ober-

heims, and the Sequential Circuits programmer. It's important to not have to fuss and waste time. Wakeman used to have to use four different Minwhere now with the programmer you've got 64 presets. I think presets are the name of the live imoogs, game.

Porcaro: The music we have now is limiting in a way, but I'm eventually going to get into as many things as I can handle live. When you get into having a lot of keyboards, it's really easy to wind up being haphazard, where some things work sometimes, and other times they don't. Something that's very important to us is not just getting stacks of keyboards there for looks, then being overwhelmed by it when we get out onstage. But there's something to be said for all the polyphonic synthesizers that are available.

Why did you buy two Minimoogs and two CS-80s?

Paich: This is to duplicate our records live. It's almost like what you'd do if you went into a studio and overdubbed a CS-80, hearing two CS-80s live with the brass sound, or even two totally different sounds.

Porcaro: I think it's fantastic having two CS-80s onstage. They create a certain sound together—the sound of Toto.

What led you to choose the CS-80?

Paich: It was a question of musicality. The CS-80 is the ultimate in terms of control. If you're playing chords on most string ensembles or any other string synthesizer, every note you're playing has the same exact effect, the same sound, but with a real string section, each instrument has its own vibrato; some are playing a little bit more intensely, some have slightly slower or faster vibratos, or whatever. On the CS-80, the harder you press each key, the more intense the vibrato on the string or horn sound.

Porcaro: One thing that the CS-80 is also very good for besides the vibrato thing is the relationship between the touch and the brilliance of the tone. The harder you hit it, the brighter it'll be. I believe the Polymoog does that too, although it doesn't have the vibrato thing.

Paich: See, I'm totally into horns. I've played things that I've taped on the CS-80 for experienced musicians, and they've said, "I love those French horns." When real French horns play crescendos, the tone gets brighter, and that's a characteristic of the CS-80. It's like having an orchestra.

Porcaro: It's also very good for taking solos, which is something very few musicians take advantage of. Eddie Jobson is one of the only people I know of who has used it as a solo instrument. Everyone is so quick to go to the Minimoog or whatever, but the Yamaha is really great for playing solos or lead lines.

Has your ARP 2600 been modified at all?

Porcaro: There have been a few things done to it. I've had two quarter-inch output jacks put on, and I'm about to have some more modifications—just the regular octave switches type of thing. I'm using the 2600 mainly in conjunction with the Sequential Circuits sequencer. A guy named Richard Mazon, who does great synthesizer work, is taking one of the speakers out of my 2600 and putting in some switches to control the routing of the sequencer, like determining which of the three oscillators it goes to. He's also doing something with the keyboard where the voltage is still connected to the rest of the synthesizer so that, if I load in a sequence and have it playing back, I can hit any key on the 2600 and it automatically transposes. That's one of the regular function of the Sequential Circuits sequencer, but the way you normally have to patch the 2600 in, it disconnects the keyboard, so I'm just setting it up so that you can use the transpose function.

Have you ever used the 2600 for bass lines?

Porcaro: I was always one of those Moog fans who liked the sound of the Moog filter. When I'm doing studio things, I have my Minimoog there for the bass. It's also hooked up to the two Expander Modules, so I can have those triggered by the Minimoog keyboard and get seven oscillators happening at one time. But I normally use the Minimoog for a foundation of bass sound.

Is there any particular synthesizer you favor for doing string parts?

Paich: This is like divulging our top secrets! We always bring strings in and mix them with the synthesizers.

Porcaro: We'll divulge something to you. We're really into acoustic instruments as well, as musicians and arrangers.

So all the string sounds on your albums are mixtures of synthesizers and real strings? Are you reluctant to talk about that for some reason?

Paich: Yes, we are reluctant to talk about that, simply because our sounds and textures are going to be our trademark. It's a special combination we've learned, so I'd rather we go on to Steve's sex life or something like that [*laughs*]. We might as well get into what kind of synthesizers we use, though. Personally, I still like getting an ARP String Ensemble out for high unison string lines, but we're into other sounds now.

Porcaro: For string parts we've used Oberheims. The funny thing about the Oberheim polysynthesizer is that the best string sounds I've gotten phonic with it have come from putting them in unison with synthesizers that aren't polyphonic, especially in the studio. What I'm really into in the studios, and as much live as I can pull off, is getting a sound that isn't just an Oberheim, Yamaha, or Chamberlin sound, but a combination of different things.

David, let's get into your keyboard set-up. What kind of Hammond organ are you playing?

Paich: It's an A-100, which is like a home version of the B-3, with a built-in speaker. I just bought this within the last year, but I've been into Hammonds for a long time. I used to play Steve's old C-3 a lot, and I did a lot of organ in the studios, but I really started getting into it during my last year in high school. I went out on the road when I was with Sonny and Cher, and all I did was play B-3 every night. I've always dug the sound of the Hammond.

What difference does the built-in speaker make when you're going through external amplification at a concert?

Paich: It's funny, because that's a very gray area. It's harder to describe in relation to live gigs than in terms of recording. When you're in the studio and they put mikes on your Leslie, you get more vibrations in it and more warmth in the sound when you turn on the speaker in the organ, almost to the point of distortion. When you start to crank the volume, the fact that the speaker is in there makes the whole box rumble a little bit more, which in turn makes that tone come out of the Leslie.

Do you ever overdub organ parts?

Paich: Usually I'll record the piano live, and then overdub the organ. I usually overdub the Hammond, because I like to distant-mike it and crank the Leslies up. We had another echo unit installed in it, so now it's got two, in addition to the normal echo that's usually in the A-100.

What effects are you using now, and on which keyboards?

Paich: Everything goes through everything live. I'm using a Roland Boss Chorus on the CP-70, and I've got an MXR digital delay.

Onstage you often play unison lines with your right hand on the Minimoog and your left hand on the organ. What led you to start doing that?

Paich: That's another example of looking for combinations of sounds. It goes back to that first Emerson concert we saw. The problem is that the whole rock and roll keyboard scene is basically producing a lot of one-handed piano players. Two hands are better than one, and if we can get all four hands going on four different instruments, you've got a lot of sound.

You have mentioned that you're interested in adding a Wurlitzer electric piano to your onstage collection.

Paich: That relates back to the fact that there's a lot of fundamental rock and roll in Toto's music. You might hear CS-80s and sequencers at first, but then you go eight bars into the tune and there's the Hammond organ and Wurlitzer piano, you know what I mean?

Didn't you also use a harpsichord on the album?

Porcaro: Yeah, we used a Neupert harpsichord. Bill Kasimov, who is the Bluthner distributor in the United States, has a whole line of Neuperts, which are the finest harpsichords in the world. It was a $50,000 instrument.

What kind of amplification do you have?

Porcaro: Dave and I have the same thing. Our speaker cabinets were made by Hard Truckers Speakers. They're great 14-ply birch cabinets. We have one that holds two 15" Gauss speakers, and a cabinet on top of that holds two 12" JBLs and six 5" JBLs. Then we have four tweeters on top; I'm not sure exactly what kind they are [piezo crystals]. Each one of us has a BGW 750 amp, powered low end. We have a BGW 250, and for the rest we have a Yamaha crossover. We use Yamaha stereo mixers.

You've mentioned your plans to broaden your musical format, but is getting another hit single out a conscious part of your plan as well?

Paich: Yes, it is a conscious thing. You have to start thinking in very corporate executive lines, you know what I mean? But it's all music, and I always try to keep my perspective as a musician first.

Porcaro: We're confident about our future because of the album. We know we can do hit singles now; we know we can put them together and pull it off, so I think we're going to be getting off more musically from now on, especially in terms of keyboards. I feel that if I can get off live, I can do all the things I want to do as far as blowin' on my axe goes, and still we can sell out Candlestick Park or whatever. We feel that we can be true to the music.
Bob Doerschuk

October 1982 — What equipment are you taking out on the road with you currently?

Paich: We practically take the whole studio. We're leaving some of the Polyfusion gear behind this time because it's being hard-wired. Steve and I always have duplicate equipment in our setups. We each have a Yamaha GS1 with a Yamaha CS-80 [polyphonic synthesizer] on top of it. I'm playing a 9' Hamburg Steinway with a Roland JP-8 [polyphonic synthesizer] on it, and in back of me I've got a little Roland VK-9 organ and a Yamaha CS-70M polyphonic.

Porcaro: I'm using a GS1 with a CS-80 on top of it, as David said. That faces the band. On the other side, I've got an Emu Emulator, a Roland JP-8, and a Minimoog. Then I have the banks [of Polyfusion modular gear] behind me. I have those configured as four stock Minimoog-type voices and one big bass drone voice that has about six oscillators in it. It's like two Minimoogs put together as far as the hardware goes. I've also got a Roland MC-4 MicroComposer and an LM-1 Linn drum machine.

Paich: I did have a Hammond, an A-100, that I was using on the road. I had some problems wit it, so I got this Roland VK-9 that I just put into a 147 Leslie speaker. It does the trick for all the things I used to use the Hammond for. I'm also using a Yamaha CE20.

How do you split up the role of playing keyboards between the two of you?

Paich: It's not the case anymore that one guy does the synthesizers and the other does the piano. We both end up swapping parts of those roles. It's usually the case that the guy who wrote the tune ends up playing the piano on it, but we stay open about it. I've got a 24-track tape recorder in my house, and after we've recorded the basic tracks, we'll take it there and sort of choreograph the keyboards. But the parts go back and forth. There are no set rules.

Porcaro: Most keyboard players are territorialistic bastards and have trouble getting along with one another. David and I work very well together.

Do you learn a lot from each other, then?

Paich: Steve's the best synthesizer teacher in the world for me, and I turn him on to a lot of orchestration things.

Do the other guys in the band critique the things you two come up with in terms of keyboard orchestration?

Porcaro: Yeah, but they're starting to catch on to what we've been trying to do. The solo in "Rosanna" was the turning point. They've had to put up with me dicking around with the banks for years. I've always had to say, "But wait until you see what I'm gonna be able to do." When we finally did the solo in "Rosanna," I was able to say, "See there. That's what all this does." It was nice to have something to show that was concrete. The guys in the group were wondering why we bothered with the modular stuff at all. Now they're at the point where they don't want to do shows without the modular gear. They've come around to understanding what it is we do with the orchestration and the modular gear.

Do you actually write out your arrangements for the keyboards?

Paich: Yeah. When I demo a tune like "Rosanna," I'll do it on 8-track for the band. Before we go in and record it, Steve and I will make up a work sheet. It's not so much for the band to use since we don't use charts when we're recording—everyone has memorized it by then; it's for our own reference. Steve will know exactly what I'm playing and I'll know what he's playing. Everything on my bass and piano parts is written down. Then we'll talk about it, and Steve will make a little score. From there we'll work up synthesizer ideas. What's going to play what, what kind of range it's going to be in so we're not doubling up voices, and so on.

How much of the solo in the middle of "Rosanna" is done with the Roland Micro-Composer and how much of it is played by you two?

Paich: It's a combination of both of us playing. It's mainly Steve, but we both start at the beginning. When we were doing that song we found we had to put a solo in the middle of it. It was a question of what do we do now. Steve has always said we should use our imaginations. So I kind of started out with trying to incorporate everything we have at our home studio. Instead of doing a regular Wurlitzer or Hammond solo we decided to try different things. We started playing lines and finally sat down and Steve wrote out the initial basis for the solo that you hear now played mostly on the modular system.

Porcaro: It's actually a hilarious story. We thought about how to do that solo for weeks, and it all came together one day at five in the morning.

Paich: When you hear the opening lines, that's Steve playing a modular trumpet sound. Then we knew we wanted a sequence running down so I programmed a little thing into the MicroComposer that Steve dropped into the solo. Then there's a Minimoog part, and at the end it's a combination of Steve and me both

playing CS-80s, Prophets, a Hammond organ, and a GS1.

Porcaro: There's even a line there that was from an older solo that David did which I forgot to erase. It was a very pieced-together solo.

Are you programming the MicroComposer by punching data in, or are you playing it in from a keyboard?

Paich: We're doing it both ways right now. I think it's according to which piece of music we're working on. If it's a classical thing or something really symmetrical-sounding, Steve will load it in from the computer keyboard. But if it's something with more phrasing and nuance, we'll play it in. But we'll always rewrite the gates on it and some of the steps and the phrasing to make it consistent.

Are you both well versed at programming it?

Paich: Steve's fastest at it. It still takes me a while to get used to it. Steve's been dealing with the MC-8 for a long time. The manual to that is ridiculous, but he stuck with it and learned it. Now the MC-4 is like a blessing, because when you make a mistake, you don't have to erase the whole thing and start over. Steve's gotten to the point where he can load numbers about as fast as you could load in notes. Because of having gone through the technical thing, I think he's becoming less technical. Our whole system has come about in order for us to be musicians. Like Steve says, as soon as he hears the right sound, he won't be messing around with the stuff anymore. It's like with the Yamaha GS1. We don't have to mess with the modular stuff getting bell sounds and celestes, because they're nailed on the GS1. But you go through the technical thing to where it becomes second nature and you can get back to being a musician. Everybody thinks Steve is a technical genius, but they forget that he spends hours and hours at at. He's mainly just a keyboardist like myself who likes playing Hammond organ and piano.

Porcaro: The thing that drew me to the MicroComposer was that my setup, when I first started, was a Minimoog and an Oberheim DS-2 digital sequencer. I got very good at the DS-2, but I wanted to go beyond that. And I wanted to go beyond what most of the polyphonic sequencers you can get these days do. As great as they all are, they seem like toys compared to the Micro-Composer. When it comes down to really trying to record something with them you run into all kinds of problems. They sound great when you're in a music store. You sort of throw something in and play it back, speed it up, and it's all very impressive, but when it gets down to having to be in sync with other things it gets to be impossible. But the MC-4 and MC-8 and the Linn drum machine and the Emulator all run on the same sync tone. Even in real time, my MC-4 and MC-8 can follow a conductor.

How do you manage that?

Porcaro: I use my sync box. It's designed to let me sync everything together. It has a momentary switch on it that if I just tap quarter notes on it the MC-4 and all that stuff will follow me, the conductor. Ralph Dyck built the sync box for us. He works for Roland. I've heard a lot of people talking about live sync, but I've never seen anyone that had it. I've got it. I've been using it.

What decided you on Polyfusion modular gear?

Porcaro: It was just one of those things. I had seen a MicroComposer hooked up to some Roland modular gear at an AES [Audio Engineering Society] convention and I wanted it from the moment I saw it. We were on the road and some guys from Polyfusion wanted to take us on a factory tour. In fact, David woke me up at 9:00 in the morning to tell me they wanted to take us on this tour and he wanted to know if I'd ever heard of Polyfusion. I knew who they were from the ads I'd seen in *Keyboard*, but I'd never seen their equipment. So they gave us a big pitch and sold us on it. I've been very happy with their stuff as far as reliability and stability go. One time we were in the studio and a guy came in with some Moog modular stuff. The sound that came out of it made me think, "Oh yeah, that's the way I got into this stuff." My father knew Paul Beaver very well when he was alive, and he used to let me mess with his synthesizers when I was younger. I didn't retain much of it, but I was in awe of it. So I've wanted to have a modular system for years. But there's so much against having any kind of modular stuff. A lot of people still don't understand it.

What have you left behind this tour?

Porcaro: I left my Prophet home. I left my MC-8 home. Some of the older keyboards like JP-4s, and 2600s, and stuff like that got left behind. We don't take Rhodeses and Clavinets out anymore even though we've got 'em at home. I really take pride in the fact that all the stuff we do bring out, we use. If we aren't using it on the road, it's loaned out to a friend who is using it. I don't get into having equipment laying around. If something is broken, I get really fanatical about it. It's gotta get fixed.

What about using an instrument like the

Yamaha GS1? You've put some of your own programs into it.

Porcaro: Actually, I mainly just modified existing programs. You load a strip into it and the programming module [there's only one in the United States] shows what the program looks like on four video screens. I would just start dicking with it, isolating different sections and seeing where different parts of the sound were coming from. I've always been attracted to those kinds of instruments because I come from being a piano player. I love the touch-sensitivity, but from a synthesist's standpoint the non-programmability doesn't bother me all that much, because some of the sounds in it are just too kick-ass to ignore.

Paich: From my point of view, I love it because of the immediacy. So many of the sounds that are in it are nailed just perfectly. Like the Rhodes and the marimba sounds. As an 88-note touch-sensitive instrument, it appeals to the piano player in me. I find myself not only playing piano music on it but writing stuff that's specifically GS1. It saves you from having to bring lots and lots of other axes on the road and into the studio.

How do you feel about the CE20?

Paich: I dig it for the same reason I dig the GS1: immediacy. It takes up where the ARP Pro-Soloist left off. The sounds it has in it are really nailed. I don't use it a whole lot live yet, because I have other synths that I use to cover those sounds in different ways. I've been using it on sessions, though. I did a thing with Kenny Loggins where he and James Newton-Howard scored out a piece for synthesizers using nothing but Prophet-10, GS1, and CE20. We put real strings with all that and you can barely tell the difference between a real orchestra and what we did.

Steve, do you use a CE20?

Porcaro: I use one, but I don't have it in my live setup right now. It changes around a lot. The way manufacturers build things these days, everything has something a little different. That's why it's so tempting to have every keyboard in the world on stage. Any keyboard player could find a valid reason for having everything up there, but it's impractical. That's one of the things I dig about having the Emulator. It lets you use sounds from instruments that you just can't have up on stage with you.

Live, do you change sounds frequently on the Emulator?

Porcaro: Yes. Ed Simeone, my keyboard tech, loads in the disks for me. I'm using the Emulator to play part of the "Rosanna" solo on now, because I've got the MC-4 playing the JP-8—I've had gate and voltage inputs and outputs put into the JP-8—and I use the Emulator to play the JP-8 brass sound.

It sounds like you have to plan each song out in a lot of detail as far as when you're going to play what instruments.

Porcaro: Oh yeah. When I'm trying to devise how I'm going to set up my equipment live I go through blocking out each song. It's like doing choreography. I have to keep track of what I have to do next after each song. I have to keep track of what sound happens next, what instrument I've got to play with what sound in it, and all that. It's something that I've gotten far better at with time. It's nice having David, because he can be a third hand for me if I need it. When it gets right down to it, and everyone's bashing out their parts, there are times when we realize that his left hand on the piano won't be missed. So he can fill in on one of my parts. I've also started getting used to teaching my left hand to play right-hand parts out of necessity.

David, how do you use your JP-8?

Paich: I use it for a number of things. Steve and I both play the horn line in "Rosanna" on them. I really get into the arpeggiator and all the different little tricks on it. I love the fact that with the keyboard split, you essentially have two synthesizers. And I love the fact that you can preset all those different combinations. Another reason Steve and I use it is because we're using the JP-8 as the main interface keyboard with our modular system at the moment.

Instead of the Polyfusion keyboard? Do you miss the touch-sensitivity?

Paich: Yes, I do. But one of the reasons why we're using the JP-8 instead of the Polyfusion keyboard is because when you play the JP-8 and use it to control the Polyfusion modules, you'll hear both sounds simultaneously.

Do you get into blending keyboard sounds a lot?

Paich: Definitely. We always try out lots of different combinations. We use a lot of acoustic instruments along with our synths too. We take orchestral instruments and combine them with synthesizers. Or we make a tape of the acoustic instrument and synthesizer combined and load the sound into our Emulator. On "Africa," you hear a combination of Steve's dad playing marimba combined with GS1.

What else is going on in "Africa"?

Paich: The kalimba is all done with the GS1. It's six tracks of GS1 playing different rhythms.

There's a high organ sound that's GS1, and I wrote the song on CS-80, so that plays the main part of the entire tune.

How do you like the CS-70M?

Paich: I'm using it mainly for its polyphonic sequencer right now. There are certain things in the show where I'll want to change parts every night and do spontaneous little sequences, so I'll load something in right then and there. I think it's an in-between instrument for Yamaha. It has a ways to go, but it does some very good things. It has a split keyboard mode which, used in conjunction with the sequencer, is pretty interesting. Its main thing is that you can memorize your own presets and play with a touch-sensitive keyboard. I think it's a step in the right direction.

You're not disappointed that it sort of replaced the CS-80?

Paich: Kind of. I love the CS-80. We told Yamaha that. They think it's like trying to compare apples and oranges. I don't know if they were trying to replace the CS-80 so much as come out with something that was on a par with other synthesizers in its category. I think the CS-70 is an in-between instrument because I think that Yamaha is going to come out with some stuff that's going to do it all.

Do you have any trouble with the modular stuff live?

Porcaro: No. As a matter of fact, the Polyfusion stuff is a lot like the way the 2600 used to be for me. I could pack that up, bring it to the next gig, and it would still be in tune. The Polyfusion oscillators are very stable. But Ralph Dyck is building me an auto-tune for them. I don't see anybody trying to build something like that into their modular system, which makes me want to get it happening.

But it's no real problem using the system live?

Porcaro: Right now, it's still keyed down to where it doesn't cause me any big problems. I don't make it that vital a part of the show right now. It's more reliable than anything else I've got on the road with me now. It's more of a bitch to have something go wrong with the CS-80.

What kind of amplification and effects are you using?

Paich: Everything goes through two Midas 24-input boards and then out to the PA system. As far as effects go, I'm using a Harmonizer, a Roland 555 Chorus Echo, a stereo Lexicon [delay line], one of the new Roland digital delays, and a Yamaha graphic equalizer. I use so many delay lines because I love slap echo.

Porcaro: I've got a couple of Roland 555

Porcaro adjusting Damius: "I don't know about other keyboard players, but I have a bitch of a time making synthesizers stand repeated listening."

Chorus Echoes, a new Roland digital delay, a Lexicon, and a great little thing by 360 Systems—their programmable EQ. I have it modified so that with a Prophet or JP-8, it'll change EQ every 3/4 octave. It takes a CV [control voltage] and a gate input and automatically switches programs every 3/4 octave. It's really helpful for string and brass sounds. I use the Polyfusion stuff to process all kinds of things. It's my all-around signal center, a big junction. I use the formant filters and the parametric equalizers in it. I'll have a control voltage input to the JP-8's filter, I'll have envelope generators being triggered by the drum machine. I do this trip with the LM-1 where I take one of the outputs from it, say the cowbell or conga, and I have it going through an envelope follower which in turn triggers an envelope generator which in turn is controlling a filter. That way, I can have my LM-1 running in sync with everything else, and have one of its drums triggering an envelope generator which is controlling a filter or a VCA in rhythm. I also get into doing things like using my MicroComposer to trigger the hold on my JP-8. All these control inputs on the back of synths . . . . The hippest things on synthesizers are the things that no one ever uses. I prove this to myself day after day. On the back of my CS-80 is a thing called the external input. Nobody uses that, and it's the hippest thing about an 80.

Doesn't doing all that interfacing make for a lot of hassle when it comes to keeping things straight during live gigs?

Porcaro: Yeah, but that's the thing. You get it all together and have snakes [cables] made. It's hard enough making synthesizers sound good on record. Making them sound good live you need everything you can get. I don't know about other keyboard players, but I have a bitch of a time making synthesizers stand repeated listening. Whether it's having a portamento footswitch, or a sustain pedal, it all takes practice, so you don't have it hooked up for the sake of having it hooked up. You have to know where and when to use it. Before we go out on the road, I like to orchestrate the show. That's something that's very hard for me to do, because when we record I set up the configuration of the keyboards in the room differently for each and every song so that I can get to them when I need to.

David, what about your piano? Why a Hamburg Steinway?

Paich: I never thought I'd be able to get a Hamburg Steinway on the road. But I went to Pro Piano in Los Angeles and they had one. I also

David Paich with a Roland JP-8 stacked atop a Yamaha acoustic grand. "You go through the technical thing to where it becomes second nature and you can get back to being a musician."

have one at my house. I've got two Steinway O's and a Baldwin SD-10, a nine-footer. One of the Steinways is a Hamburg and the other is American. I think Hamburg Steinways are the hippest, because they are the meatiest-sounding pianos around.

Do you have any trouble getting them to reproduce through a sound system?

Paich: I've got the hammers slightly doped [a process that hardens them, making the tone of the piano brighter]. I'm using Helpinstill pickups and a new thing from England called the Seducer. It has two contact sound strips that go across the bottom of the keyboard. It picks up all the harmonics that Helpinstills don't.

What piano do you use for recording?

Paich: I mainly use the Baldwin SD-10 for recording. I bought it three years ago. I needed a piano to bring into the studio with me.

What kind of action do you prefer on your piano?

Paich: At home I prefer heavy for practicing. I love a heavy action because every hour you put in on a heavy action is like putting in three hours on a light action. When I'm on the road I love a light action. I almost like the GS1 action better than a piano's action. It's so similar to a piano action, it's ridiculous. But pianos don't have any after-touch [pressure sensitivity, used to alter the tone by beating down on a key after it is fully depressed].

That added touch-sensitivity is really nice.

Porcaro: I can't wait until I have that kind of sensitivity in a general synthesizer keyboard. I'll be able to have my Emulator sounds going through VCAs that are controlled by the velocity-sensitive output of the keyboard, so the harder I hit, the more the Emu is let through. So when I'm doing string sounds I can have more of that real bow sound kick in the harder I hit it. Things like that are the reason you need modular systems.

Is much of the equipment modified beyond what we've spoken of?

Paich: Certain things have been modified. We probably have the most up-to-date Emulator on the market, in that we have it synced up to our Linn drum machine. We will shortly have it hooked up to our JP-8 so that the JP-8's keyboard will play the Emulator. In general, we don't believe in having things modified that much. We don't believe in having this or that put on a Prophet because it wasn't there to begin with. That's why we've got the modular stuff. We do have little things here and there, like unison switches on our CS-80s. We've had CV gates and triggers put in our Prophets—which we've left home. We have a whole bunch of keyboards that we don't use live.

Do you feel that Toto has a Southern California sound?

Paich: I guess it might. I don't think there's a definite southern California band sound except for the fact that we've played on a lot of records that have come out of Los Angeles, so it may seem like there's a definite sound that comes from down in L.A. I could play you a bunch of records where you wouldn't be able to tell who's on them. We're on a lot of records where you'd swear it was some black guys from Chicago or New Orleans. One thing you do get into when you make records is that you get to be radio-oriented. Not that you're catering to that, but there are certain variables that make something more radio-worthy than others. I think that may be the way we play. I don't think we have a definite Southern California sound. I was more influenced by English stuff. There aren't that many American bands that have a sound similar to the one we have.

What about in terms of production quality?

Paich: Right. I think there's definitely more production work that goes into our sound than is usual for bands. I think that's one of the ways we separate ourselves from other bands. The ability to do overdubs and certain production things without getting to sound really over-produced. It's funny. When something sounds better to us, like a double on a vocal or an orchestra overdub, we just do it. We don't have any rules about it and say, "Oh, people are going to say this sounds over-produced." We just go with it because it may sound better. Same with the Beatles. They used a lot of doubling and tripling techniques. Everybody's so conscious of the production, of it sounding like it's in the studio. Sometimes things like that sound better. I just know that when you double something, when something's tight, it sounds real good. But I know what you're talking about. I think we're getting better at it. I think we're loosening up. We're getting less slick. There are a lot of albums in the top ten right now. The whole industry is very oriented to slick-sounding records, in my opinion. You listen to a lot of records—Steely Dan, Supertramp, Foreigner; those records are slicker than ours. So that's kind of the name of the game with radio right now. You can't get away with a whole bunch of loose, raw stuff now because they would be tearing your record contract up.

Dominic Milano

VI. Cold Fire

Not everyone jumped on the romantic bandwagon. As Journey, Toto, Styx, and other one-word supergroups milked their equipment for lush sounds and effects, a younger generation of players watched from the sidelines. These dissident rockers sensed that the gritty grain of their music was being pasteurized and sterilized. They watched uneasily as the new romantics, like the progressives before them, developed a Barnumesque approach to performance, with intricate props and stage designs, breakneck instrumental cadenzas, immaculately rehearsed arrangements, and predictable "Do-you-feel-all-right?" raps. All of these elements either lent a Nuremberg-like drama to each concert, or interrupted the crucial rhythmic surge, depending on your point of view. To growing numbers of musicians in the Seventies, the romantic revival added up to a betrayal of the music, a sell-out of spirit for showbiz.

These suspicious observers, most of them in their late teens or early twenties, were the driving force behind punk, new wave, and related rock phenomena that began shaking up the mid-Seventies music landscape. On the surface they seemed a bizarre aberration to many media observers, but in fact it was the new romantics and the progressives who had left the mainstream of rock in search of more arcane tributaries. The resurgent new wave was a predictable demonstration of rock's regenerative power. The fact that bands like the Sex Pistols, the Clash, and Blondie began grabbing headlines in the Seventies, and inspiring countless imitators far beyond

Electronics and the Classical Ethic

Previous page: Gary Numan's elaborate staging helped him become one of the first synthesized classicists to enjoy commercial success in the States. Below: Thomas Dolby streaks through a surrealistic video.

the English working-class ghettoes that spawned the original punk movement, indicates that raw, gut-level rock is a phoenix, rising again and again from the ashes of its own commercial excess.

One problem with the new romantics, according to the new wavers, was their preoccupation with equipment. Keyboard players who lost themselves in the electronic mazes within their synthesizers were, to borrow a phrase from

Thomas Dolby, blinded by science, often cut off from the bare-bones formula of beat and attitude that sparked rock in its natal days. Some reacted to this perception by abandoning modern keyboards for low-budget relics of the Sixties; by resurrecting the Farfisa and Vox electric organs, Jimmy Destri of Blondie and Steve Nieve of Elvis Costello's Attractions followed this path. Many others preferred working with state-of-the-art quipment, but in a less florid fashion than the new romantics. Where Steve Porcaro, for example, might search his Polyfusion modular unit for subtle shadings of tone and expression that reflect the orchestral evocations of progressive rock and the old romantic use of Leslie vibrato, the new wave synthesist chose steely sounds, more obviously electronic and less orchestral in texture, with no expressive modulation, pitchbend, or vibrato whatsoever. Even the tuneless *wack* of drums took on an eerie sheen when digital drum machines came on the scene in the late Seventies; in their perfect regularity of timbre and tempo, they upstaged the hypnotic monotony of disco music at its own game, and gave dancers a vibrant alternative to that exhausted style. The overall effect was similar to the electronic fantasies of Vangelis and Tomita in its other-worldliness, but with less impressionistic gauze and a much more relentless beat.

Exhibitionistic solos were anathema to the new wave keyboard player. No Emersons, no Claptons, would emerge from this school. Chord voicings were stark, with lots of open fifths, and even long single notes whenever possible. The idea was to get as far from progressivism and romanticism as you could, and to merge essential rock and roll in all its primitive anti-virtuosic glory with the sounds of the Eighties. As Andy McClusky, a founding member of England's influential synthesizer band Orchestral Manouevres In The Dark, explained to *Keyboard,* "It goes back to the rock and roll thing. Most of the keyboard music we heard in the early years was this flash sort of Jon Lord soloing and arpeggiating stuff. We just weren't interested in that. You *can* make different kinds of music on synthesizers. You don't have to play heavy organ chords, or be ethereal like Tangerine Dream. You can actually make more pointed, somewhat angular music."

In their adherence to the traditional elements of rock, these keyboardists paralleled Stravinsky's return to Mozartean classical form in symphonic music some fifty years earlier. Long after the words "punk" and "new wave" had lost their shock value, this idea persisted and continued to grow in rock. It is accurate to describe the proliferation of keyboard-oriented dance bands as a classical reaction to the new romanticism, and to recognize the musicians in these groups as the new classicists.

Though it flowered in the late Seventies, this movement was already taking seminal form in the Sixties. Amidst the thunder of Hammond organs gushing out gospel licks, lost in the crowd of Felix

Cavaliere, Mark Stein, and Lee Michaels clones, a handful of dissatisfied keyboardists shook their heads and withdrew to concoct an alternative approach. Premonitions abounded—in Al Kooper's work with the Blues Project, in John Cale's haunting organ drone in the Velvet Underground's "Heroin." But the style crystalized in 1966, when the Doors, with Ray Manzarek at the keys, released their debut album. Unlike Alan Price and the other early Vox Continental players, Manzarek didn't attempt to approximate the Hammond sound on his tiny electric instrument. Instead, he discarded the hyper-emotion B-3 cliches and began concentrating on more understated goals—thoughtful melodic construction, sensual smooth tone, and complex musical interaction with the rest of the band, especially singer Jim Morrison.

Manzarek's Vox solo on "Light My Fire," from *The Doors,* marked a historic moment in rock history. of the LP, Manzarek demonstrated that you could create exciting rock and roll from behind a keyboard without relying on whirling Leslie horns and screeching registrations. But with his lesson there came a challenge. Organists, and later synthesists, found a new standard in Manzarek for improvised melody—indeed, improvised structure, free of 12-bar blues straitjackets. New vistas were opened by "Light My Fire," but it took a while for others to forge into these uncharted territories and return with substantial innovations of their own.

There were a few stirrings. Not long after *The Doors* was released, the Iron Butterfly, an L.A.-based group that had shared several bills with the Doors at the Whiskey-A-Go-Go, put out their first album, *Heavy,* featuring the Manzarek-like Vox Continental work of Doug Ingle. The title cut of their follow-up, *Inna-Gadda-Da-Vida,* unleashed Ingle in an even longer solo than Manzarek had undertaken in "Light My Fire." Recorded in one take as a studio sound check, "Inna-Gadda-Da-Vida" was dominated by his spooky organ improvisation, in which contrapuntal lines snaked through intricate patterns and masked quotes from "God Rest Ye Merry, Gentlemen." Though not quite as groundbreaking as "Light My Fire," Ingle's "Inna-Gadda-Da-Vida" still stands as one of the all-time great rock keyboard solos.

But the immediate catalyst for the classicist resurgence was a German quartet called Kraftwerk. The name translates as "power station," which offers an insight into the band's anti-romantic philosophy. All four musicians—Ralf Hutter, Florian Schneider, Karl Bartos, and Wolf-

Devo's Mark Mothersbaugh demonstrating his
iconoclastic view of music technology on a Minimoog and other assorted hardware.

gang Flur—were trained in formal music, with an emphasis on electronic composition and performance. Hutter and Schneider established their own recording studio in 1970, and began acquiring synthesizers in 1971. From the start they steered away from conventional instrumentation and the spacey tone-wash style already emerging in pop electronic music. Instead, they built their own instruments, including synthesized percussion devices because, as Hutter explained to *Keyboard*, "Our drummers didn't want to turn electronic," and developed an approach based on sequences of biting staccato tones, spat forth like sharp pins from a staple gun. With the cold world of machines as their inspiration, Kraftwerk replicated the cyclic rhythms of the assembly line in its steady electronic beat, and the soulless wails of shortwave interference in its robotic solos. Through the use of vocoders, devices which translate spoken words into electronic pitches, they even gave machines one leg up on human singers in expressing verbal ideas. "Technology as an art—technology as it is," Hutter proclaimed. "We have nothing to hide."

The peculiar outcome of their experiments was that Kraftwerk became known simultaneously as pioneers of a detached and dispassionate pop synthesizer style, and as the most popular European disco dance band of the Seventies. Beginning in 1975, with the release of the album *Autobahn,* and on subsequent LPs like *Radio-Activity* in 1976, *Trans-Europe Express* in 1977, and *The Man-Machine* in 1978, they fused synthesizer technology, then the more-or-less exclusive property of romantics like Isao Tomita, Vangelis Papathanassiou, and Jean-Michel Jarre, with powerful repetitive rhythms and the unemotional stance of the rock classicists. Their impact was immediate, particularly in Germany, where it would galvanize punk derivatives like Deutsche-Amerikanische Freundschaft, and in England, where their innovations were expanded upon by an equally important classicist hero.

Originally a conceptual artist, Brian Eno brought his brilliant creativity and unorthodox intellect into rock when he formed Roxy Music in the early Seventies. He had had virtually no contact with keyboards up to that point, so his synthesizer work with Roxy Music was unencumbered by the traditional perceptions that piano training often imposed on other performing synthesists. For the same reason, he had little effect on other musicians as an instrumentalist *per se.* But through his inspired solo albums which spanned the widest ranges of electronic rock from chaotic tape collages to blissful trance

music and stretched into the avant-garde fringes of classical music, and his extensive work as producer of records by other experimental artists, Eno stimulated countless young artists to liberate themselves from the musical conventions in which they had been raised, and to follow no dogma—including Kraftwerk's techno-rock gospel—blindly.

Many of the most gifted synthesizer virtuosi in the classicist rock movement, like Bob Casale and Mark Mothersbaugh of the American group Devo and Billy Currie of Ultravox, picked up tips by working directly with Eno. Others, like most listeners, took their cues from his recorded work. A few, like Gary Numan, one of the first English synthesized classicists to enjoy commercial success in the States, would stubbornly refuse to acknowledge him a a direct influence, yet Eno's pervasive presence throughout rock in the late Seventies cannot be denied. He and Kraftwerk laid the foundation on which the classicist reaction was built.

On the following pages we offer excerpts from *Keyboard*'s interviews with some leading lights of this ascendant movement. Eno's wide-ranging comments have been heavily edited to preserve our focus on only one of the many subjects that interest him, rock keyboards. Jimmy Destri of Blondie speaks for the low-tech wing of the classicist school. Mothersbaugh and Casale explain Devo's iconoclastic view of music technology. The Human League, whose all-synthesized album *Dare* topped European and American charts in the early Eighties, represent the triumph of rock's hallowed unlettered mentality in the complex labyrinths of electronic instrumentation. Thomas Dolby, perhaps the most promising new face in the classicist community, offers a glimpse at even newer classicist vistas. And a panel of electro-pop innovators discuss their stylistic similarities and differences.

More than any other chapter in our book, this section is incomplete, for the classicist revolution is just taking off. It is rife with potential not just for further variations on the Kraftwerk-Eno formula, but for infusing the romantic element in rock with fresh insights and stimulus for a different kind of romantic backlash at some future date. As long as rock continues to communicate, this give-and-take of ideas will extend from generation to generation *ad infinitum.* And as long as instrument designers keep finding ways of expanding the expressive and sonic resources of their synthesizers and other keyboards, the musicians who play them will stand at the forefront of every important new trend.

Bob Doerschuk

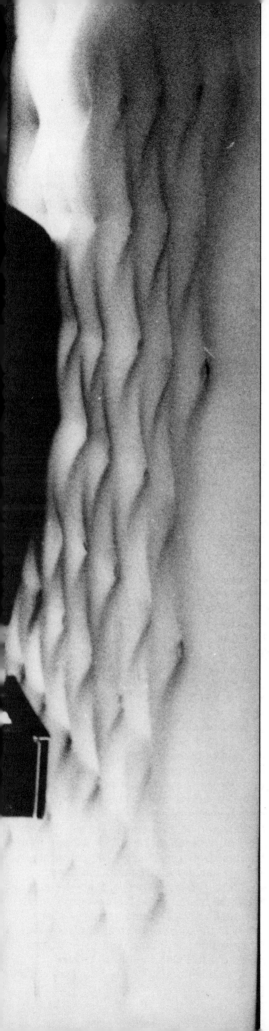

The New Synthesizer Rock
A Round-Table Primer

June 1982 — Rock is a constantly regenerating phenomenon. When one generation of artists gets a little too flabby, or starts straying a bit too far from the basics of the music, it gets elbowed aside by impatient newcomers, eager to get back to the sound, beat, and stance of rock at its simplest. A mellow Elvis Presley, tamed by the Army, led to the Beatles, whose successive cuteness and artsiness stimulated the psychedelic movement, in whose burned-out ashes the anti-romantic seeds of punk and new wave were sewn.

But while styles change, while the cycle spins on, the tools stay roughly the same. Rock means guitars, drums, and, thankfully, keyboards of one sort or another. The current revival of essential rock involves, if anything, a greater use of keyboards than any similar return to rock roots. But in almost every other respect, a refugee from the '60s or even the mid-'70s would find huge differences between the rock of those days and what is happening now. This means, in turn, that the use and function of keyboards, especially synthesizers, has undergone some breath-taking changes in the journey from Tomita to Deutsch-Amerikanische Freundschaft.

What many post-new wave bands have in common with earlier stripped-down rock groups is an interest in playing more for dancers than for listeners. Where older acts as diverse as the Who and Styx tend to appear before sedentary, sometimes demurely seated, crowds in stadiums and vast concert halls, performances by Orchestral Manoeuvres In The Dark, Depeche Mode, and their brethren usually work best in the more traditional rock setting—hot sticky clubs jammed

Previous page: Soft Cell in a soft cell. The problem is that it can be difficult to draw the line between image and reality.

wall to wall with bodies leaping about to an irresistible 4/4 rhythm.

These new bands pursue a familiar formula—heavy on the second and fourth beats, with compelling counter-rhythms from the bass and as little adornment as possible. In short, the tried-and-true rock and roll blueprint. In fact, their subservience to the beat is more complete than was the case with Little Richard, Creedence Clearwater, and other oldies, because of the disco influence. Most disco records center around the drums, in some cases almost exclusively the bass drum, with orchestras, guitars, and everything else except vocals mixed down to nearly a subconscious level. Although the ideology of the music hasn't much relevance to the young synth rockers, they are children of a radio era that has saturated the airwaves, street corners, and brain cells with disco's merciless pulse.

Inevitably, this has had its impact; even the dreariest, most nihilistic lyrics shout out in post-new wave ensembles over a bedrock beat that should set the most danced-out feet tapping. But though the lyrical focus differs, with disco composers seldom searching beyond sex and neo-wavers often dipping into anger and alienation for inspiration, the impact on dancers is nearly identical. Both Donna Summer and Soft Cell's Marc Almond have an ability to project a kind of detached desperation through their vocals, but much of that projection is due to the hypnotic power of the unsyncopated repetitive electronic riffs over which they sing.

To further this effect, many new bands have turned from live drummers to rhythm machines, which allow for unvarying sequences of identical percussion sounds and eliminate any possibilities of trance-breaking irregularities in the less dependable hands of human drummers. Some groups, like Orchestral Manoeuvres, do use drummers onstage, though even then the impact of electronic rhythm units can be heard in the steady beat the drummers are assigned. But more frequently, in the work of Soft Cell, the Human League, Throbbing Gristle, Tuxedomoon, and the now defunct Suicide, digital boxes have replaced trap sets.

Sound familiar? This is the approach pioneered by the German techno-rockers Kraftwerk. Their straight-forward beat, minimalist textures, and use of pointy razor-edged synthesizer sounds awakened many young keyboardists to the fact that keyboard electronics did not necessarily have to follow the color-washed soft-focus footsteps of Tomita or Jean-Michel Jarre. Any consideration of the new style must acknowledge Kraftwerk, especially in their fusion of disco and techno, as the movement's musical godfathers.

Of course there are other branches in the music's family tree. Spiritually, the lineage stretches back to the early '50s. In its pure state, rock and roll has always been iconoclastic, with certain inseparable and generally anti-establishment connotations. Little Richard's manic antics were beyond the comprehension of the adult world in the Eisenhower era; the fact that white kids listened to black music, let alone music played by a black man wearing mascara and suggestively writhing all over a piano keyboard, caused perhaps more dinner table anxiety than the prospect of nuclear war.

As society loosened up in the liberal '60s, rock performers had to probe further into the dark corners of parental fear for equivalent effect. The faint hint of androgyny in the Beatles, the delinquent scruffiness of the Rolling Stones, the flamboyant communism of the Haight-Ashbury bands, all measured this escalating assault on grown-up standards. But when the heavy artillery rolled out in groups like the Doors, the Fugs, the Velvet Underground, the New York Dolls, and the MC5—groups that cultivated vaguely occult, sleazy, arrogant, anarchistic, and/or sexually bizarre facades—anti-establishment posturing blossomed into a fine art. The music had finally hit America's funny bone. Shock rock was born.

Image-wise, the ramifications are still being felt today. In traditional showbiz, performers smile, laugh, and dance for audiences. Because of the shock rock ethic, these entertainment techniques are frequently abandoned by bands who get their energy by mobilizing their audience's instincts for rebellion. The problem is that it can get difficult to draw the line between image and reality; no doubt many old-time vaudevillians were genuinely happy people, and as the Sid Vicious and Joy Division legacies demonstrate, many shock rockers seem to be genuinely strange as well.

But it would be a mistake to dismiss the new bands as pure shock rockers. A close listen to the best of their work reveals a growing musical sensibility, a feeling for orchestration and linear composition, and an overall discipline frequently absent in the best of some highly regarded progressive rock artists. The singers may appear to wrestle with the ideas of pitch and melody, but this is a stylistic issue; just as early jazz singers dismayed oldsters with their neo-African melisma, so might today's Barry Manilow fans be distressed by the emotional yowls of Jim Morrison's and Johnny Rotten's vocal progeny.

It follows, then, that technical virtuosity is not an especially relevant attribute in this style. Since much of the impact of neo wave synthesis stems from machine-like repetition—a technique also employed by the equivalent anti-romantics in classical music, the minimalists—the keyboard flourishes of the Keith Emerson school would be definitely out of place in this context. Solos in the traditional sense, improvisations realized on the keyboard, are a rarity; at most you might find occasional four-bar single-line passages, more fills than solos, such as at the end of the Units' "Bugboy."

Instead, the focus shifts to the arrangement. The droning organ sounds and underplayed fills of Ray Manzarek in *The Doors* and John Cale in the Velvet Underground's "Heroin" are the real rock antecedents of the new synthesists. Like Manzarek and Cale—both technically adept keyboardists—they are more interested in integrating into the whole than in standing out front. This attitude is also reflected in the early work of Jimmy Destri with Blondie and Steve Nieve with Elvis Costello's Attractions, the most prominent figures in the new wave revival of Farfisa and Vox organ sounds. But aside from a few adherents here and there, among them Joe "King" Carrasco, the Insect Surfers, and Tex-Mex nostalgists like Augie Meyer of the Sir Douglas Quintet, most new keyboardists who want old-timey electric organ effects find it easier to store them into their synthesizers as one of an array of possible programs.

The fact is that the new-wavers are just as concerned as Tony Banks or Patrick Moraz with orchestrated sound, but they tend to work from the background. Even when Wakeman is only laying down synthesized strings, he does so with such panache that there is no mistaking his identity. His younger counterparts prefer sublimating themselves to the beat, inserting short riffs or patterns of subtly contrasting colors. Case in point:the tiny tonal variations in the riff that constitutes DAF's "Liebe Auf Den Ersten Blick," from *Gold Und Liebe*. If you want to listen, you must listen carefully to appreciate synthesist Robert Gorl's meticulous touch.

But if you want to dance instead, you can do that too. And so the cycle is once again completed. For listeners who are used to sitting back and letting orchestral synthesized chords or a string of lightning-bolt licks wash over them, neo wave synthesis may be an acquired taste. But

once again something different is happening in rock, and as the first swing back to basics in the synthesizer era, there is as much in it for the head as there is for the feet.

Partly because of the relatively low-key roles they lean toward, there are no superstars, no Hendrixes or Emersons, among the young synthesists. Their bands have followings, but sometimes the most devoted fans have trouble remembering the names of the players whose records they consume. This is true especially in the States, since many pioneering new wave groups are English, and some of the most important of these have never played any American engagements.

For this reason, *Keyboard* indulged itself in a series of trans-Atlantic phone interviews with some of the leading lights in this still fresh movement. We also talked to the keyboardists in three American bands whose work ties in with that of the European pioneers. While no two of the artists in the following assembled interviews should be considered clones of one another or anyone else, they all share at least one thing in common:an interest in using the synthesizer in rock as it's never been used before, in part to get back to where the music in its essence belongs.

Some of the people we spoke with—Martin Gore of Depeche Mode, Layne Rico and Scott Simon of Our Daughters Wedding—are close to the mainstream of pop music, using rhythm machines and sequencers to pound out a disco-derived dance beat. Others—Scott Ryser and Rachel Webber of the Units, David Ball of Soft Cell—also adhere to a steady rhythm, but with darker overtones more clearly reminiscent of punk and new wave, while Richard Barbieri of the English group Japan, Chas Gray and Stan Ridgway of Wall Of Voodoo, and Peter Principle of Tuxedomoon all shy from the tyranny of the sequencer and pursue freer forms in their own ways.

What it goes to show is that even at this early stage of its development, the new rock synthesizer vanguard is branching beyond stereotypes and finding room to create in ways unforeseen by the rock trendsetters of a decade ago.

Let's begin by finding out about your musical backgrounds. Did you take a lot of piano lessons, for example, or were you mainly self-taught?

Richard Barbieri (Japan): I was self-taught, really. I was never taught how to play by anyone, and I didn't start off on the piano. I've never felt comfortable with acoustic piano. It was really only when I started using synthesizers that I felt I could be useful and do something interesting, or put over what I wanted to do.

Had you had any electronic music experience before you got into synthesizers?

Barbieri: Not really, no. It was a very naive kind of thing. I just started, and carried on from there. I was just lucky that I had the right people around me from whom I could gain influences and who I could influence in turn, and that's really how Japan came about. I joined probably six months after the band was formed. We're all self-taught. I'd say there's probably only one real musician in the band—Steve Jansen, the drummer.

Scott Ryser (the Units): We got together about three years ago. Rachel and I met at a Tuxedomoon concert at the Mab [Mabuhay Gardens, a San Francisco club]. We were both hauling some equipment for them, and we just got to talking. It turned out that Rachel was doing an experimental performance in the windows at the abandoned J.C. Penney building downtown. We wound up collaborating. Rachel painted the windows black from the inside, and as I played some synthesizer music while films were being shown, she'd gradually scrape the stuff off the windows so people could start peeping in.

Were you both visual artists before getting into music?

Rachel Webber (the Units): I was, but Scott has more of a background in synthesizer. He bought the first synthesizer to come into San Francisco. I started singing with Scott, then I ended up playing synthesizer too because it was more gratifying to help write music.

Layne Rico (Our Daughter's Wedding): We also started off as friends in the San Francisco Bay area. About two years ago we had a band that was similar to the Cars, a rock-style guitar band. We had no synthesizers at the time, but finally we incorporated a couple of keyboard players—Scott [Simon] and someone else. Then we got tired of that guitar-drum lineup, so we all moved to New York, I traded my drum kit for the new percussion synthesizers, and Keith [Silva], the lead vocalist, dropped his guitars and learned to play keyboards. We thought that would be more interesting, because most of the music we were listening to at the time was more or less electronic, European things that American bands weren't playing.

Martin Gore (Depeche Mode): When we got rid of our guitar players, it was mainly because we

didn't have any transport at the time. We had to get one of our friends to take us everywhere in a van, and it was very difficult to get in touch with him all the time. It was far easier for us to just play synths, because they are very portable. Everywhere we played we just showed up with our synths in suitcases, then hired a PA and played through it.

But wasn't there also a musical reason for scrapping the guitars?

Gore: The guitars were getting rather boring. They've got just one sound all the time, and though you can flange it and do things like that, it's still basically the same sound.

David Ball (Soft Cell): I originally started with guitar too, but I got bored because there really wasn't much you could do with it. I was interested in different types of sound, so I got rid of the guitar and got a synthesizer.

Was Soft Cell always a duo, as it is today?

Ball: We did start out as a duo. Marc [Almond, singer] and I started working together in 1979, when we were both in college at Leeds. Mark was in a performance that was more like a cabaret, and I was doing soundtracks with him. Then we decided to do something more commercial. We came up with about ten songs and played our first gig in the autumn of 1979.

Chas Gray (Wall Of Voodoo): We also started out doing soundtracks. Stan, our guitar player, Marc Moreland, and I rented an office off Hollywood Blvd. in late '77 specifically to do film soundtracks. We had a couple of two-track tape recorders, a file cabinet, a desk, and a light—no typewriter, and we were kind of low on clients too. But we made a lot of tapes.

Stan Ridgway (Wall of Voodoo): Eventually the company turned into a band.

Do you feel that keyboard virtuosity is not as important to new styles of synthesizer playing as it was in the past?

Ridgway: Yeah, and I think I understand why. When the synthesizer first came out, it was looked upon pretty much as a crazy organ. You had players like Chick Corea and Jan Hammer trying to make it sound like a guitar. But in formal music people had been using the instrument for a long time before that, and it just took some time for the two ideas to catch up with one another.

Barbieri: I think people tend to use synthesizers in a more subtle way now.

Ball: The technical skill now lies in actually programming the synthesizer, rather than in playing the keyboard. I don't think of synthesizer players as keyboardists, actually. There are keyboard players who play piano and organ, and there are synthesizer players who are more like technicians. Of course there are really good piano players who can do great things on synthesizers too.

Ryser: It's more a matter of good taste now, or just generally being creative. I don't think it's as necessary as it used to be to have lots of impressive licks. Some of these new synthesizers, like the Sequential Circuits Pro-One, will play arpeggios for you. My sequencer is Sequential Circuits too, and I can program it at a snail's pace then just speed it up to whatever tempo I want.

In that sense, you really differ from the bands of the '60s, with their extended solos.

Ryser: Yeah. It's more important to me to contribute to the sound of the band than to play a solo. When any of us do solo, it's more to create a dialog between the instruments, as opposed to just sticking one player out in front.

Simon: Exactly. Solos should be pertinent to the vocal line and the message you're trying to get across. When you have singing involved, belaboring an instrumental section just takes away from the song. And the kids get a little bored; even if someone is excellent on an instrument, all the licks start to sound the same if it goes on and on.

Ryser: In the '60s people got outside of the structure more, and now it's a thing of getting back into the structure, making the players in the group work really well together.

Simon: As soon as synthesizers came along, everyone said, "Oh, wow, outer space!" and that type of thing. That lasted until the players matured, and then synth started to take on a different meaning: horn lines, guitar lines, background noise, or what have you, rather than the Keith Emerson "Lucky Man" standard glide.

What are your thoughts now about people like Emerson and Rick Wakeman?

Simon: They were very good keyboard players, that stands by itself.

Ryser: For my part, I think my style is a reaction against guys like Emerson and Wakeman. When they first came out, I really liked them, but after a while it got too pretentious.

Ball: I really used to hate the kind of things they were doing, because it was like just impressing people by how fast they could play a riff. To me, that doesn't mean anything. There's no feeling there; it's just technical brilliance.

Is having that kind of technical skill in any way a liability in your music?

Principle: No, not at all. I couldn't imagine anything that would be a liability if it comes from talent. It's not what you have, but the way you use what you have, that makes good art.

Ridgway: But in a lot of ways I think having a knowledge of music has helped us out a lot more than just having a knowledge of the keyboard. It's interesting to be talking to a keyboard magazine, because we've never really considered ourselves keyboardists at all.

Yet there is a lot of synthesizer on your albums.

Ridgway: I know, but it's still funny. We've played them, but our area of expertise is different. The idea of a monophonic synthesizer, where one note is played at a time, opened up a whole different approach to the keyboard. For centuries being a keyboardist was a two-handed thing. You worked in an orchestral sense. Then when a keyboard came along that was just a trigger to generate sounds out of a synthesizer, that completely changed things.

Gore: When you use a lot of sequencers and things like that, you don't really need much technical playing ability. But you still need some sort of know-how, some sort of musical knowledge to know what sounds right. When a note sounds wrong, you should know how to change it accordingly. When people talk about just leaving a sequencer running to finish a song, it's not that simple.

Ball: Groups that are dominated by sequencers I find a little boring, actually. I think a lot of people are possessed with the idea that because machines can do that kind of thing you've got to let them steal the limelight. Those people seem to be into the idea that the medium is the message. Kraftwerk is a perfect example.

Principle: We started out as a drone group, but we've never really used the sequencer trip, maybe because it's sort of a familiar sound. A lot of sequencer music really makes me angry. We've never had one. If somebody gave one to us, maybe we'd do something intelligent with it.

Ryser: The sequencer does take a lot of the fun away from playing. Now that our percussionist, Jonathan Parker, plays keyboards, he'll play some of the old sequencer parts. It's just more fun to not use it in a live situation, and it creates more interplay. You feel there's more energy happening. For composing it's great to use rhythm machines and sequencers, but onstage I think it's just a little more exciting to do the live thing. It's more like an orchestra when you see all these different people playing different parts, as opposed to just having a machine do them.

On the Digital Cowboy *record, Scott, you included a note reading "No Sequencer Used." Why?*

Simon: I think a bit of the humanity is lost, and we're trying to get the fact across in our music that we are human beings. We're not machines playing machines. Also we're trying to state that we are different from a lot of other bands that do use sequencers. Take that bass pattern on "No One's Watching" [from *Digital Cowboy*]. That's a traditional sequencer pattern, but I played the whole part through with my fingers. When I do it live, sometimes I make a mistake, but I can also make it sound more energetic without the sequencer. I can accent different notes and change the feeling in a way the sequencer can't.

Still you must hear the similarity between the patterns you play and the sequencer lines of Kraftwerk.

Simon: Oh, sure. They're great. I've been listening to them since 1976 or '77, when I first met Keith and Layne in California. But they are a bit different from us. We are a band that plays on electronic instruments, whereas they are an electronic band. We're not just using tape loops and feedback and stuff; we're striving to write *music* on electronic instruments because they are more interesting than conventional guitar and drums.

Ball: Kraftwerk had my favorite sound in electronic music. That's what first attracted me to synthesizers.

Was Kraftwerk an influence on Japan as well?

Barbieri: I suppose we were inspired by them in a way because we work with sequencers, but only to that extent.

And your sequencer work is much less a factor in your music than in theirs.

Barbieri: We use it for a much sparser kind of rhythm than they do. We play it against the drums as well, as opposed to adhering to a strict four-bar thing. It plays between the intervals of the drum pattern, rather than having the drums following the sequencer pattern. We tend to split them up into two separate things so that they play against each other and create different rhythms.

Webber: Kraftwerk is obviously someone we get compared to a lot, because they've been around for a while. But when we started, one of the slogans 415 Records hyped us with was, "Humans playing synthesizers." The whole thing was that we were human, we weren't machines. Now it seems like there's a definite trend away

from synthesizers as machine-oriented noise creators. If anything it's turned in the other direction, with bands like Orchestral Manoeuvres and Soft Cell.

How much of a challenge is it to get past the electronic framework of your music, especially given the influence of Kraftwerk, and make it seem more emotional, if that's what you're trying to do?

Gore: I don't think we've had that problem. There are a lot of bands around who do play synthesizers very coldly, but I think we've gotten away from that.

Principle: That's why we're interesting to a lot of people. We use electronics for a lot of what we do; we use saxophone and violins too, but a lot of times it's a heavily treated violin, and even so we still manage to cut it and the emotions somehow come through. This is one of the enigmas of Tuxedomoon as compared to our peers. I'm pro-emotion. I'm pro-everything that's human. I don't think the way of the future is to close off certain circuits in your nervous system, by drugs, will power, religion, or whatever. We have to open them all by these same means!

But even bands that don't rely on sequencers often show their influence in how they use cyclic repetitions of notes. The fact that they're played by hand may escape the notice of the listener, who just hears something that obviously was inspired by machine-like sequencer patterns.

Ball: But Brian Eno once said, "Repetition is a form of change."

Webber: I know that my bass lines are usually pretty repetitve, but I think it's kind of nice and a little more free to have something like that going on with a percussionist doing things on top.

Ryser: In fact, we're always thinking we're not repetitve enough. Repetition is nice for dancing, and since we like to dance ourselves, that's one way we get into a good groove and stay on it.

Simon: But you know, I think dancing is less important now. I have a feeling that people want to listen a little bit more to what's going on. They want to be able to move their bodies a little bit, but it's not necessary to go out and go crazy on every song. If there's a message there, people want to hear it. Rock in the middle and late '70s didn't have much of a message, the way there was in the '60s. There is a need for that now.

Principle: I don't argue against dance-oriented music with lyrics like that, because one of the blessings of rock and roll is the fact that it describes your problem and also gives you the solution, which is to dance away into a dervish

Billy Curie of Ultravox playing a Yamaha string synthesizer, stacked on a Yamaha electric grand next to an ARP Odyssey.

delirium. A lot of the world is in that mood right now.

And you feel the new synthesizer rock addresses that need?

Ball: Sure. It's hypnotic as dance music. That's the whole essence of it. People are so limited and restricted, crammed into offices and trains. They can't move around, so they just want to shake and go wild. Dancing is what they do rather than hitting or killing somebody.

Principle: There is a lot of soulful, fiery dance-oriented music in New York, but I think that kind of inspiration has drifted away from English music. When I was a kid English music was very interesting but now it's very flat.

Webber: The English bands really go for an extremely simple drum sound, just four to the bar, if they have a drummer. In a way that's what separates us from all the synthesizer music that's happening right now in England, especially with our percussionist and drummer. We try to remain simple in what we do, but it's still a little more creative than that.

Gore: Well, I'm a bit biased, but I think a bit more thought goes into our rhythm than just laying down a disco track. Most disco records sound very much the same to me. We do use a powerful bass drum and snare sound, and they are mixed up loud, but we don't start by saying, "Let's make this a dance record," although most of them are.

Doesn't it seem like the use of drum machines by many new bands contradicts claims that they're trying to get closer to human feeling?

Ball: Well, we use drum machines because they're convenient. I couldn't play a drum kit, but with the Roland TR-808 or the Linn you can program as you go along; it's like live playing. You don't just type out a rhythm part and let it play; you can actually put in fills as you go along, and that enables me to play drums using a keyboard or switches rather than drumsticks.

Do you try to approximate a drum sound as closely as possible?

Ball: Yes. I always thought the snare sound on drum machines was a little thin, so when we record the drum machine, with each drum sound on a separate channel, we take the electronic snare signal and feed it into a small speaker which is placed on top of a real snare, then we record that. So the drum machine is triggering a real snare drum!

Principle: But the whole idea of using electronics for rhythms instead of a drummer is to get something that sounds different from real drums!

That's one thing I don't like about rhythm machines: They have imitation drum sounds on them. Look at the Roland: You can treat it with a fuzz box or flanger or echo, but you never get away from that drum sound.

On the other hand, it sounds like the Depeche Mode bass drum sound is not even remotely an attempt at imitating the tone of a real bass drum.

Gore: Since we've started making records we've always used an ARP 2600 for the bass drum because we've never found a drum machine with a powerful enough bass drum sound. We run it through the sequencer. We like the snare sound on our Roland TR-808. Our Korg KR-55 also has quite a good snare. We chose them both mainly to get a good snare drum.

The snare sounds on Soft Cell's "Sex Dwarf" and on "Talking Drum" by Japan seem to be cut off at certain points. Did you use a noise gate on it?

Barbieri: That's exactly what we used. It took quite a long time, because there's a lot involved with the special type of delay you want, but on "Talking Drum" we used the noise gate on the snare and on the toms.

Ball: We had some sort of limiting amplifier that clipped the sound so that it died very abruptly, leaving a kind of ringing reverberation.

Layne, why did you move from regular drums to electronic percussion with Our Daughters Wedding?

Rico: I like the drums, but I couldn't get some of the sounds I wanted from them because all you can do is hit a stick against the skin, so I used my knowledge of drumming and syncopation and changed it all over to playing keyboards. My drumming was where I got all my rhythm machine ability.

You also do mix rhythm machines in with your electronic drums, don't you?

Rico: That's exactly right. We like the sound of a rhythm machine, but they can get too repetitious, just going *click clack click clack* all night.

Ryser: We definitely made a decision to have drummers as opposed to just electronic drums, but we'd like to start using electronic drums to augment the percussion.

What do you like about them?

Ryser: The textures, the tones. They'd be nice to intersperse with real drums. When we record we use a vibraphone, but our percussionist now plays keyboard instead because the vibes are so hard to mike onstage. I really like the slight tonal variation between the keyboard and a percussive instrument like vibes. It's the same with electronic and real drums. To have the two textures together would be nice.

Ridgway: Our drummer is into experimenting with textures too. He devised this set of frying pans attached to a practice pad that he plays along with the sequencer at the end of "Back In Flesh" [from *Dark Continent*]. You can't tell which is which!

Martin, what do you get in Depeche Mode from playing with a rhythm machine that you don't get from a live drummer?

Gore: That's a difficult one for us to answer, because we've never used a drummer. Even when we first started, with a guitarist and bass guitarist, we used a small drum machine. We've never felt limited by it, though.

Principle: We just recorded a 12" 45, three songs with heavy electric guitar and not one drum beat on the whole record. I'm really proud of that [*laughs*].

There's a cut on the American Japan album, titled "Ghosts," that has no drum track either.

Barbieri: It is very difficult to play without a drum track because there is no real timing. The only timing we could follow was the bass synthesizer, which kind of denoted the chord changes. I think it came over quite well. That's probably one of the best examples of my keyboard work. The arrangement is what's interesting about the track. It's a very straight vocal line, but we decided to make the arrangement a bit strange.

Do you feel that different kinds of synthesizer sounds are popular these days than were popular in the progressive rock era?

Gray: I think so. When they were used on a more traditional level people tried to approximate the sound of a real instrument with a synthesizer, so they didn't come up with as many jolting sounds.

Like the one you used on "Back In Flesh."

Gray: That was an Oberheim mini-sequencer plugged into two holes in the back of the Minimoog that it wasn't supposed to be plugged into, according to the manufacturer, but it's also run through this little gizmo box I built at home.

Ridgway: Then you turn all the filters off on the Moog, fiddle with the box and the sounds come out.

Ball: In the early days most synthesizers sounded the same. The Moog sound seemed the most popular. It's developed now to the point that you can use a synthesizer and people won't realize that's what it is, which I really like. It's not that you're trying to deceive anyone; it's just that you can get the feel that you've dreamed about. People can't say the synthesizer is just a gimmick that makes silly little sounds, because it isn't doing that anymore.

Ryser: In the '70s they were going for more of a guitar sound. It was more of a Jan Hammer thing. Now I'd say synths are used either more percussively or with longer melodic tones.

Webber: And new possibilities will come along as time goes on. Kids who play video games hear a lot of weird sounds, and when they go hear a synthesizer band they'll be able to relate to it on that level.

Simon: To me it goes back to the desire to have a raw edge in music. People who are playing string synthesizers now prefer to hit chords and pull off rather than keep it down, because it's so convenient an instrument that players I know instinctively back off from it.

That is a major change from the way progressive rock synthesists used string lines in the past.

Simon: That's the fun thing about it. The beat is very important. You have to define it first. Once that's done, then you have all the room in the world to color a song.

Gore: We don't make conscious attempts to imitate the sounds of real instruments, but a lot of times the sounds we're looking for come very close to conventional instruments. They might not be perfect replicas, but they sound very much like the originals.

Barbieri: We try to make almost every single sound as acoustic as possible. If we knew how to play those acoustic instruments well enough, we'd drop synthesizers altogether. I much prefer the sound of traditional instruments. We're merely using synthesizers to create that.

Ridgway: But to me, there really isn't any point to that. I like the way synthetic strings sound. If I wanted to have a real-sounding violin on a record I would get someone to come in and play one.

Principle: We only use machines to give us more possibilities to make mistakes.

Do you feel like you're involved in a significant trend that's changing the direction of rock and roll?

Ryser: I think so. We're doing it in a reactionary way. It's like, there's been enough of this other stuff; how about something different?

Simon: Yeah. Sometimes we'll be sitting around talking, and someone will say, "God, it feels good that something we just happened to be doing is working, and besides that it's new and important." Bands like the Human League,

OMD, and the Units are all in a new thing, and as it matures, as artists who are presenting the music grow up, kids who are 15 now will start using these instruments to play something different too.

Principle: Well, I don't want to paint the picture either way, because it's too romantic. I don't expect to be the mainstay of a new revolution. I'm not on that much of an ego trip.

Do you have any apprehensions that synthesizers may simply fall into a new kind of cliched use?

Principle: I think they already have.

What can you do to avoid that in you own music?

Principle: I don't worry about it.

Barbieri: It does sound to me like something new is happening, but everybody does seem to be doing the same thing. It's all going into another style again.

Ridgway: I would only say that it sounds as if a lot of musicians have figured out that less is more.

Ball: That's what I hated about a lot of the '70's rock bands that had synthesizers. They overcomplicated things. The return to simplicity is good.

Gray: That seems to be what a lot of other people are doing right now, and as a result everyone has sort of stumbled onto a certain basic style of using the synthesizer.

Webber: There are a lot of similarities among synthesizer bands. You really have to be original and creative with what you do with a machine, because it's really easy to get into a quirky little synthesizer sound. It doesn't take much to come up with that kind of thing.

Barbieri: It's just a matter of choosing your influence, and if you choose the current music scene as your influence, then I don't really hold much hope. If you tend to pick your influences from something more diverse, whether it's Erik Satie or Frank Sinatra or traditional Chinese music, then you could come up with something original.

One last question. If you had to explain what's happening now in music to a rock fan who had somehow fallen asleep in the late '60s and slept through the '70s, what would you say?

Simon: I'd ask him to go back to the '50s and listen to the kind of steady keyboards that Fats Domino played in "Blueberry Hill."

Webber: I'd tell him not to go shopping, not to take out any loans, and to try and survive.
Bob Doerschuk

Ray Manzarek
Passion and Objectivity

September 1977 — When did you begin playing keyboards?

When I was seven years old, my parents bought an upright piano, put it in the recreation room, and said to me, "Well, Raymond, it's time for you to learn the piano." At my first lesson, my piano teacher opened a book to a little exercise on the first page. He played it, and then said, "Now you do it." I looked at the little lines and dots and said, "This is impossible!" But after a few weeks I finally figured it out and I stayed with that piano teacher for a couple of years.

Did you practice a lot as a child?

I never really got into it, although I had to practice for half an hour after school and half an hour after dinner. We lived right across the street from the schoolyard, so when I could hear the guys playing baseball over there in the afternoon after school, that half hour seemed like an eternity.

When did you know that you wanted to be a keyboard player?

It was when I was 11 years old and I heard the blues for the first time. I grew up in Chicago, and up to that time all I had known about was "How Much Is That Doggie In The Window?" and "The Shrimp Boats Are A-Comin'." But one day at a playground, somebody had a portable radio tuned to the right-hand side of the dial—the ethnic side—and when I heard the blues there, it just blew my mind. I'd never heard music with such a sense of rhythm and such a minorish, strange overtone to it; the harmonies, the way the singer would sing, and the whole approach to the music was just totally different from white

Previous page: Ray Manzarek at the apex of (l. to r.) an ARP Odyssey, a Hammond B-3 organ, an ARP string ensemble, a Hohner Clavinet, and a Rhodes electric piano.

popular music. From then on I was hooked on Muddy Waters, Jimmy Reed, John Lee Hooker, and the Chicago blues school.

When did rock and roll come into the picture?

It happened one day when one of those stations played a song called "Mystery Train" by a new guy named Elvis Presley. They didn't know he was a white guy because he didn't sound like it, and I didn't know he was a white guy either. But it was different from the black music because it had acoustic rhythm guitar patterns with a country kind of feel. That was rockabilly, or rock and roll and hillbilly music. Little by little I got into white music and then rock and roll hit. Chuck Berry, Little Richard, Fats Domino, and Jerry Lee Lewis were very big influences on me.

Did all this new music inspire you to go back home and practice?

That's exactly what it did. I'd try to learn to play the songs the way those guys did. Then I got together with a couple of friends—a drummer and a quasi-guitarist—and we'd play little rock and roll gigs around town. Also, my brother had a rock band called Rick And The Ravens; they'd do surf-rock and I'd come on and sing some blues songs, like "Little Red Rooster," "King Bee," and some of Muddy's tunes.

What keyboards were you playing then?

I was still just playing piano. I played a Wurlitzer electric piano when that first came out, but I didn't play organ until the Doors got together. I used a Vox Continental on the first two albums (*The Doors* and *Strange Days*) and on the road for a long time. It was the perfect instrument to put the Rhodes piano bass on because it was as flat as a pancake.

Why did you play keyboard bass with the Doors?

We never found a bass guitarist we wanted to work with. We had guys like Harvey Brooks and Douglas Lubahn playing bass on the sessions with us, but when the band was forming we looked around for bass players and never really found any. Then one day we were auditioning at some place—we didn't get the gig because we were too weird—but they happened to have a piano bass on top of an organ, and when I saw that I said, "That's perfect. I'll just play the bass with my left hand and play the organ with my right hand." The Rhodes keyboard bass didn't record that well since it didn't have an attack, but in person you could turn it up real loud and it was fine.

Who influenced you keyboard bass style?

My left hand influences came originally from boogie woogie pianists like Pinetop Smith and Albert Ammons when I heard their left hands repeating those figures over and over, so when the time came for me to play the bass lines for the Doors, I had those two things going; I was able to keep a repeating line going with my left hand while being free to improvise with my right. In the course of modern popular jazz there have been a lot of guys who have done this; Lennie Tristano was the king of the left hand during the 1940's.

Who have your other influences been?

It's a combination of the blues things and Russian classical music of the late nineteenth and early twentienth centuries. Stravinsky's sense of harmony really blew me away and appealed, of course, to my Polish soul too. So what I try to do is to add that Eastern European ethnic minor sense of drama and heaviness to our good old American rock and roll beat; it's Africa and Eastern Europe, the steppes of Central Asia, the Ukraine, and Warsaw. Lately I've been getting into African and Brazilian rhythms, too.

How do you think your playing has changed since your days with the Doors?

Well, I've gotten better. All those years of playing and practice and stretching your mind and attempting different things has an effect. When I really start repeating myself and getting into ruts is when I'll quit for sure. Harmonically and melodically, strange things are starting to go on in my mind that have never gone on before.

What equipment are you using now?

Onstage I use a cut-down Hammond portablized B-3 organ, with an ARP Odyssey synthesizer on top of it and the mixer on top of the Odyssey. The other equipment is an ARP String Ensemble, a Clavinet, and a Rhodes.

How do you like the Rhodes?

The Rhodes is the perfect American keyboard; like the American car, it's good for six months, then it just falls apart—although I've been lucky . I've had one that's been worked on and it's lasted about three years. I don't know what kind of work has been done to it; I'm terrible at that kind of stuff.

Did you ever use a Hammond with the Doors?

No. I used the Vox for about two-and-a-half albums. Then Vox was sold to somebody and the organs started falling apart. I'd go out on a gig and in half a set I'd break about six or seven keys. I eventually got a Gibson Kalamazoo. It had a little more versatility than the Vox; it could make the sort of piano-ish sound I used on "Backdoor Man" [from *The Doors*], plus it had a little knob sticking up on the volume pedal which could bend the note a half-step down. We used it on "Not To Touch The Earth" [from *Waiting For The Sun*]. Even synthesizers don't really do that.

Are there any specific drawbar settings you use on the Hammond?

Yeah. Full out! Let it rip! I like to have the low and high ends of the drawbars out and the middle ducked down or do just the opposite by ducking a little of the low and high ends and featuring the middle drawbars. But for the most part I just play it full out because I'm not looking for variations in the sound of the Hammond. I'm much more concerned with getting the purest organ sound I can.

Do you enjoy working with synthesizer?

Yeah. They are a lot of fun. Unfortunately, when I started working with synthesizers I had to become technical, so I sat down with the little ARP book and started to go through it. It was like learning to play the piano with all those unfamiliar terms, but there's no other way to talk except in terms of oscillation and waveform modulation.

Did you ever use a synthesizer with the Doors?

We used some synthesizer on *Strange Days* in 1968. The late Paul Beaver came down with his Moog synthesizer, and that was probably one of the first times it was used in rock and roll.

Can you describe the Ray Manzarek style of improvisation?

Of course I like to hear a guy play fast and clever solos and all that kind of jazz stuff, but I really like the idea of inventing melody lines with logical figures that have a beginning and build to some sort of climax before the solo is over. I think some people tend to run changes too much in solos. A lot of players really get hung up on their technique; guitar players are really guilty of this. But it doesn't matter if you have the worst technique in the world if you can just play a couple of interesting notes per eight bars that lead to other notes that all go together to make up a melodic whole. That, not technique, is the art of music. Technique is just something that gets you there. I think all musicians should think of the notes they are playing rather than their fingers going over the notes. Forget about your fingers; play what's in your heart. On the oher hand, God knows I wish I had better technique.

But do you ever find yourself stealing licks from other musicians? Does that sort of thing reflect "what's in your heart" if it fits in with what you're playing?

Well, I don't just say, "Hey, I'm going to steal this lick." What I like to do is make the lick very obvious and give an inkling of where my likes and roots and all that business come from. I like to stick in something from Miles Davis or cop something from Coltrane. And that's not stealing; it's saying, "Hey, this is what I like and has anybody else out there heard this? Wasn't it great when you first heard it?" On the album I did by myself for Mercury, *The Golden Scarab,* there's a song called "Downbound Train" where the piano passage at the beginning of the solo is from part of Wynton Kelly's piano solo on "So What" from the Miles Davis album *Live At Carnegie Hall.*

Did Jim Morrison's singing with the Doors shape the way you played then as opposed to the way you play now?

Yeah. If you're going to be in a band, you have to modify your playing to fit into the framework of the other musicians you're working with. I think a band is four or five guys who have gotten together and each one sublimates his ego to the total ego of the band. The Doors was an accumulation of all my influences up to that point but even as I got them all out with the Doors I was in the process of accumulating a whole new series of influences, yet I always play Ray Manzarek.

Steve Rosen

Jimmy Destri
Recycling the Sixties

March 1980 — What kind of music were you first attracted to?

Well, I grew up with an affinity and passion for the sciences, so naturally when I turned to music, it would be something with a lot of buttons, something that was one step beyond the guitar. It's funny that it worked out like that, because originally I was a bass player, and to this day I write my songs on the guitar. The keyboard is the instrument I'm most advanced on but I want to keep my songs simple and have the vocal melody be the main thing. So I just sing and write on the guitar and keep basic chords going.

How did you get into keyboards? Did you take any lessons as a kid?

My sister is a concert pianist and she's the one who studied. I never did. I just looked over her shoulder: "Oh, that's a *B* and that's an *A*?" It just came like that. When I was about 15 or so I bought an old Farfisa organ for a lark. That was '69 or something, and the organ was a '64. I loved it, and I bought a Leslie off a friend of mine too. You see, I come from Brooklyn, and in Brooklyn we used to barter equipment: "Whaddya got? Got a Gibson guitar? I'll trade you for my Leslie." Finally you build up what you got. So I got the Farfisa and kept it in my basement.

What kind of groups did you play in back then?

I never played in any real bands except Blondie. My interests in music were always very self-contained. I never cared to go play the high school dance or the local club or things like that. I was just in my basement with my Farfisa and my Revox tape recorder, making weird tape loops, using my voice, my bass, and the acoustic piano

Previous page: Jimmy Destri winging it with (left, top to bottom) an Oberheim 2-Voice, a Tapco board, and a Polymoog; (right, top to bottom) Roland Chorus and Space Echoes, a Farfisa dual-manual organ, and another Polymoog.

upstairs. This was when I was a teenager, living with my parents. And then my sister got me into the kind of rock and roll that I fell in love with. She was always a flipped-out, spaced-out kid, and one day she came home with this [David] Bowie album, *Images*. And I said, "What is this? It sounds like Anthony Newley gone bizarre!" I started following his path, and at the same time I was getting into T. Rex. I think new wave music is a bastardization of glam-rock. It all came out of Bowie and T. Rex; a tangent off of that was the New York Dolls, and that started the whole thing. We were one of the first post-Dolls bands, one of the first to be signed, but we still had all our pop roots behind us.

If you weren't playing in bands, what were you doing during those early years?

Before I joined Blondie, I was just in Brooklyn with my Revox. I went to art school for two years after high school, like every other musician on earth. Then I got bored with that and went to pre-medical school for two years. I was making good grades, working in a hospital and making a lot of money, and being bored out of my teeth. By this time, I was living in a flat in the East Village, and every night I would just go home to my Revox. Next, I quit my job, went totally broke, and had to move back into my mother's attic. I was looking for a gig, any kind of gig, and I began hanging around CBGB's, Max's, and other clubs in the area. I became friends with Debbie [Harry, singer] and Chris [Stein, guitarist]; this was maybe six years ago.

Were they playing in the Stilettos at that point?

Yeah, and they were just starting to form Blondie, not knowing where to go or who to play with. We had a vibe going as friends, I never even mentioned I could play anything. I think my sister told Debbie, "You know, he plays piano." And I said, "But I don't have one. I have this natty old organ, and I can fill in on bass if you need that." There were no auditions; we just got in a studio and it clicked.

And your first tour followed shortly thereafter.

The first actual tour we ever did was very beneficial to me and to every other member of the band because we were exposed to two really good artists: Iggy Pop and David Bowie. We were kids off the street but instead of treating us like that, they took their time and showed us things. David would get Debbie and show her things about staging and technique and talk to me about production and how things are done. He was really good about that. Their crew and sound people helped us out. They sort of took us under their wing. That was the time that David was very intrigued by anything new wave, running around in a black leather jacket, trying to hang out with us. We were going, "Why is this superstar trying to hang out with us?" Then we realized he was going to try to rip us off for our whole style and do *Heroes*. But I love him for it. He does it so much more artistically and unabashedly than someone like Nick Lowe, who does it tackily and cheap. I don't like the way he puts his hand in things and then says, "I was the originator." I think Nick is a nice guy, but on a lot of occasions I think you have to wonder about him. He said, "I like the way you copped Steve Nieve's sound through your set with the Farfisa." [*Ed. note: Nieve plays keyboards with the Attractions, singer Elvis Costello's backup group, whom Lowe produces.*] I said, "Nick, the Blondie album was out a year before that." How could I have copped his sound when he says he's a fan of ours and listened to it?

So you were the first to bring the Farfisa into the new wave?

Well, it was like an accident, it's not like it was planned. I never took the credit for taking the organ and bringing it back, but these other guys after me did, so it upset me a bit. It's not a real important thing to take credit for; it's bullshit. Whatever sounds I achieve are because I'm into production and I know what I'm doing behind a board. But I consider myself primarily a songwriter, and anyone who is gonna put their fist into the air and say, "I brought the tinny organ back into the new wave scene," doesn't know what he's talking about. But that's Nick's problem, not mine [*laughs*]. I started out playing the CBGB's/Max's circuit with the Farfisa and a smaller Roland synthesizer, the SH-1000, which I still use to this day because I haven't found a substitute machine to do the little "dugga-dugga-dugga" bits.

Is that the one you had on top of the Farfisa last night?

Yeah, and on my left side is the Polymoog; that and the Farfisa are the main keyboards. I play the Polymoog with my left hand. I use it for all my color textures. Whatever basis I'm gonna lay down for the Farfisa on my right is done on the Polymoog. It's an amazing machine; I love it. It's more a programmer's synthesizer than it is a player's synthesizer. Like the Yamaha CS-80, you punch in, you got it. But with the Polymoog, you can have attenuation after you punch in and you can play with what you get. You can play with the strings and make them sound strange. It's got a ribbon controller right by my fingers, so it's also very good for a keyboard player to use. The pedals are fantastic. Mixing that with the Farfisa, I've created something that just sounds like Blondie.

What did you have on top of the Polymoog?

Roland Chorus Echoes. The new models have this chorus thing and the regular tape loop echo with the various speeds. Those are real nice units, probably one of the few nice units Roland makes. The little SH-1000 is pretty awful. The only reason I use it is that I'm used to it, and I've got a commitment to so many of the songs where I used it on the album, that I have to keep it until the next album, when I can just dump it. The SH-1000 goes through a line driver, then through an MXR flanger, then into a Chorus Echo and out through my Kelsey mixer, which takes a direct balance input/output to the board. And the Polymoog again goes through the line input into the Chorus, into the other Chorus machine, and out to the Kelsey mixer. The dumb thing about the Roland Chorus Echoes is that they're mutual outputs, the A & B, so if you put a Roland and a Polymoog in them, when you play them at the same time, they get the same output. You can't individually balance them, so you have to use two machines.

You keep one of them on top of the other?

Yeah.

And you have the Kelsey between the two keyboards?

Yeah, it's a good model. And the Farfisa I run through a beefed-up Leslie rack using Yamaha heads and everything. We just gutted the Leslies, took all the old tube amps out and put in solid-stage Yamahas, with police siren drivers so I could crank it all the way up. The Farfisa has a lot of highs, and I was blowing drivers left and right because the highs were going through the power amps and the Yamahas were boosting them and blowing diaphragms and drivers. The only thing that we found that would work were police siren drivers and diaphragms and when we got them we put them into Leslies; we have two Leslies for the Farfisa alone. Every now and then, I pan the Moog into the Leslies, because I like the effect of the strings starting out in a little twin amplifier, then moving over to the Leslie going fast, and then back again.

How did you get hold of the police equipment?

One of our roadies just has a connection. This guy can get you anything to do with gear. He got the police siren drivers from the company that makes them for the police department, but it took a long time. I just added an Oberheim Two-Voice with a sequencer into my rig, but I'm not using it yet. I use most of this stuff in my studio at home; I've got a little 12-track studio in my apartment.

Has your equipment changed as you've become more successful?

The only thing that's changed is that I can go into Manny's or someplace like that, in New York, and they don't get on my back when I try out everything in the store for six hours. No, monetary success hasn't mattered, because we realized we needed the right equipment from the start. I bought a Polymoog when we were selling 14 records. I had it four years ago; I took it all over and it was the only one. It was expensive for me at the time and I just couldn't afford to get another one. So I took it all over America, to England, all over Europe. Then we took it to Australia, and at one point it broke down. We couldn't understand why. The only thing wrong with it was that one of the handtrucks for moving the gear ran over the output wire and slashed it a bit, so we resoldered the wire. At the end of our Australian gigs, we went to this island for a vacation and there was no place to store our equipment. So they put all our equipment in this World War II landing barge, one of those things where the front goes down and the soldiers come out. They came up to the beach with my keyboards and this umpteen thousand dollar synthesizer, and put it down on the beach with all this sand. I was just standing there aghast.

The Marines landed with a Polymoog?

Right. The roadies put it away all right, but it was pretty scary. Then we brought it to Japan; this is really funny. We forgot to switch the power to Japanese, which is closer to American power, so we just fried the voltage converter in it. And there we were, far away from any American equipment. We called up this Japanese guy, an electronic genius. He took out his meter and fixed it, no problem. He goes, "Very good, just like Yamaha." And I go, "Well, I think it's better." And he goes, "Yamaha big Japanese company, make motorcycle, make everything." He went into this whole trip; the guy was a Yamaha rep. I'm going, "No, no thanks." Then he showed the guitar roadies Yamaha guitar pamphlets [*laughs*]. When we came back to the States, we needed new stuff. At that point, we had a manager, who we've since gotten rid of, who wasn't really into it. We got together and made the decision that we needed about 30 grand worth of equipment. We bypassed the manager, went straight to the record company, and bought new equipment. We're at the point now where we can get what we need to work. We just get what we need to work and that's it.

Why haven't you put together a bigger collection of keyboards, then?

I could go totally nuts. I'm very proud of myself that for the past three years, I've used the same instruments. My effects lines change every now and then, but I would rather use a versatile instrument with different effects than six different instruments. And when you have a versatile instrument, you can punch things in.

Do you still use the original Farfisa?

I've got several of them. The first one is in pieces; that's gone. The one I'm using now I got in Sweden at a pawnshop. The roadies find them and they buy them; we get them for two to three thousand dollars. There's a guy in New York, Mickey Adams, who just opens them up, looks at them and susses them out right away. He just has this affinity for fixing Farfisas. I buy 'em, send 'em to him, and I get 'em back in good shape, sounding like shit, just the way I want 'em.

Why do you play only the old Farfisa, rather than the company's newer models?

The thing is, Farfisa had a sound of its own. Then they tried to become like Hammond. When Hammond made a portable, Farfisa incorporated the tone wheel to make it sound like a Hammond. Then when Hammond found the digital way to go portable without the tone wheel, Farfisa did the same thing. When ARP came out with the string thing, Farfisa did the same thing with the Soundmaker. [*Ed. Note: A Farfisa spokesperson told us that his company has never produced a tone-wheel-driven instrument.*]

So you feel that Farfisa was so concerned with keeping up with the times that it missed the chance to revive its old sound for the new wave?

Yeah. Vox is a smarter company because as soon as it started happening, they came out with the Continental again. When they see that guitarists are leaning toward a cleaner guitar sound, they come out with the AC-30s again, the Beatle amps and the Super Beatles. Instead of imitating Marshall or Fender or Mesa-Boogie, they have their own distinctive sound. Farfisa could have had that but they blew it.

One of your early heroes, Felix Cavaliere, sometimes had an organ sound similar to yours when he was with the Young Rascals.

They probably EQ'd it with a lot of high end.

It was a Hammond but it was EQ'd. I think Felix also used some Fender twins with his Leslies and that made it sound so roller-rinky.

But his sound wasn't something that moved you towards Farfisas?

No, like I said, the Farfisa was an accident. I just fell in love with it after I got it. In retrospect, after listening to all those bands for years and then playing in a group, I'll listen to bands like Shocking Blue and the Doors and think that maybe I'm achieving that now. I was influenced more by the Rascals as a songwriter, not for sound. I never liked Gene Cornish's guitar sound. I thought that he was a good player but I never liked the way they miked it, and I always thought they mixed too much keyboard. As a keyboard player, I was more interested in Procol Harum.

And Procol Harum were almost the quintessential Hammond band.

Soundwise, King Crimson was the band that I preferred. With Procol Harum, it was not Matthew Fisher's organ that I was listening for; I loved Gary Brooker's style of playing the piano behind the songs he wrote. I'd say I didn't like about 50 percent of his songs, but the way he played piano on the ones I did like really influenced the way I play piano on a lot of Blondie songs.

Could you name some of those songs?

Sure. "No Imagination," off our *Plastic letters* LP, is like a synopsis of all of Procol Harum's *Shine On Brightly*. It's a cross-ripoff between that and "Lady Day," off Lou Reed's *Berlin*. "Fan Mail" [from *Plastic Letters*] has a very heavy Brooker/ Fisher feel in the piano/organ chording underneath. Brooker had a very heavy thing about using sus4th chords, like in "Homburg" [from *Best Of Procol Harum*]. "Fan Mail is a similar type of trip. On a keyboard level, "Fan Mail" could have been a Procol track. As a matter of fact when Terry Ellis [head of Chrysalis records] heard it, it was real funny. He said, "You wanna meet Gary Brooker?" Actually, I did, and I was real impressed by him; he's very brilliant. He just wants to do other things now, like music for movies, which I think he'd be great at.

How do you approximate the King Crimson sound without a Mellotron?

Polymoog through a bit of tape echo. The Polymoog strings have the frequencies of real violins, and a Mellotron has a tape of real violins, so you put those frequencies through tape echo and you get a Mellotron. I did that on "Fade Away And Radiate" [from *Parallel Lines*]. I said, "Hey Robert [Fripp, ex-King Crimson leader], if you're gonna be on this, I may as well do a Mellotron [*laughs*]." It worked great with him.

How did that track come about?

I met Robert at the Palladium in New York when we played a gig. He came up to me and said hello. He said he was a fan of ours and listened to our stuff. We just had a great time talking. I invited him down to one of our rehearsals the next day and introduced him to Chris, and they hit it off instantly. They're both space cases and they both have the same ideas on the guitar. Chris asked him to collaborate on guitars on "Fade Away And Radiate." And he loved to do it. He's just a real good guy to work with; he's a real good musician and he's got great ideas. He'd make a brilliant producer if some big record company would give him the bucks to do something good. Because he's in such an artistic vein, they don't want to haggle with that format.

What do you use in the sequencer-like intro to "Heart Of Glass" onstage?

A Roland rhythm machine, Compu-Rhythm. It's a real good one because it's got an external clock input where you can get them really in sync. I got that awhile ago; it's the same thing that's on the record.

Didn't you do a two-week European tour before starting work on Parallel Lines *?*

Yeah. We went over there and were totally bored for two weeks. There is nothing worse for a musician than to do lip-syncing.

Did that boredom translate into extra energy once you got into the studio?

That's what happened. The album has got at least seven singles on it. The writing is so concentrated, it works perfectly. There are twelve original Blondie songs on it, no covers, the majority of them written by Chris, Debbie, and myself. We spent a long time on the sounds of this record, as opposed to the arrangements, because [producer Mike] Chapman didn't have to pull them out of us. We did it at the Power Station, which is the state-of-the-art studio in New York now. They have everything you need; it's real comfortable. We had the Kinks next door. They came boppin' back and forth because we've become friends with them. Actually, their keyboard player broke his arm and he went back to England, so [singer/guitarist] Ray Davies was stuck in the studio. I walked in one day and he said, "Hey, how you doing? Would you . . ." And I said, "No, I gotta go next door." And he said, "Well, I'd really love you to play." And I said, "Ray, if you want me, you get my sound. I'm not gonna play Ray Davies piano parts." So I guess he got some studio guy

and Ray did some himself. I told him if he wanted to do it, he could move his session into our studio where my rig was and build Kinks music in our spare time and I wouldn't do it any other way. I wasn't even interested in the money. I just wanted to be on a Kinks record, but on my terms. They're real great guys, and it was a nice inspiration having them recording next door to us. Then they left and Springsteen came in. Bruce and Frankie [Infante] are from the same neighborhood and they became real tight, trading guitars back and forth; we used Bruce's Country Gentleman. We had a good time with those guys.

Do you record the keyboard part with the rhythm section?

Basically, what I do in the studio a lot is lay down my left hand with Nigel and Clem before anything else, and I'll double up, use two hands to do the left-hand part. We have a lot of that on the last album: keyboard, bass, and drums. "Heart Of Glass" was done real strange. We did attempt after attempt after attempt. Finally it was my idea to throw everybody else out of the studio. I said to Chapman, "Let's put a click track and synthesizer down." And that's what we did, looking at the lyrics as we went. We went through the whole thing like that. Then we put the Poly on after that, doing the swells and everything, and then put the levels down. We put all the other keyboards on, keeping the levels down, the organ solo and everything. We brought Clem in to play with the first dugga-dugga-dugga part, then put the guitars on. Now the guys didn't know that I had played on the whole thing already. Then we put the levels of the keyboards up and they said, "Whoa, what's going on here?"

You felt it would be easier for them to get the rhythm parts down without hearing the swells.

Yeah. It was fun to do—real clinical, but at the same time, fun. It was *real* fun watching their faces when we brought the keyboards up from the background.

Any plans to do a live album?

I'd love to do a live Blondie album. This morning I was doing a mix of a show we did in Dallas with the 24-track mobile unit, and after we're done with it I think we'll definitely have a good live Blondie album. We may need a couple of more tracks to flesh it out, but the sound is amazing. I found a real good studio last night for the mixing—Kendum Studios in Burbank [CA]. It has a fantastic computerized board; when I came in it said, "Hello, Jimmy. Would you like some coffee?" I felt like I was mixing with HAL.

Michael Davis

Devo
The New Classicism

August 1981 — You're using three separate keyboard setups onstage now. Is that a Minimoog that Jerry plays in the back?

Mark Mothersbaugh: A Minimoog, yeah. He went through a lot of things to arrive at the Mini. At first, we were using a Wasp, which turned out to be real unpredictable. Sometimes that heat from the stage lights would make the thing start playing these riffs before anybody even touched it. It was really funny; it would sound like Stanley Clarke on Ex-Lax.

Mark, what is that synthesizer set at right angles to your main keyboard arrangement?

Mothersbaugh: That's a stock ARP Odyssey, and I only use it for three or four songs.

Bob Casale: When we go on the road, we try to stay with things that can be found and fixed.

Mothersbaugh: We learned some things in the past about exotic, homegrown equipment.

Casale: It doesn't make it.

Mothersbaugh: Things that couldn't be repaired were horrible. We had one of the first Prophets and took it on a tour. It was the worst, a total headache, breaking down every second or third night. We carried a full-time technician with us, and we were still constantly on the phone, screaming at the Sequential Circuits people. We even paid to fly some of their people to Boston to repair them, because we couldn't find any replacement instruments in the area.

Casale: Plus, they hadn't perfected their memory circuits, so we had to sit down, 15 minutes before a show, and try to program the thing from scratch if something went wrong.

Have your impressions of the Prophet changed since then?

Previous page: Devo's Mark Mothersbaugh as Bijou boy, fiddling with a Wasp synthesizer. "I found the exact same sound on an eleven-dollar toy ray gun that we used a five thousand-dollar synthesizer to get on our third album."

Mothersbaugh: This tour, we used it again. We tried out every other programmable polyphonic synthesizer on the market, and we just preferred the versatility of the Prophet. So we went out with a backup one and we only had a few minor problems. They started getting senile near the end of the tour, after about 90 shows, but those were about the first problems we had.

How many units do you have in the main keyboard setup?

Casale: Four—the Prophet, Odyssey, Minimoog, and an EML 500 and Poly Box.

What about the Minimoog?

Will you interface it with a Sequential Circuits programmer too?

Mothersbaugh: Right now I'm not sure. We might just have a tech person work out settings on it with us. Since only the keyboard actually has to be onstage, we might have someone programming synthesizers for us offstage. We had a Minimoog from the beginning; it was a very early one, with oscillators that drifted. When we played "Mongoloid" [from *Are We Not Men?*], for instance, I'd tune it up and set up the oscillators to a full chord for the synthesizer break in the middle of the song. And the minute-and-a-half it took to get there was all it took for the three oscillators to go out of tune. So we were trying to find a way around that, and we found a Poly Box. What that does is take the first oscillator as its source, and it splits the notes off like an organ keyboard, so you can play full chords on it. Then there's a memory switch that holds it, and it'll follow this oscillator so it will simulate a polyphonic synthesizer sound.

Any other keyboards?

Mothersbaugh: We also had a Clavinet, which we used to use with a lot of devices to mutate the sound. At one time we used Electro-Harmonix frequency analyzers on every instrument and voice. It was one of those things that came out for guitar players, and nobody liked them. It wasn't like a wah-wah or fuzz tone; it just destroyed the pitch and made everything you played sound weird. We used really cheap devices like that. Then my brother Jim, who was our first drummer, left to experiment with electronics. He worked with electronic drums; at the time, there were no Syndrums or Synares available. He'd do things like put pickups on the drumheads, so we'd get an acoustic drum sound plus this noise that he would put through ring modulators and Echoplexes. He successfully made his cymbals sound like trash can lids being banged together.

Is that what led you into getting involved with electronics more seriously?

Mothersbaugh: Yeah. We got into experimenting with tape recorders and buying all the toys that were available on the market, like Radio Shack organ kits for eleven dollars, and Optigons. That was one of my favorite instruments. I had one about four years ago; it got stolen, but I've just purchased another one, so it's one of my favorite keyboards again. It's one of the most perverted instruments ever made. They had optical disks; you could throw two of them in at once and have two instruments playing at the same time, like a piano and guitar which weren't even in the same key. You could put the disks in upside down and make the banjos play sucking sounds. Every time I sit down and play it, it makes me laugh.

Where did you ever find one?

Mothersbaugh: They're easy to find in L.A. I think I bought one for a couple hundred dollars. I even saw one selling for twenty dollars when I left for New York. You know, people who bought them have left them sitting in their basements, and now they're thinking, "Boy, why did I spend $450 for the thing?" They don't want them anymore.

Do you remember the Vako Orchestron?

Mothersbaugh: Yeah, it was basically like the Optigon. I wasn't interested in it, though, because I never wanted to do voices and strings and pretty stuff. I was more interested in hideous sounds. I liked the ones that made you think of someone wearing madras and plaid and a polka-dot tie all at the same time.

Casale: We had a Mellotron.

Mothersbaugh: For a while, but we could not keep up the payments on it.

Casale: So we took it apart [*laughs*].

Mothersbaugh: We did a lot of experimenting with things that weren't even instruments, including electric appliances, gated TV noise, and early PAIA setups where we tried to play modules that were laying all over tables. It was like having a Gilbert chemistry set. Then after we did a record, our problem became one of doing the same sound two nights in a row. When we had all week to prepare for a gig, it was okay. We'd drive to CBGB's or Max's Kansas City in New York with two weeks before we had to play, so we'd get all our junk assembled before performing for a night or two. But when we had to play every single night, we couldn't keep working on equipment maintenance ourselves. We had to find a way to stabilize our equipment so that we could play the same songs twenty nights in a row.

Did you use any of your homemade gear on your first album, Are We Not Men?, *which was produced by Brian Eno?*

Mothersbaugh: We used a little bit of everything, but at that time we mostly used a Clavinet, an ARP Odyssey, and the Minimoog with the senile oscillators.

Casale: We also used a Reverbrato on a lot of stuff.

Mothersbaugh: It was sort of a reverb/vibrato effect that Acoustic built into its amps about ten years ago, then quickly dropped. I don't exactly understand the setup, but there's something like a tin can that spins around inside this thing and makes this really horrid sound that we like. We also had an all-manual drum box that Vox made. You couldn't program it; you just played it by pushing this little punch board.

What kind of drum machines do you own nowadays?

Mothersbaugh: I have a couple of Rolands, the SPV-355 and SVC-350, a Vox drum box, and the Linn LM-1 drum computer. Before I found out about the Linn machine, I was just trying to do synthesized drum tracks that sounded good, and the Roland sounded real good. It has an envelope follower that just trails whatever pulse changes are happening into a synthesizer sound, so it gets crazy. The Vox drum box is kind of nice because it's manually controlled. There are a couple of foot pedals you can hook up too; you can assign two functions to your feet and play the others by hand. The Linn has separate volume controls and outputs for each of the drums, which is important when you use a drum box a lot, like I do; usually you just have one output, so if you put on a high-hat, you've got to equalize it off the same pots you use to equalize the bass and snare drums. The problem with all the drum machines is that they are all basically gated noise, and that's what they sound like. Even the Linn doesn't sound *exactly* like real drums; it's at some nice spot in between. You have the visceral gut hit you get with a kick or a snare or the toms, but then you also have the capability of muting it electronically.

Have you modified the Linn at all?

Mothersbaugh: The one I have has been modified, and I've changed the chips in it a couple of times. We've made our own chips. I think I took out the cowbell and tambourine; I only used the tambourine on one song on the new album. It was highly affected, so it didn't even

come out sounding like a tambourine. Anyway, in their places I put in pulses, which I used on about five of the songs. They trigger two different sequencers, so where I would normally be programming in the cowbell line, I end up programming or triggering the sequencer. I mean, like any other high technology stuff, it's really scary, and we've got to have a technician around all the time in case things go wrong.

Do you still shy away from using the drum machine onstage?

Mothersbaugh: I don't think it's really together enough yet to take it onstage. We've been working on some prototypes for drums, where we burnt the real sounds of Alan's [Devo drummer Alan Myers] drums onto digital chips, and now we've got them on Synare-type pads. We might use them on tour if all the bugs are worked out by that time.

Who did the modifications on your Linn machine?

Mothersbaugh: Basically, my brother Jim, who's our tech person in residence. Roger Linn was helpful too. He visited the studio, and when a chip wasn't working he showed me how to make it work. Jim also modified all of our synthesizers and some of our other equipment.

Are there any other keyboards you're interested in exploring?

Mothersbaugh: Well, this may sound awfully jaded, but I think I have all the keyboards I'm interested in having. My biggest gripe about all this equipment, though, is that so little of it is modular and interchangeable. The only sequencer that really works right with a Prophet is the Sequential Circuits sequencer. Roland makes a really good digital sequencer, but it only works right with a Roland synthesizer. You see, the way the Prophet keyboard is set up, the first key on it is almost one volt, where on most keyboards it's zero. For the first couple of octaves, it'll sound like it's in tune, but by the time you're in the upper register, the tuning gets weird. Normally, if you set the sequencer on the keyboard voltage add, you can change the pitch of the sequence with the keyboard, but because it's one volt off, when you hit a G on the keyboard, it plays an F on the sequencer. Since this is polyphonic, you get the G and the F both. The sequence will stay one note flat of what you're doing on the keyboard.

Why do you use tapes instead of sequencers onstage?

Mothersbaugh: We've had problems with the technology. We're afraid to take sequencers onstage. They're either really complex and delicate, or they're too crude and untrustworthy. The only way we can deal satisfactorily with this is to put it on tape. The tape tracks are pretty minimal. It's usually either just the sequencer, or the sequencer plus a click track of some sort that only we can hear onstage.

Do you use the click track to cue yourselves with the films and other effects you use in your show?

Mothersbaugh: Yeah. We'll have maybe four clicks. We spend probably as much time as anybody working with the monitor man. There's a lot of work for him to do, what with movie cues and where to send the sound off a tape or off a board. We leave our amps offstage, and some of the instruments go directly into the monitor board, so that puts a lot of weight on his shoulders.

What kinds of amps do you use?

Mothersbaugh: The keyboards and the bass don't use any. Only the guitarist uses amps. He goes back and forth between Music Man and a small Fender. We have mixing consoles so the monitor mixer gets a sub-mix from us. On the last tour the monitor man got three or four mixes from the keyboards, and on the next tour he'll probably get a couple more.

Do you handle all the effects onstage?

Mothersbaugh: We do almost all of them onstage. There's a sound man out in the hall who does some of the vocal effects.

Do you still use the Echoplex?

Mothersbaugh: Not any more. On the new album we spent a lot of time trying to get the same effects using studio echo chambers that we had gotten on our demo tapes. We even used the reverb in Bob's Music Man guitar amp for a couple of songs, because the only way to get that chintzy reverb sound I like from our demo tapes was to use a chintzy reverb unit, although the studio was loaded with great echo effects. We finally had to go out and buy a cheap little Tapco.

Did you learn a lot in your work with producers Ken Scott and Brian Eno?

Mothersbaugh: Yeah, we learned not to overwork the songs. Some of our past songs were overworked, and the productions were overdone. I don't think either of the first two albums sounded as good as they could have. They were either over-produced or under-produced. When the first one [*Are We Not Men?*] was recorded, it had a great sound, but when it got mastered, it sounded a lot like a transistor radio. We were more careful with *Freedom Of Choice*, so we

oversaw the mastering of it.

Which one was under-produced, and which was over-produced?

Mothersbaugh: You could probably get into it cut by cut, but it gets real obvious if you just play the songs we recorded on a TEAC tape recorder in our basement, which were released on Stiff Records, and compare them with the versions of the same tunes we did on our first album: They get drained of their essence. Those songs turn out consistently better live and on demo tapes. A lot of it comes down to conflicts with outside people who don't understand what we're doing.

Why did you get involved with them?

Mothersbaugh: It was almost by accident. David Bowie came to see us at Max's Kansas City, before we were signed with Warners, and said he really liked the band and wanted to produce us. Brian Eno loaned us money to fly to Germany to do the session with Bowie, so we went there, not knowing whether he'd be able to produce us or not, because [his film role in] *Just A Gigolo* was starting to take up a lot of his time. He did show up at the studio a few times, but he was sick and he just laid in the back of the studio, semiconscious, so Eno wound up producing us. We were floating around like some sort of virus. Our record company had no faith; they didn't know what the hell we were doing, and they thought we were crazy to begin with.

When you record nowadays, do you go in knowing exactly what you want, or do you just have basic sounds in mind that your engineer helps you realize?

Mothersbaugh: It depends. We usually have strong opinions. We've had problems in the past wrestling with the people at the board, but we were careful in looking for the engineer we work with now, Larry Alexander.

How did you find him?

Mothersbaugh: We sent postcards to all the engineers at the major studios, with 25 fill-in-the-blank questions, like: "Are we not (blank)?" and "You must (blank) it." Larry was the only guy who got them all right.

Were there any technical criteria?

Mothersbaugh: We wanted someone who could get good drum sounds. We've been looking for a different drum sound than we had on our first albums. Also, Bob 2 [Casale] has come forward as the resident engineer in the band. He did a major portion of the engineering on our demo tapes, and he's doing a lot of work on our next album.

How are your present recording techniques

different from what you were doing earlier?

Mothersbaugh: For one thing, we don't use headphones for microphones, which was one of our earlier techniques, except on rare occasions. You'll probably think that's how everything was laid down on the second album, but in fact we only did that on a couple of guitar tracks. We do most of the keyboard work with most of us standing in the control room, except for the drums and vocals.

Do you feed the signal out to the amps while you're in the control room?

Mothersbaugh: Yeah, even after it's down on tape.

What about the keyboard feed?

Mothersbaugh: Our biggest problem in the past was always how to make the keyboards sound as good in the studio as they did on our crummy TEAC tape recorder. It took us a long time to figure out how to make a synthesizer sound as dirty and distorted in a studio as it does on our cheap equipment. We had to find a way to make high tech sound like low tech, and I think we achieved it by running it back to the speakers. Whenever we could we used SM58 microphones.

How did you do the whip crack in "Whip It" [from Freedom Of Choice]*?*

Mothersbaugh: That was on the EML. We had to mess around to get it.

You're using synthesizers more in your music these days than you did on your first albums. Are you using them more for writing material as well?

Mothersbaugh: Yeah, definitely. In the process of experimenting, I find some sound I like, then I write a song, kind of as an excuse for the sound to exist. Often all the parts are written on synthesizer and taped on a TEAC 4-track before we work with them as a band. But then we'll also take a sequencer pattern that Bob put together, and play it with a sequencer pattern that Alan wrote, and lyrics that Jerry wrote, and then borrow other parts from other people. There's no set pattern to how our songs come about. Usually all it takes is a good nightmare to get things going.

Casale: A lot of *Freedom Of Choice* was written entirely on synthesizer.

Mothersbaugh: We spent a lot of time on that album writing with everybody together in the room, which wasn't always the case in the past. Because of that, everybody had more of a say in the writing. On the first album, all the bass parts were bass guitar, except for a couple of doubled lines. On the second album, about a third of the bass lines were synthesized, and on *Freedom Of Choice* it was all synthesized bass except for one track. That's the direction we want to follow. It's just that when you're doing it for more than just a rap, you have to have sounds that you feel are really better than the bass or guitar or drum sounds to replace those instruments with.

Did you make a conscious decision to avoid pursuing the traditional orchestral synthesizer route?

Mothersbaugh: We just ignored all the horrible aspects of how companies package their own synthesizers so that you can't patch them together. Their whole idea is to try to get you to collect all these synthesizers and waste all your money on multiple keyboards to get the effects you want. We tried to ignore all that and just go for sounds. As a matter of fact, I found the exact same sound on an eleven-dollar toy ray gun that we used a five thousand-dollar synthesizer to get on our third album, so I ended up using the ray gun onstage. That was one less synthesizer we had to take on tour.

Casale: We take a reductive approach to the use of keyboards. Rather than using many layers of textures, we just use a few and make them physical. It's more direct.

Mothersbaugh: It's easier to come up with equipment now than it ever was. There are all sorts of great toys out there. The Muson, for instance, is an incredible little fourteen-dollar Japanese instrument. It's got a single-note tuneable mono electric organ keyboard, and you can make four-note, six-note, eight-note, or ten-note sequences, with control of speed and pitch. You can have either organ mode or organ and sequencer, while playing the organ along with the sequencer. And there are a lot of toys like this out there, like ray guns with a dozen sounds for six dollars. So getting into electronic music is easier than ever, but at the same time, I don't think having more equipment necessarily means you're going to make better music. In fact, I think it's really obvious that when most people get more money and equipment, they lose sight of what it was all about in the first place. But there are kids out there with incredible ideas. We think it's time that they should be aired.

Michael Davis

Human League
Salvation through Synthesis

October 1982 — *Looking back on the first version of Human League, what are your thoughts on what the band was trying to do, and how successful it was at doing it?*

Philip Oakey: Well, it's amazing to me that I could have made two records with a group without knowing about hi-hats. Pathetic, isn't it?

Adrian Wright: We all liked pop songs with words you could sing along to and choruses you could remember. We wanted to write a song that would be as good as a song written by Carole King and Gerry Goffin.

Yet your methods for composing were somewhat unusual. How did you put your songs together?

Oakey: Instead of doing a simple rhythm, writing a song and then maybe adapting the rhythm so that it bolstered the song a bit, we'd do a very complicated rhythm and say, "That's fantastic! Let's put some tunes over that," which is no good at all because the rhythm is really the last thing to consider, I think, in a song. We're not African drummers; we're trying to write pop songs, and pop songs are about melodies and chord changes. So we'd end up with these horrible crashing noises that sounded good on their own and these things that just didn't fit over the top. Although it was sort of interesting and very intellectual, it didn't get us anywhere.

But you did create an impact, as reflected in the number of British synthesizer bands that popped up after your first recordings.

Wright: Oh, yeah, we were about the trendiest thing in the world for a week or so in 1978.

Previous page: Susan Sully, Phil Oakey and
Joanne Catherall of the Human League. Right:
Oakey, Adrian Wright, Catherall, Sully, Ian Burden,
and Jo Callis in a publicity still.

Maybe that inspired a lot of bands to take up
synthesizers.

*Why exactly did the first Human League split
up?*

Wright: We split up for personal reasons, not
musical ones. We just got sick of each other.
They [Ian Marsh and Martyn Ware] left and we
had to do a tour, so we got loads of people in. In
England, everybody wrote us off and said we'd
had it.

Oakey: Yeah. Me and Adrian [Wright] would
not have made any good records, it's as simple as
that. It's possible that we could go on and make
some good records now, but it's only because
we've learned from the people we've been working with.

*Your current lineup seems to have assembled
in a most haphazard way.*

Oakey: I can't imagine how it came off. I'd
seen Ian Burden in his group Graph in Sheffield. I
always thought he looked good onstage. After
the first Human League split up and we went on
tour, we had to use tapes of the old band
because we had only two weeks before the tour
began to put a new act together, and we couldn't
do it in that amount of time. We wanted to swing
toward the visual and just admit that we were
using tapes as much as we always had. Ian
worked the tape recorder, and we agreed that if
he wasn't doing anything on a song, he would
just sit in a chair onstage and let the tape
recorder roll. We got the girls [Susanne Sulley
and Joanne Catherall] at the same time for backing vocals and to make it look a bit more interesting. We got back from the tour and then Ian
dropped in at the studio.

Ian Burden: I was going to come down and
help because you said you had to record an
album [*Dare*], and I said something to you about
helping with the playing on it.

*You wound up playing synthesizers, mainly
for bass lines, on* Dare *and joining the band. As a
guitarist at the time, how did you wind up on
keyboards?*

Burden: Having a guitarist play keyboards
leads to a different approach to things. If you play
an instrument you're not used to, you come with
different ideas.

Oakey: He was the first person I knew who
would be impressed more by the bass lines of a
song instead of by the general effect, so he seems
to be our bass line player.

*How did your most recent addition, Jo Callis,
join up?*

Oakey: Jo and Adrian got friendly because

they both like to collect toys—spin-off toys from
TV shows, comics and that sort of thing. So Jo
came down to visit Adrian and we just picked up
from there. The only problem with Jo is that he's
got so much energy, you can't turn him off
sometimes. It astonishes me that he's playing
keyboards with us. The first time he ever played
keyboards onstage times. was when we were
number three in the charts; that puts a hell of a
lot of pressure on someone. And he's not just
playing one note here and there, but chords with
both hands on every song.

*Then why do you sometimes hire Mike Doug-
las, who tours as a spare keyboardist with Orchestral Manoeuvres In The Dark, to augment your
keyboard parts onstage?*

Burden: On the album there are so many
overdubs that there are more parts in each song
than there are people to play them, so we get in
an extra keyboard player.

Oakey: So what do you want to know about
keyboards?

What happens when you push the keys down?

Oakey: Just exactly what you're not expecting
a lot of times. Jo's been known to punch up the
wrong program for the start of "Things That
Dreams Are Made Of."

Jo Callis: I used to do that a lot. On the first
tour, all my presets were in alphabetical order.
Then we changed the running order, and it took
me ages to get used to the fact that we went, like,
from G to F and then to H. Another good one is
leaving the arpeggio going in "Circus of Death"
[from *Reproduction*].

Oakey: Always good for a laugh.

What kind of drum machines are you using?

Oakey: We use the Linn, which has a limited
memory capacity, so we have a cassette machine
which reloads it halfway through the set. While
we're reloading it, we use the Roland 808 drum
machine, which is good for programming patterns, but not for programming a whole song,
and it doesn't have as nice a sound. And when
we do encores, we use the 808 again. We drive a
lot of stuff off of it. We've got the pulse line,
which comes out of one of the drum tracks on
both the Linn and the Roland, driving the
Yamaha CS-15. To get the Syndrum sound, we
use a Simmons SDSV drum synthesizer, which is
quite a nice machine, but a bit slow in triggering.
We did a whole show with Ian [Burden] bashing
the pads on it, and we couldn't understand why
the rhythm track wasn't in time. It actually takes a
little bit of build-up time to trigger. What else do
we have?

Wright: We have your old Korg with the two keys missing.

Oakey: Which we use on one number, "Darkness" [from *Dare*]. It's a Korg 770. I don't think very many of them were made. Everyone got the K-700S [Minikorg] because it looked nicer.

What does each member of the band play?

Oakey: Jo's got a Roland Jupiter-8. Mike [Douglas, auxiliary keyboardist] has a Jupiter-8, the drum equipment, and the Korg, and he has the SDSV on his stand. Near Ian [Burden] is the bass unit, which is the Roland GR-33B bass guitar synthesizer, and the Yamaha CS-15. I have a microphone, and the girls each have one too.

Aren't you playing anything on stage?

Oakey: I'm just playing those little runs on "Love Action" [from *Dare*] on the Yamaha. We trigger it, and it does all this noise all the way through; I make it change pitch when it's supposed to. I've got a feeling that our sound man turns it off at the front anyway, and just leaves it in as an indulgence to me.

Were you playing more in concert in the original Human League?

Oakey: No one was playing anything onstage then; almost everything was on tape. Martyn used to play certain things that were already on tape. Ian [Marsh] used to put the occasional white noise crash into things, and he had one tune to play in one song that he used to get wrong. The rest of it was on a Sony 2-track tape recorder. I was singing live, and Adrian [Wright] was doing his slides live. It was horrible.

What sort of equipment did the original band have?

Oakey: The original Human League only started because of the availability of the original Roland System 100. It looked like an old radio—great big units with one oscillator and an expander unit. Ian Marsh got it on credit, along with two analog sequencers. We did our drums by using white noise filtered with a lot of resonance. He used the second bank of pots on the analog sequencers to time the first bank. We did all our drums like that, and it was rotten. The bass drum sound is critical on a record. You can't sell anything for dancing nowadays without a good bass drum.

What specifically was the problem?

Oakey: As soon as the oscillators got low enough for the bass drum, they became unstable and began fluctuating all over the place. You'd get maybe two really good beats and five rotten ones. You couldn't have a bass and snare on the same beat because you'd get a step where your voltage was so high that it opened your filters up and let the white noise through. We wouldn't touch a drum machine on two albums because we didn't like how they sounded. Around that time Martyn got the Korg 700S. It was very popular; you couldn't sequence it, but it was very cheap and usable, and very adaptable, with two oscillators, ring modulation, and everything you could want out of a keyboard synthesizer. But he got bored with it really quickly, then went out and got a Roland SH-3A, which was absolute rubbish, just a rotten synthesizer, made for disaffected keyboard players or something. Then we got the Roland JP-4, which was potentially good but very unstable. It had only eight programmable memories and eight presets. I had my 770, which we still use. Then the group broke up.

How did you use your tape recorders?

Oakey: We used them a lot to record bass lines at half speed and things like that. I think using tape recorders and sequencers was at least as important as using synthesizers at all. They enabled us to get around the fact that we were very bad keyboard players, and to get our ideas over a little bit. Then there was the problem that we never had the money to buy the devices to sync the synthesizers to tape.

You did your syncing by ear?

Oakey: We did a bit of that, but I guess our biggest problem was that our complicated rhythms never varied. We couldn't even, say, go into a bass drum section while someone sings, or leave off the hi-hat cymbal. We were stuck. The song would start and end with the same rhythm, and it wouldn't change anywhere in between, which is dull. When we're live now, we work with one basic rhythm for each song, one variation on it for the chorus, and maybe a fill for both of them. It's not complicated—we don't use up too much memory on the Linn—but it's enough. You've got your fills there, and you can go from a swing rhythm of some kind to something a bit less swinging.

Burden: You find that the least is the most effective as far as the drum machine goes.

Oakey: When you're recording with the Linn, you can program up to a hundred different things. And it's very good for people who haven't had a lot of experience with computers. Do you know the little Roland 808s and 606s? They've got 16 divisions in each bar, so you can turn it to, say, snare, press 5 and 13, and you've got the snare at those positions. I like that. I like being able to see that, because I haven't got the feel for rhythm that Ian has. Ian does it by ear, and it's very good for that too.

Burden: That's the great thing about the Linn as far as being a musician goes: It's all real time, rather than on sort of computer terms.

Phil, do you play anything on the recordings?

Oakey: I don't play anything on the recordings, do I?

Wright: You played the entire "I Am The Law" [from *Dare*] on your own.

Oakey: That's because there's not much in it. We program a lot of things on the [Roland] MicroComposer; that does a lot of the more difficult parts.

You just store the parts you need in it, then punch up the program in concert?

Oakey: Or the whole song from start to finish, if you're careful with it. It's a matter of juggling it around and wondering which things suit the songs. At the moment, we're thinking that maybe you can microcompose things too much.

Burden: Especially after we've played live.

Oakey: I was all for the MicroComposer until Jo and Ian started pointing out that sometimes things sound better played by hand.

Burden: Sometimes you go back into the studio to hear what's been programmed, and you're really disappointed. All the beats are in the right place, it's all logical and correct, but it doesn't feel right. That happened on "Sound Of The Crowd." The bass line was programmed up, but I thought it just didn't feel right, so we did it again. You can't play it perfectly, like a machine.

Oakey: And that's good. Ian, didn't you play most of the bass lines on "Don't You Want Me" yourself on the keyboard?

Burden "Seconds" [from *Dare*] was done entirely by hand, I know that. No MicroComposer on that one. There was quite a lot of manual playing on "Don't You Want Me." Didn't we use the Korg for the bass on that one?

Oakey: You do whatever seems best at the time. If it's not sounding right, then you do it some other way. We were in a rush when we recorded the album.

Wright: Even though it took months, we were in a rush.

Oakey: We were worried about studio time. We'd spent all the money on the studio, so we sort of panicked when, say, Jo couldn't get his elephant sound exactly right on "Hard Times" [from *League Unlimited Orchestra*.]

Callis: I think that was the saxophone preset of a JP-4, but it sounds nothing like a saxophone. They should just say "elephant" instead.

Oakey: Why did you want an elephant there?

Callis: Well, I pressed the button thinking it was going to be a saxophone, like a Junior Walker thing. Then I thought, well, that doesn't sound much like a saxophone, but it's a real bitchin' elephant.

How much synthesizer programming does you co-producer, Martin Rushent, do?

Oakey: He did all of the programming on *Dare*. We'd never seen a MicroComposer before. We've since bought our own, and I can program it now, so I'll be doing a bit of that in the future. Normally, when we used Martin's equipment, he'd program it and I would very often modify it a little bit. When we worked on our equipment, it would be the other way around. Martin's not very interested in getting accurate or wonderful sounds; all he's interested in is getting enough to support the melodies. Melodies and song structures are his basic interest. Because we didn't have much time on that album, we didn't spend more than a few minutes programming anything. We'd just come up with the first sound, then he'd use his effects units to turn it into exactly what he wanted. Next time around, I think we'll be more careful.

Do you try to imitate horn and string textures in your programs?

Callis: There are quite a lot of obviously stringy or brassy parts on our records, a simulated horn sound, for instance, with maybe the attack of a horn. Then for some things, you just get a sound that works, whatever it is.

Oakey: If we want something that sounds like a trumpet, we put in five or ten minutes' work and come up with something that sounds adequately like a trumpet. If you're going for the cliche real trumpet sound, why mess around? Go get a trumpet.

Burden: One of the interesting things about synthesizers is, if you want something that's got the feel of a trumpet, you try to achieve that with a synthesizer, but you don't quite get it. You come up with something new, something you wouldn't have deliberately set out to get—an approximation.

Oakey: And if you're using the MicroComposer, you can combine sounds in a very accurate way that you could never otherwise have done. If we wanted a trumpet, but with a hard attack that trumpets don't have, we could, say, hit a bell, but you could never hit the bell at just the right time to combine with the trumpet sound. But with the MicroComposer, you can set up the trumpet, set up the bell, and play them together perfectly for a new sound. The horn sound on "Don't You Want Me" has a lot of string parts in it that are a mixture of *pizzicato* strings and horns. Martin and I kept going back and adding sounds to it. I think it's really a good sound, and one that's never been on a record before. The problem with MicroComposers is that they are in time all the time. You just have to send them a little bit out of time occasionally. Say you set up a string section on a Fairlight and do it with a MicroComposer. Instead of having a string section of seven violinists, you get the sound of one violin that you go back and record again; it'll be so close that it'll actually phase. No violinist is going to start at exactly the same time as another violinist, so you can't get that real, rich sound

unless there's something slightly "wrong" with it. All the effects in the world won't make up for that.

Burden: If you do a series of passes on one sound, you can slow the tape down slightly the second time you record it, then do one with the tape sped up slightly the third time. You can get a nice spectrum of sound that way. But when you're using the MicroComposer, you still have that business of having every note start at exactly the same place. Detuning helps, but what needs to be done beyond that is to delay and push things just a bit further.

Will you be using primarily synthesizers for the foreseeable future?

Oakey: Primarily, I'd say yes. But I think that we will very likely be admitting other instruments if we think they're necessary. We've proven what we had to prove, that we could get the hit records only using synthesizers, and now that we've done that, we're taken very seriously, and we've got to compete in the same market as everyone else. The gimmick will hold you for one album; after that, you have to work for excellence. No one's going to be impressed with a gimmick for very long. There's a lot of music coming out of England now, a lot of competition.

Burden: But I don't think it's a gimmick. I don't think we'd have gotten where we've gotten except that we chose to do it by a different route.

Oakey: But I think we did go overboard to a certain extent, and people were right when they said, "Don't be stupid." We made it a selling point that our music was only synthesizers, and that we wouldn't have a drummer, and *those* were the gimmicks.

What makes you different, in your opinion, from most of the synthesizer bands you mentioned coming out of England now?

Oakey: We're a song band. We believe that song bands will make it, and the rest won't. You can push it so far on silly things like having a pretty face, and there are bands that use synthesizers just because they're synthesizers. But the song bands will push on through—the ABC's, the Imaginations, the Police. We're lucky because this band has a bunch of guys with melodies in their heads.

Burden: The thing is, the people in this group have all had a go of it in previous years. We've all had previous attempts at success and made a lot of mistakes. So the new Human League got together afresh after learning from those mistakes. We've just managed to get a few things right this time.

Michael Davis

Thomas Dolby
Echoes from an Electronic Future

August 1983 — There are more chord changes in your tunes than one might expect to find in contemporary pop music.

Oh yeah. I think that traditional changes are rather boring. When I was first starting out, I quickly became taken by the jazz innovators. I was really into the slow stuff. Moody jazz piano is what really interested me. People like Bill Evans, Thelonious Monk, Dave Brubeck, and all the way back to Art Tatum. I used to copy their records by slowing down the turntable. It was their chords that interested me, not the runs. I never liked fast things, and I could never get into the discipline to practice scales or any of that. It was always the chords for me. Certain chord sequences made me feel certain ways. So I built up a vocabulary of chord changes that said something to me emotionally. That's the vocabulary I draw on. It's far easier to be individual with those kinds of chords. If you're just using straight fours of major and minor chords with the occasional 7th, it's very difficult to make a chord sequence sound good in and of itself unless you're playing electric guitar with a thousand watts of power.

You traveled quite a bit when you were younger. When did you actually get a chance to start playing an instrument?

My father was an archaeologist, so we moved around the Mediterranean quite a bit. My first music experience came when I'd play percussion using my mother's cutlery along to the Shadows. I suppose the next stage was singing in a choir at school. I was the only kid in class who could sing alto, although my voice wasn't particularly well suited for it. I started playing piano and guitar by

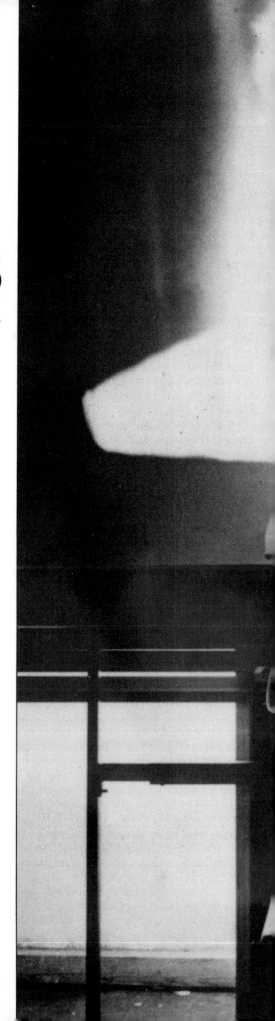

Previous page: Thomas Dolby, overcoming science for fun and profit, with his PPG event Prozessors and Generators.

ear when I was 11 or 12. I could hear my favorite tunes in my head and I learned to pick them out. I used to play a lot of folk music on the guitar. Things by Woody Guthrie and Joan Baez. On piano, it was always jazz. I played a little in restaurants and bars. On guitar I busked a bit, playing the Metro [the subway], doing Dylan and other things familiar to people so they would pay money to hear it.

When did you start to develop your own style?

It wasn't until I discovered synthesizers, when I was 16 or so, that my music became individual. I had this terrible tendency to mimic things, which I've finally overcome. I can tell now when I'm being myself and when I'm mimicking something. But I never discovered the original side to myself until I started playing synthesizers back in '75 or '76, just about when the punk thing was starting. I was back in London with no job and very little money. I used to go to a lot of the punk clubs; I was a punk for a while. But what was interesting for me was that the kids who were up onstage had been through the same things as me. Musically, it wasn't stimulating because it was just three chords and they were badly played. But there was an energy in it, and there was an empathy between the people in the audience and the people onstage. I thought that was great, because for so long, pop stars had been like aliens from outer space. But it was only when the more interesting new wave bands came around, like XTC and Talking Heads, that I had any idea that I wanted to be involved in something like that. So I started to play in a couple of bands.

What instruments were you playing then?

A Rhodes, a Micromoog, and a little thing I built from a kit called a Trancendent 2000. It was very odd. Things always went wrong with it. It had a spring reverb built into it, which made some great sounds when you banged it. But it was all bad timing, because we were wearing futurist gear about two years before the futurist thing happened.

Didn't you do a live one-man show at one time?

I started out doing a one-man show because I felt that it was the most sensible way to reproduce onstage what I was doing in the studio. Though I have guests from time to time, a lot of my studio work is just me working in the studio. I felt that it would be a shame to hire session musicians and have to dictate the parts to them in order to play the things live. I also thought there was a certain kind of intimacy that comes from watching one guy onstage. I remember seeing

Bob Dylan when I was 11 years old, and obviously what I do is a completely different style of music and I couldn't do any of it without all the technology, but I thought it was about time someone did a one-man show with technology. The problem withit was that in computer technology there are so many variables and so many ways for things to go wrong that I became too preoccupied with keeping my machines running. It became difficult to perform to an audience.

How is playing solo different from playing with a band?

Playing solo was fun in its way, you know, but what it amounted to was me doing onstage what I do at home playing songs and improvising around a bit and having fun. The audiences were sort of voyeurs into my own fantasy dreamland, which I don't think is the same as a performance. It doesn't demand a response from the audience. There are still sections of the new set that I do on my own because certain songs feel wrong when I do them with other players.

Can you give us an example?

"Airwaves." It has a fairly lush arrangement on the album that isn't easy to reproduce note-for-note without a studio facility because, obviously, these sounds depend on the way they are layered and textured. Live, I prefer to do a simpler arrangement, just two or three instruments, the computer, and me standing there and singing it. Sometimes I do that as the last number in the set, although it seems strange to do a slow number last. I send all the band off and do it with just a spotlight on me. It works very well that way.

When you started working with sidemen, did you change your setup or did the sidemen adapt to the equipment?

They adapted to what I had already. Since about the time I was halfway through making *The Golden Age Of Wireless*, I've been using a drum system based around the PPG, which besides being a digital synthesizer is also a very complex sequencer. It occurred to me that the system would be very useful for triggering Simmons drums. I prefer writing drum parts using the keyboard of the PPG as opposed to using the little switches you see on systems like the Linndrum. Also, I can take parts and put them in different places of the memory with maybe one change in them or something. The PPG has enough memory for me to fit my entire set into it. I couldn't do that with a Linn.

You use video in your live shows. How do you sync it up to what's going on onstage?

If you've got some lip-syncing going on in the videos, you don't want it to be five seconds behind what's going on onstage. What I used to do was run the video on three screens that were all slightly out of sync with one another and with the song. I found that that was a more interesting effect than just one screen because you didn't quite know what you were watching. What I tend to do now is put an audio track on the U-matic [the projectors], which contains codes which are fed to the PPG. That way the PPG runs in sync with the videos.

There are also a lot of effects going on—Vocoders turning on and off in an instant, echoes doing the same thing, and so on. Is the PPG controlling the effects too, or have you got a really good sound man?

The PPG is doing it. It turns the echoes on and off, the vocoders on and off. It also does things like change the sounds on the Simmons drums and stuff like that. I did all that programming myself.

What kind of disadvantages are there to doing live gigs where everything is tied into the PPG?

Precarious business. It keeps you very tense because your whole livelihood is dependent on this incredibly fragile bit of machinery. Occasionally, it makes me wonder whether I'm cheating a bit. I'm not somebody who can stand up on a musical stage and just entertain people without any props. I wasn't born with that. I'm very much an activator. Right from running a film co-op, through being a meteorologist, to working a P.A., I'm the kind of personality that stands at the center of it. The show goes on around me. I'm kind of pulling the levers. It's my best talent, I suppose. But it's a dangerous business, because voltage isn't particularly reliable, especially in old theaters and on sweaty club stages.

What other instruments are you using onstage at the moment?

I'm playing a Roland Jupiter-8 interfaced to the PPG at the moment, and that's all I use myself. The guitar player and bass player I work with also have keyboards.

What made you decide to use just the JP-8?

It was a conscious decision. When I stopped being a one-man band, I wanted to get rid of as much equipment and as many personal responsibilities onstage as possible as far as the gear went. I didn't think I had to prove to anybody that I was capable of twiddling knobs. Having gotten that off my chest, I was free to perform and wanted a simple system. The Roland had a split keyboard and was programmable. That was everything I needed. The other two guys in the band actually learned synthesizers when they started working with me.

How technical do you think a good keyboard player has to be these days?

I don't feel a need to be state-of-the-art as far as being a part of any particular musical movement. And I regard all these machines as being just the means to create the sounds I want to hear. But I think a keyboard player has to be as technical as a producer and a producer has to be as musical as a keyboard player.

There are very few solos on your records.

There's a reason for that. I'm not really a very adept keyboard player when it comes to the finger department. Maybe I was when I was 14, but I spent so much time thinking about sounds and textures and composition in general that I've had very little time to practice. Anyway, I think that individual virtuosity and bravado is completely out of place for the age that I'm doing things in. It's never been that important to me, so solos don't seem appropriate.

How do you do most of your writing?

Primarily, away from any instrument, in my head. I'll get an idea for lyrics or something and just write it down. Sometimes I'll just work from a bass and drum groove. I carry around a Roland Drumatix and Bass and I'll take them on planes and use headphones. Then I'll just get a groove going and write something around it.

Did "Science" start out with dancing in mind?

Sure. I was rather surprised when a lot of the songs off the album began getting played in dance clubs, because they weren't written with that intention. You run into a dilemma when you try to pack as much information into a song as I like to pack into mine, and still make a good dance record. One of the basic ingredients of a good dance record is a certain level of hypnotic blandness. It shouldn't be too demanding except rhythmically. It should be very economical and just have a minimum of information. Just a very good groove. I was surprised when those things got played in clubs. I've got a preoccupation with R&B, but it's always been difficult for me to use that influence in my music. "Science" is probably the closest I've come to sounding black, although I hate those categories.

What comes first for you? Is it the arrangement of a tune, or the visualization of it as a video?

Well, the concept behind a song is very visual anyway, and I can almost picture the film that the clip comes from before I start working on the song or the video. It's kind of there in my imagination, and all I have to do is sniff out ways of articulating it. Video is my main medium; that's where I've got the most to offer because it covers all the fields I'm best at.

Dominic Milano

Index

More Quality music books for Quill from GPI Publications. . .

MASTERS OF HEAVY METAL
Edited by Jas Obrecht

Unique musical techniques, personal creative insights and valuable technical detail from the greatest metal artists of hard-core rock and roll. From Jimi Hendrix to the Scorpions, Judas Priest, Def Leppard and Eddie Van Halen — here is the ultimate documentary of intense, high-energy, guitar-dominated hard rock taken to the full extreme. Profusely illustrated. From the pages of Guitar Player Magazine.

paperback/$8.95 0-688-02937-X

THE BIG BOOK OF BLUEGRASS
Edited by Marilyn Kochman
Foreword by Earl Scruggs

Interviews, playing hints, note-by-note solos for guitar, banjo, mandolin, fiddle and dobro. The history, the personalities, the greatest artists and their music, including Bill Monroe, Earl Scruggs, Lester Flatt, David Grisman, Ricky Skaggs, Sam Bush, and many more. From the pages of Frets Magazine. Music and photos throughout.

hardcover/$22.95 0-688-02940-X
paperback/$10.95 0-688-02942-6

GUITAR GEAR
Edited by John Brosh

A comprehensive, practical guide to buying, maintaining, repairing, customizing all guitar equipment, accessories, and effects. How gear works and how it's made. Amps, bass guitar, guitar synthesizers, strings, fuzz boxes, chorus machines, analog delays, graphic equalizers — the latest developments, information, insight, and inspiration from the pages of Guitar Player magazine. Illustrated with photos and diagrams throughout.

paperback/0-688-03108-0

THE ART OF ELECTRONIC MUSIC
Compiled and with Commentary by Tom Darter
Edited by Greg Armbruster
Foreword by Dr. Robert A. Moog

The first definitive book: the creative and technical development of an authentic musical revolution. From the Theremin Electrical Symphony to today's most advanced synthesizers. Scientific origins, the evolution of hardware, the greatest artists — in stories, interviews, illustrations, analysis, and practical musical technique. From the pages of Keyboard Magazine. Completely illustrated.

hardcover/0-688-03105-6
paperback/0-688-03106-4

From your bookstores or directly from the publisher.
Quill
A Division of William Morrow & Company
105 Madison Avenue
New York, NY 10016